Quentin Tarantino

Shooting from the Hip

Wensley Clarkson

True Romance
Rs 100 ;125

PIATKUS

First published in Great Britain in 1995 by
Judy Piatkus (Publishers) Ltd of
5 Windmill Street, London W1P 1HF

Reprinted 1995, 1997

The moral rights of the author have been asserted

*A catalogue record for this book is available
from the British Library*

ISBN 0–7499–1555–2

Data capture and manipulation by
Phoenix Photosetting, Chatham, Kent
Printed and bound in Great Britain by
Mackays of Chatham PLC, Chatham, Kent

To Toby,
who is critic enough to know

*'Fame is like
cocaine – people
think they can control it,
but they can't.'*

William Goldman, *Adventures in the Screen Trade*

*'I am a racist.
I am a killer.
I don't give a fuck,
alright?'*

Quentin Tarantino, May 1995

'Wait a minute,
wait a minute.
You ain't
heard
nothing
yet.'

First words spoken on screen.

Al Jolson, *The Jazz Singer*, 1927

Contents

ACT II – The Confrontation

ACT III – The Resolution

Notes of Gratitude – In a Nutshell

I owe many individuals who have helped make this book possible, my deepest thanks. All told, I interviewed more than 100 people, among them friends, acquaintances, writers, directors, producers, editors, artists, lawyers, publishers, video store clerks, salesmen, college students, cops, ex-convicts, agents, hookers, private eyes, reporters and down-on-their-luck dropouts.

Some of these sources have chosen to remain anonymous. To them I offer a note of appreciation for the help they provided.

However, there are a lot of others who don't mind being thanked out loud. First and foremost, my heartfelt thanks must go to Quentin's mother, Connie Zastoupil, whose help and guidance have been unswerving. Quentin's onetime best friend Craig Hamann was a source of many great stories about Quentin, especially from his years at the James Best Acting School and during the long and troubled shooting of *My Best Friend's Birthday*. Hamann stayed close to Quentin for several years and clearly remembers the problems and frustrations they both faced.

Cathryn Jaymes was Quentin's personal manager for almost ten years and she kindly revealed some fascinating details about the years when Quentin was really struggling. Cathryn patiently endured many hours of questioning and, unlike many people in Hollywood, always returned my calls graciously and swiftly.

Scott Spiegel provided marvellous descriptions of Quentin's struggle through the seedier areas of Hollywood. His off-the-wall movie geek mentality gave me a unique insight into the life that Quentin was leading in the late eighties and early nineties. The Spiegel bedroom must be the envy of movie and horror comic fanatics across the globe.

Film Threat magazine were wonderfully helpful and I have a number of people to thank, including Paul Zimmerman, who met Quentin on the way up. Now editor of the magazine, Zimmerman generously shared his memories of those early, heady days of *Reservoir Dogs'* success. His colleague Brian Williams talked at great length about his more recent encounters with Quentin and provided a fresh appraisal that was of enormous benefit. David Bourgeois' account of how he stalked Quentin at Cannes was highly amusing and incisive.

A number of Quentin's friends from his days at the Video Archives store in Hermosa Beach came up with details of Quentin's film addiction years. Most helpful in this regard were the Martinez brothers, Chris and Jerry.

The section on the build-up to actually shooting *Reservoir Dogs* owes a great deal to Monte Hellman. He welcomed me into his home and provided the inside information that lies at the heart of this book. Crew member Jamie Beardsley made an equally vital contribution with her marvellous photographs and extraordinarily accurate recollections.

On the editorial front there are a number of people to thank, particularly my editor at Piatkus Books, Sarah Hannigan, whose enthusiasm from day one has been magnificent and inspiring. The unique design of the book owes much to her efforts and the skills of designer Jerry Goldie, who came up with suggestions that made it look genuinely fresh and pacey. Many thanks also to Kelly Davies for all her work.

Others who deserve many, many thanks include: Tina Mascara, Don Murphy, John Glatt, Joe Paoella, Cathy Griffin, Stanley Margolis, David Thomas, Alex Stone, Paula Eileen Eckert, Rand Vossler, Mike White, Mark La Femina, Paul Bartel, Rich Turner, Joe Carabello, Jack Lucarelli, David Stein, Jeff Burr, Vinnie Mizzi, Tom Duckweed, Rupert Maconick, Jon Ryan, Martin Dunn, Mark Sandelson, Jason McCue, Toby and Karim.

The Academy of Motion Picture and Science Library (Los Angeles), the *Charlie Rose Show*, the Knoxville County Office of Records, the Torrance Library, the BBC's *Omnibus* programme, the Lincoln Center (New York) the *L.A. Times*, Associated Newspapers, News International, the *New York Times*, the *Boston Globe*, *Vanity Fair*, *Entertainment Weekly*, *Los Angeles Magazine*, the *Village Voice*, the *New York Daily News*, *Variety*, *Interview Magazine*, *L.A. Weekly*, *Premiere*, *Empire*, *TV Guide*, *Playboy* and the Mirror Group provided much of the background material.

Author's Note

The central figure in this story, Quentin Tarantino, has changed his name twice through his life. In an effort to avoid confusion, throughout the book he is referred to as Quentin.

Some of the dialogue represented in this book was constructed from available documents, some was drawn from tape recorded testimony, and some was reconstituted from the memory of participants.

Hip, *hip*, n. The fleshy projecting part of the thigh; the haunch; the joint of the thigh; the fruit of the dog-rose or wild brier.

2. **Shoot from the hip** *v phr* To act or respond impulsively and aggressively; be recklessly impetuous.

Robert L.Chapman, Ph.D. The Dictionary of American Slang.

Introduction – The Path of a Righteous Man

Reader beware. This is a book about a ninetics' icon who has never shied away from speaking his mind. It does not reveal all of Quentin Tarantino's most secret or outrageous thoughts but it is the most fascinating account of his life you are ever likely to read.

Who is the man behind the public face of the world's premier movie maker? Whence comes his love of life's darkness, his apocalyptic drive? How is it possible for someone with so little formal education to become the ultimate twentieth-century artist?

I first came across Quentin Tarantino when we were both struggling scriptwriters in Los Angeles in early 1991. My agent suggested I read a 'really wacky' screenplay entitled *Reservoir Dogs* because she reckoned it was one of the funkiest scripts she had ever come across. I read it from cover to cover in one sitting.

No one had bought the script at that stage, but I knew it would only be a matter of time before its author became a force to be reckoned with.

I later encountered Quentin at a horror festival in an airport convention centre near Los Angeles Airport, not far from where, as a teenager, he had been woken by the constant thunder of jets taking off and landing. I got a feeling for my subject by watching the way he performed in front of hundreds of adoring fellow movie geeks. He worked the crowd brilliantly.

I also consulted the person who knows Quentin best – his mother Connie Zastoupil.

'He's riding on the crest of a wave,' declared Connie. 'But I'm worried that he is going too fast.'

For the sake of this book, Connie agreed to open up old wounds and disclose the life she has shared with her only child. I spent many hours interviewing her, finding out about Quentin's strange habits as a child and their occasionally volatile relationship. She told me that in her opinion this book was going to be the only truthful and balanced account of her son's life. She said she was sure Quentin would 'appreciate that you are trying to get it right.' Her decision to sanction my efforts above all other books on Quentin deserves my most heartfelt thanks. Much of the early part of this book reflects her courage and determination in bringing up a child as a single parent.

Quentin's brilliant screenplays were my other vital source. They tell so much of his life that they provided the thread I needed to sew the narrative together. Quentin's life is his movies and his movies give us a glimpse of his life.

When we last met, in May 1995, Quentin was quick-witted and sharp as ever, giving the answers to questions almost before I'd asked them. I greatly appreciate that he did not to try and block my efforts to write this book. Although he never came on board officially, he never stood in the way of any of his friends when they decided to help me. I think the book is better as a result. With their generous contributions, a picture with words has emerged that fully conveys the unique stature of the man. All of it is here, straight from the hip. . .

Quentin is the first movie director in Hollywood history to be treated like a rock star. Screaming adolescent girls – not legally old enough to see his films – mob him everywhere. The seventies had teenyboppers; the nineties, apparently, have Tarantino-boppers. Even rock icon Kurt Cobain thanked Quentin Tarantino on the album *In Utero*, following the release of *Reservoir Dogs*.

The celebrated hamburger exchange in *Pulp Fiction* is one of his trademark scenes – a gangster delivering a lecture on an arcane aspect of popular culture. The characters discuss the question of what a McDonald's quarterpounder hamburger is called in France. The answer is a 'Royale' because, as all Tarantinoboppers know, France follows the metric-system. The way things are going, a Paris quarterpounder will soon be officially renamed a 'Tarantino'.

There is no simple way to explain this worldwide mania. Perhaps as in *Pulp Fiction*, the question is best explored from different points of view.

In the past only one young director has generated so much fuss on such a limited output – and that was Orson Welles. Some are even suggesting that *Reservoir Dogs* is another *Citizen Kane*. Both are all-time great films but other factors must surely be involved in Tarantino-fever.

In general, the surest way for an artist to achieve adulation and visibility beyond the limits of their chosen discipline is to have extraordinary sexual charisma. Youth and an air of danger will, if the artist is lucky, invite comparison with rock stars. Brett Easton Ellis and Damien Hirst are obvious examples from the worlds of literature and art.

Yet Ellis and Hirst are never actually mobbed by screaming teenage girls, whereas Quentin Tarantino has been. Youth is certainly part of his mystique – he was only twenty-eight when he made *Reservoir Dogs* – but there is far more to it than that.

Unlike Scorsese, Coppola and Spielberg, Quentin has achieved his amazing success in a frighteningly short time. Also unlike them he has yet to make a flop. To date, his oeuvre includes *Reservoir Dogs* and *Pulp Fiction* (which he created and directed), and *True Romance* and *Natural Born Killers* (written by him but directed by others).

Yet Quentin is the sort of guy who, before 1992 – when *Reservoir Dogs* put his geeky face on the cover of every magazine in Christendom – would probably have gone unnoticed in any gathering of more than two people. That is part of his appeal. Quentin may be God to his more extravagant fans, but he is also Everyman.

Young audiences lap up everything he has to offer. Many of them would no doubt love to write like him (hence the extraordinary success of his published screenplays).

Quentin's 1995 tour of Britain, to promote those screenplays, was sold out. His scripts have been bought by more than 100,000 people in Britain alone, even though paperback screenplays usually only sell to passionate film buffs and would-be scriptwriters.

His astonishing success may be at least partly due to his unusual name. Quentin Tarantino sounds half English-aristocrat, half Italian-American. (He is actually half-Italian, quarter-Cherokee and quarter-Irish). Yet, however much Tarantino may sound like a brand name, his films definitely have a style all their own. Woody Allen is probably the only other director whose work is so easily identifiable. Despite what his detractors say, there is a great deal more to Quentin than diligence, a solid grounding in movie culture and a knack for exploiting this generation's insatiable appetite for sex, drugs, rock 'n' roll and startling violence. His use of violence is actually the most commonly misunderstood aspect of Quentin's work. His average body count is, in fact, much lower than in most Schwarzenneger movies. More importantly, his approach to violence is invariably more subtle than his critics are prepared to admit.

His skill lies in coaxing the audience into thinking they are seeing gruesome violence without it actually happening on screen. A true cineaste, his control of the viewers' imagination conjures up infinitely more terrible scenes than anything the camera can show them.

Quentin's work as a director and screenwriter is all cut – or rather, hacked – from the same cloth. Combining the offbeat humour of seemingly irrelevant dialogue with designer violence is the gimmick that has raised his profile so far so fast.

Suddenly Tarantino gags are appearing everywhere, from Steve Bell's 'If. . .' cartoon strip for the *Guardian* to Garry Bushell's TV column in the *Sun*, where the critic assumed that his millions of readers would understand a joke about tempestuous soccer star Eric Cantona signing to appear in 'the new Tarantino movie, Reservoir Frogs'.

Then there is the fact that Quentin – unlike many other so-called legendary Hollywood directors – so far has insisted on working with his own screenplays. This gives his movies a strong visual character. Tarantino believes that directing 'other people's material puts you in handcuffs.' Acting in such movies is fine but directing them is an entirely different matter.

Tarantino's scripts have a way of reworking classic genres. The plots and characters are familiar, but Quentin's structure and dialogue transcend category. His style is firmly rooted in a world of seventies cool-guy pop culture that may never have existed except in movies but has resurfaced in the nineties.

Although it is his distinct pure blend of comedy and violence that appeals to critics and cinephiles, it is probably the violence that accounts for Quentin's status as a youth icon. There is a sense of danger in his work. His films have in many ways been treated like a banned substance: *Reservoir Dogs* waited more than two years to get a video release in Britain and there was much debate about whether *Natural Born Killers* would be allowed cinema exhibition in the same country.

This outlaw status is a crucial part of the Tarantino myth. What troubles critics about his work – his lack of moral perspective – is precisely what most appeals to his young fans.

Although in person, Tarantino may resemble a harmless trainspotter, it is the blank-eyed violence of his movies, their callous laughter at the dark, that has made him Hollywood's first rock star director. Yet he has remained approachable and exudes the easy charm of one completely unaware of his status as the world's hottest film director. It is as if he's saying, if I can do it, so can you. . .

Main titles

cast of principal characters

Avary, Roger	Film maker
Beardsley, Jamie	Assistant Director/Producer
Bender, Lawrence	Actor-turned-producer
Buscemi, Steve	Actor
Gladstein, Richard.N.	Executive producer
Hamann, Craig	Actor/writer
Hellman, Monte	Film maker
Jackson, Samuel L.	Actor
Jaymes, Cathryn	Personal manager
Keitel, Harvey	Actor/producer
Lovelace, Grace	University lecturer
Lucarelli, Jack	Actor/ drama coach
Madsen, Michael	Actor
Margolis, Stanley	Personal manager/producer
Martinez, Gerry	Film geek/video store clerk
Murphy, Don	Producer
Roth, Tim	Actor
Scott, Tony	Film maker
Spiegel, Scott	Film maker
Stoltz, Eric	Actor
Stone, Oliver	Film maker
Tarantino, Quentin	Film maker/actor
Tierney, Lawrence	Actor
Travolta, John	Actor
Turner, Rich	Actor
Vossler, Rand	Producer/director
Weinstein, Harvey	Miramax
Weinstein, Bob	Miramax
Willis, Bruce	Actor
Zastoupil, Connie	Parent
Zastoupil, Curtis	Step-parent
Zimmerman, Paul	Movie magazine editor

'I'm telling a story you've seen over and over again. We're going to follow the oldest set-ups in the world, but then we're going to go to the moon.'

Quentin Tarantino

'I don't care what you write, just so you get it right and just so it sells.'

Serial killer Ted Bundy to his biographers as he awaited the death sentence

Act I

The Set Up

'*Fate just stepped in and fucked me over*'

Quentin Tarantino

'It's a hard world for little things'

Lillian Gish, in *The Night of the Hunter*, 1955

Connie – The Lone Ranger

KNOXVILLE, TENNESSEE, MARCH 27, 1963

Connie Tarantino, a pretty, young trainee nurse at the Tennessee State University Hospital, hurried out into the cold rain from her tiny one-bedroomed apartment on the edge of town to the waiting ambulance. She was worried. The pains in her stomach indicated that her pregnancy might end prematurely. She wanted to have her baby like all the other mothers she had attended during her training. But life never seemed to go smoothly for Connie. Here she was, pregnant at sixteen and abandoned by her actor husband, who had jumped ship within a couple of months of their wedding not even aware that she was expecting a baby.

No one in Connie's family had seemed all that surprised when she had announced her marriage at fifteen, and then that she was pregnant two weeks before her sixteenth birthday.

Connie was born in Knoxville, Tennessee, in the mid-1940s, when her mother was just seventeen. (Connie did not want the specific year of her birth made public: 'The day and the month are September 3 – a

gentleman shouldn't ask a woman her age.') Her father died when she
was a baby and at the age of two she was adopted by the man who married her mother and the family moved to Ohio. Connie's relationship with
her stepfather and mother rapidly disintegrated and at the age of twelve
she moved in with her Aunt Sadie in Pico Rivera, California. Aunt Sadie
had no children of her own and provided her young niece with more
encouragement and support than she received from her parents. Connie
has specifically requested that none of her immediate family should be
named in this book because she is estranged from her mother and says,
'I do not want any of my relatives to find me. I don't want them to know
about Quentin.'

The root of the problems between mother and daughter lay in her
mother's penchant for alcohol. She would go on enormous drinking
sprees during which she would lose all sense of parental responsibility.
She blamed much of that alcohol abuse on something that Connie was
very proud of – her family's Cherokee and Irish ancestry. By an odd coincidence, Connie's maternal grandfather had been full blooded-Cherokee
married to an Irish woman and her paternal grandmother was Irish,
married to a Cherokee.

From the age of ten, Connie had been like a mother to her mother.
Her problematical stepfather had taken the family to Ohio from
Tennessee. Connie continually found herself mopping up the chaos and
distress that went with the Bourbon her mother kept drinking. At the age
of ten she moved in with her grandmother in Ravenna, near Cleveland,
in Ohio. Then she decided to flee her entire family to head for California
at the age of twelve. Now, at sixteen, she refused to let her mother help
look after the child she was expecting, even though she intended to continue working after the birth.

At her aunt's home in Pico Rivera, Connie had to work from her
early teens to pay her way through school. At one stage she worked at an
Orange Julius fast-food joint, but anything was better than being back
with her parents.

Connie had only just turned fifteen when she met twenty-one-year-old matinée idol lookalike Tony Tarantino while taking horse-riding lessons near her home. Tarantino – a part-time actor and law student – was appearing on stage at the Pasadena Playhouse, near Los Angeles, at the time. He was entranced by this half-Cherokee Indian, half-Irish girl. Connie was unusually tall, with long, dark, flowing hair, large deep brown eyes and a trim figure. She also looked at least three years older than she really was. Tarantino, with his Italian features, neat buzz cut and liking for well-fitting clothes, cut a smart figure.

Connie – who had graduated from high school at just fifteen with a major in microbiology – had been seriously considering going to pre-med school to train as a doctor. When she met Tarantino she decided to do a nursing course first, with the intention of going on to pre-med school later.

To Connie – ever the daydreamer – the marriage and her subsequent pregnancy seemed to offer the perfect escape route from her mundane existence. By marrying Tarantino she immediately gained emancipated minor status, which meant her parents no longer had any legal authority over her.

'I don't know if I ever truly fell in love with Tony. It's difficult to tell because I was so young,' says Connie now. She pauses, then adds, 'I guess I still don't know what love means.'

Connie and Tony's marriage in Los Angeles in the summer of 1961 actually provided nothing more than a brief respite from drudgery. Connie's family saw the wedding as an ideal way to get her off their hands. In their eyes, she was a troublemaker who had constantly skipped school and been sullen and unhelpful. In her eyes, she was the neglected and abandoned child who had always played second fiddle to a bottle of booze. Her mother even told Connie she was relieved that she appeared to be settling down to raise a family.

But, as usual, Connie's happiness was shortlived. Tony Tarantino moved to Tennessee with Connie when she enrolled to train as a registered nurse in Knoxville. But, after failing to get a job, he departed for his home state of New York. Connie had not even discovered that she was carrying his baby. They had been together less than three months and she was still just fifteen years of age.

So it was that six months later Connie found herself working sixteen-hour double shifts as part of her gruelling training to be an angel of mercy back in Knoxville. And now all those incredibly long hours were threatening to turn her pregnancy into a disaster.

The day before Connie went into premature labour, she had worked yet another double shift at the hospital. In many ways, the relentless grind helped her avoid thinking about her situation: all alone, about to become a mother at a ludicrously young age, and barely able to survive on her salary of a dollar and a quarter per hour. Her pride prevented her from moving into her mother's trailer home, thirty miles north of Knoxville. Nothing was going to faze her. She would make it on her own.

As the ambulance pushed through the suburbs of the city towards the hospital, Connie felt no fear.

'I was completely alone. I had no one to turn to and I was too young to really know how serious it was to bring a child into the world. There was no choice for me, I had to just get on with my life,' she says now.

The hospital was like a home from home for Connie, who had spent more of the previous three months there than at her cramped apartment. As she was wheeled through to the maternity wing, doctors and nurses greeted her. It felt reassuring to the sixteen-year-old. It was almost like being famous. The people in that hospital truly cared for Connie, which was more than could be said for most of her family.

The birth itself was remarkably easy, but then the child did weigh under five pounds because he was so early. Connie really did not give it much thought. She'd got married, got pregnant and now she'd had a baby. It was no big deal. It went on all around her during her working hours, so why should it be any different for her?

'It's a boy,' announced the midwife, holding up the tiny infant with his mop of black hair. 'What you going to call him?'

Connie looked up bleary-eyed, and forced a smile. 'Oh, I'll think of something.'

In fact she had thought it through very carefully during those endless, lonely evenings watching television at her apartment. She didn't do much else except eat, and that was usually in front of the TV. Connie had few friends. Girls of her own age had very different interests and older women tended to disapprove of a virtual schoolgirl getting pregnant.

During those solitary evenings at home, Connie would let her imagination take over while she tuned into different programmes. She had a particular penchant for a Western called *Gunsmoke*.

Her all-time favourite heart-throb was a young, rugged half-breed cowhand called Quint Asper, played by handsome stud Burt Reynolds. Connie would swoon every time he came on the small, flickering black and white screen of her secondhand TV. Sometimes she would dream about riding off into the sunset with Quint. Her real life cowboy, Tony Tarantino, had ridden off into the sunset by himself, so Quint seemed a safer option. Fantasy figures never abandoned their loved ones.

Connie's other important influence in choosing a name for her son was one of her favourite books, *The Sound and the Fury*. One of the characters, Quentin, was the progeny of an ill-advised seduction and a hasty, loveless marriage. There was a clear parallel with her own situation.

The nurses in attendance at the hospital were concerned that mother and child should bond instantly. Adoptions were not as common in those days. When a woman – however young – had a baby, she was expected to keep it.

But, as Connie lay there recovering from the birth of her premature son, she found herself feeling incredibly detached from everything that had just occurred. It was as if all those dramatic events had happened to someone else. Initially, it was impossible to see the tiny creature who had popped out into the world as her child. It wasn't until the baby started crying and the nurses showed Connie how to feed him, that it actually dawned on her that he was *her* baby. She had long since blotted Tony Tarantino out of her mind and here was a reminder of Tony. Perhaps that was why it took her a little time to accept him as her flesh and blood? But Connie was determined to raise him herself. She had no father for him, so she thought back to *Gunsmoke*, the programme she had so frequently watched in her lonely apartment.

'I'm gonna call him Quentin,' Connie proudly announced to the nurse. And so Quentin Jerome Tarantino was named.

Connie later insisted that, besides her interest in the two Quints, she also wanted to ensure that her son's name would fill up an entire screen. 'A multisyllabic name, Quen-tin Ta-ran-ti-no. It's a big name and I expected him to be important. Why would I want to have an unimportant baby?'

Connie had no time for post-natal depression. She did not even have an opportunity to breastfeed her child. He went straight on to formula because she had to get back to work to keep them both. Connie was all alone with a baby to bring up. By the time she left hospital, with tiny, milky-white Quentin wrapped in a blanket in her arms, she had already worked out a game plan. This child was going to be her inspiration. He would spur her on to succeed in life.

Soon after the birth, Connie was back working sixteen-hour days at the hospital and attending classes in-between. She took Quentin over to an English nanny called Mrs Breeden, who looked after a number of children of working parents in Knoxville. For the first year of his life, Quentin spent more time under the watchful, caring eye of Mrs Breeden than in the company of his mother.

Connie had reluctantly decided that she had to make work her priority if they were to survive financially. She would drop her baby son at Mrs Breeden's one-storey house on a quiet tree-lined street a few blocks from her apartment, then take the bus into work every Monday morning. Quentin would not see his mother again until Friday evening.

Connie was working so hard that she hardly even had time to stop and think about the assassination of John F. Kennedy on November 22, 1963. While Americans wept in the streets of Knoxville, Connie just got on with her life. JFK may have seemed half messiah, half movie star to the young all over the free world, but this teenager's priority was keeping a roof over herself and her young son. Mourning the death of the President wasn't going to pay the rent.

'I didn't have time to worry about those sort of things. We had to survive and there wasn't a waking moment in every day when I didn't put that at the front of my mind,' recalls Connie.

Not surprisingly, Connie's mother felt enormous guilt over her young daughter's lonely and gruelling existence. However, Connie steadfastly refused to involve her mother in the life of her baby son.

But by the time Quentin was a year old, Connie's mother seemed to have turned over a new leaf. She convinced her daughter that she had conquered her drink problem and pleaded to be allowed to look after little Quentin.

Connie – extremely suspicious of her mother's motives – put her to the test by letting her look after the child at her home on a number of occasions. She actually did a fine job and there was no sign of any alcohol in the house either. Connie began to believe that perhaps her mother was a reformed person.

With her work commitments at the hospital increasing, Connie allowed her mother to look after Quentin full-time at her mother's mobile home on a trailer park.

For the next year and a half, Connie should have been able to lead a fairly normal teenager's life, as she spent at least five days each week as a single person. But her low wages and exhausting work schedule forced her to flop in front of the television on her rare nights off. She did not even have enough spare cash to make it to the movie theatre to watch her idol Elvis doing his thing in classics like *Viva Las Vegas*. Connie would have loved to have seen the film, as she particularly adored the idea of a sports car racer having fun in the gambling capital of the world.

'It was a strange existence, I guess. I had few friends and my life was wrapped around Quint and work when I should have been out having fun,' explains Connie.

On her days off, Connie would change buses twice to get to her mother's home thirty miles away. The bus trip there and back would take practically all day, but it was worth it to spend a few hours with baby Quentin in the back yard of the rundown trailer.

Connie read books occasionally, but she was almost addicted to superhero comics. She would sit and flick through them for hours before falling asleep. *Spiderman* was her favourite. Why couldn't she find a man who was the perfect combination of Spiderman and Quint from *Gunsmoke*? But not many guys were likely to come knocking at the door of a quiet, shy teenage girl, with a baby in tow.

'I guess Quint and I grew up together in more ways than most mothers and sons.' she goes on. 'Comics were as much an escape for me as they were later for Quint. I didn't have much else in those days.'

The fact was that Connie enjoyed spending time imagining a fantasy life with one of her fictional heroes. In real life, up to that time, men always seemed to have betrayed and abandoned her. Her father had left her by dying, and her adopted father had made her life miserable by failing to curb her mother's excesses. The heroes of television and comic books didn't drink or neglect their children. They were kind, thoughtful and brave.

Connie kept thinking about California where she had spent her three happiest years living with Aunt Sadie, in Pico Rivera. In California, the sun shone most days, there was a feeling of optimism, and heroes like Quint and Elvis seemed to grow on trees.

'I call him the boy with the ice-cream face'

Emile Meyer, about Tony Curtis in *Sweet Smell of Success*, 1957

Curt – The Archer From Heaven

PIANO BAR, MONROVIA, SAN GABRIEL VALLEY, NEAR LOS ANGELES, SUMMER 1965

Curtis Arnold Zastoupil, twenty-three years old, prematurely balding, five feet ten, with a penchant for goatee beards and archery, charmed his way into the lives of Connie and Quentin like a latter-day Robin Hood. Zastoupil was a versatile musician who played regularly at small clubs and Ramada Inns. Connie first set eyes on Curt when he performed a solo gig at My Old Kentucky Home, a piano bar in Monrovia. Curt, with his laid back attitude and warm smile, reassured Connie – now nineteen – that good men actually did exist in the real world.

Connie had travelled to California earlier that summer after she'd qualified as a registered nurse. Tennessee had proved a depressing place to try and bring up a child singlehanded and she genuinely felt that Los Angeles might provide more opportunities.

Connie left Quentin with her mother and, once in California, had even briefly linked up again with Quentin's father Tony Tarantino, who had returned to the state to work. They dated a couple of times after she told him that he had a child back in Tennessee. But the romance did not re-ignite and both rapidly decided it would be better if they went their separate ways. Connie never once asked Tarantino to play the role of father and he showed little or no interest in the child. She was used to coping on her own so what difference did it make?

Curt Zastoupil and Connie fell in love within weeks of being introduced at the piano bar and she decided it was time to bring little Quentin back from Tennessee and make a life for herself in California. Connie was so taken by Curt's close family that she even recruited his brother Cliff to drive with her back to Knoxville to collect the child and their belongings.

On the three-day drive back from Tennessee, two-and-a-half-year-old Quentin tried to read every billboard and advertisement they passed. 'He even recognized logos. It was a real pain, but I guess it showed what way he was headin', explains Connie. The drive was also her first chance to get to know her young child. She soon discovered that Quentin would not eat anything except hamburgers and hot dogs, and she had to call every item of food by those two names in order to get him to eat.

Once they arrived in California, Curt Zastoupil took the young Quentin under his wing and provided the boy with a genuine father figure for the first time.

Connie and Curt married later that same year. It seemed like the beginning of a real life for Connie. Curtis introduced her to a world that was a million miles from Tennessee. He took her to jazz and folk clubs and restaurants in the racially mixed downtown area of Los Angeles. He brought her out of her private world that had – until that point – revolved around Elvis, comic books and *Gunsmoke*.

The couple purchased their own hunting falcons and went horse-riding in the nearby San Bernadino mountains with their birds, which were kept at a friend's ranch. Other weekends they would find deserted,

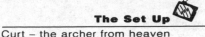
open spaces, set up their archery targets and play Robin Hood and Maid Marian for hours.

Connie and Curt even took to fencing, but they ended up being kicked out of their first apartment when they decided to have a sword fight on the balcony.

Connie worked for a short time as a fully qualified nurse, but then decided to seek a more traditional nine-to-five career as a manager in the healthcare industry. She was still so young that she got her first management job by lying about her age on the application form.

Curtis was Cool with a Capital C. Nothing bothered him. When the family moved to a larger rented house in Alhambra (a bedroom community on the edge of the South Bay, in the San Gabriel Valley) Connie announced that her kid brother Roger was going to come and live with them because their mother had taken to the bottle once more. Curt's only response was, 'Sure. No problem.' He was that kind of guy.

Connie's brother Roger was thirteen at the time and seemed destined to end up home-hopping just as his sister had done before him. But for Quentin, Uncle Roger's appearance was a marvellous development. In the space of a few months he had gone from having no father to gaining a father and a big brother. Roger was so overwhelmed by the atmosphere in the house that he told his sister that living with her and her family was like growing up at Disneyland.

Curt even officially adopted Quentin just before his fourth birthday and the boy was called Quentin Zastoupil for the rest of his childhood. His birth certificate was legally changed and has remained that way ever since.

The next few years were the happiest in Quentin's childhood.

The harpoon was darted; the stricken whale flew forward;
with igniting velocity the line ran through the groove; –
ran foul. Ahab stooped to clear it; he did clear it; but the
flying turn caught him round the neck, and voicelessly as
Turkish mutes bowstring their victim, he was shot out of

> *the boat, ere the crew knew he was gone. Next instant,*
> *the heavy eye-splice in the rope's final end flew out of the*
> *stark-empty tub, knocked down an oarsman, and smiting*
> *the sea, disappeared in its depths...*

Connie watched the excitement in Quentin's eyes as she read the climax of *Moby Dick*. To make it more exciting for her four-year-old son, she would imitate the sound of the waves hitting the side of the boat, then the huge splash as the giant whale crashed down into the surf.

> *Now small fowls flew screaming over the yet yawning gulf;*
> *a sullen white surf beat against its steep sides; then all*
> *collapsed, and the great shroud of the sea rolled on as it*
> *rolled five thousand years ago.*

Moby Dick, first published in the 1840s, completely captured young Quentin's imagination. The story of the cunning whale, which becomes the focus of hatred and superstition, appealed to the young boy. Quentin became obsessed with the fearsome, yet courageous whale winning out against the loathsome Captain Ahab.

Connie could not stand 'all the sugary nonsense' that most people tended to read to their children. The realities of life had hit her hard between the eyes and she couldn't help passing on that gritty approach to her beloved son.

'I read him hard, real stories that came alive on the page, not some crap about stupid fluffy toy animals,' she recalls. Other books read to Quentin included *Gulliver's Travels* and *Treasure Island*.

At that time, Quentin started to develop a talent for mimicry. He also had a remarkably good memory for such a young child. He was forever reciting things around the house. Although Connie recognized this as evidence of some inbuilt talent, she also found it incredibly irritating.

Quentin would drive Connie particularly crazy by memorizing both sides of long-playing albums. She had one comedy album by a stand-up

called José Mendes and the youngster would recite every joke verbatim. It was like having a demented, highly intelligent parrot in the house. Other times Quentin would listen to one particular Fats Domino record over and over again. His taste was already proving rather eclectic.

There were also musical albums like *Dr Doolittle*. Quentin knew all the songs from *Doolittle* and would constantly sing them – out of tune. Unlike most children, he wasn't remotely interested in being a policeman, fireman or pilot when he grew up. His only desire was to be an actor. The bug had already bitten.

One diversion was when Connie bought Quentin a ragged, friendly mongrel puppy which the little boy immediately named Baron. The spaniel/terrier mix instantly captivated Quentin and he lavished love and attention on the animal.

A few days after getting the dog, Connie had to forcibly drag Quentin away when she found him banging the puppy's head against a wall in the back yard. Quentin thought he was being playful and had no idea he might be causing brain damage to the animal. Connie reckoned that Baron got 'real slow' after the little boy had battered his pet's head against that concrete.

Quentin gradually started to appreciate that a gentler approach to the dog was preferable and the two became inseparable. Quentin would faithfully take the dog for a walk around the block at least twice a day.

However, after the family moved to another house in Alhambra, which was fifteen miles south-east of Los Angeles, Baron became very disorientated and started disappearing with alarming regularity, only to show up in a local dog pound a few days later. It was all extremely distressing for Quentin, who couldn't understand why the dog he cherished seemed so intent on running away.

A very emotional Quentin would frequently call Connie at work after he got home from school and discovered that Baron had gone missing yet again, and the dog pound had called to say they had him.

'Baron's in jail again, Mom,' Quentin would tell his mother, before collapsing into floods of tears down the phone. Connie would then leave

work early, pick Quentin up and rush round to the dog pound, where they'd retrieve Baron once again.

The only other friend Quentin had at this time was a boy called Todd who lived three houses up from their home on Sixth Street, in Alhambra. The two little boys would play together in each other's back yards. But Quentin was very possessive about some of his toys and often found it difficult to share them with other children.

By the age of four, Quentin had developed a virtual obsession with G.I. Joe dolls. (In Britain, they were called Action Men.) It was slightly ironic that he should take such an interest in these warlike toys, as Connie and Curt had very liberal views on the Vietnam war which was still raging at the time.

California was probably the most divided state in the nation when it came to American involvement in Vietnam. Draft-card burnings and peace marches were becoming commonplace; a few American pacifists had even burned themselves to death in sympathy with the self-immolation of Buddhist monks in Saigon.

Woodstock was about to happen, and a strong counter-culture – with its roots in the anti-war movement – was growing. In California, hippies were appearing everywhere, from San Francisco's Haight-Ashbury district to Hollywood's Sunset Boulevard. Tie-dyed T-shirts, sandals, beads and bell-bottomed jeans were the uniform of the day.

Both Connie and Curt supported the anti-war effort so strongly that they wore the bracelets of American POWs in memory of servicemen taken prisoner by the Viet Cong. Connie had the bracelet of an army captain who thankfully was eventually released and made it back to the United States. Her brother Roger was even posted to the Cambodian/Laotian border towards the end of the war.

Curt Zastoupil was entranced by anti-war troubadours like Bob Dylan and Joan Baez. He definitely swung in the direction of jazz, blues and folk music. Peter, Paul and Mary and a band called Scotch and Soda were amongst his favourites.

Connie had more varied taste in music, ranging from Tom Jones, Engelbert Humperdinck, Jack Jones and Frankie Avalon to certain Beatles tracks and even Isaac Hayes, Janice Joplin and Curtis Mayfield. Connie also liked some Rolling Stones tracks, despite her overall preference for the sweaty ballad school of singing. Her favourite group was a little-known ensemble called, aptly enough, The Crooners. Sometimes she persuaded Curt to play his own version of the Beatles' 'Day Tripper', but only when he was in the mood.

A sprinkling of bubble gum music followed in the early seventies, including Steeler's Wheel's 'Stuck in the Middle with You'. Connie was immensely proud of the fact that she liked everything from opera to Country and Western to soul to blues to rock and roll.

Meanwhile, Quentin and his mini-army of G.I. Joe's fought on in deepest Alhambra and poor Connie spent much of her son's early childhood on her hands and knees, trying to put the little black plastic combat boots back on his toy soldiers. Her other task was to keep reassembling the dolls after Quentin had torn them limb from limb, during particularly gruesome battle scenes. Connie still remembers how aggravated she would get because she and Quentin could never find the tiny black plastic bayonets that were forever going awol.

Quentin would set up vicious hand-to-hand combat scenes all over the house, usually after he had seen that evening's television news containing harrowing footage of the real fighting in south-east Asia. The little boy's voice could often be heard directing entire battle dramas, making sure that each scene worked in relation to the next.

'KEEP YOUR FUCKING HEAD DOWN, SOLDIER!'

Connie could not believe her ears one evening as she settled down on the settee with Curt to watch *The Untouchables*. Her young son was swearing like a ... trooper.

'Quentin, come here this instant!'

The shy little boy appeared at his mother's side.

'Don't you let me hear you using that kind of foul language ever again. Do you understand?'

Instead of looking down solemnly at the carpet, Quentin was burst-
ing to explain. 'I didn't say that, Mom. G.I. Joe said it.'

A wry smile appeared on Curt's face and he nudged his wife. But
Connie was in no mood to laugh. The boy had to be taught the difference
between right and wrong.

'You just tell him not to use that kinda language in this house.'

'But, Mom...'

'No buts. D'you understand?'

He walked away with his tail only just between his legs. How could
he tell a platoon of tough guy soldiers not to swear...

Quentin also had superhero dolls like Spiderman, Aquaman,
Superman and Batman. But Connie noticed that he was reluctant to
allow any interaction between his G.I. Joe's and the rest of the figures,
apart from Spiderman. Well aware of his mother's keen interest in that
particular superhero, Quentin occasionally permitted his soldier dolls to
get into scraps with Spiderman, but he had a problem: he did not know
who should win.

The only other doll Quentin got attached to was a Sindy doll left at
the house by one of his cousins. One day Connie caught Quentin trying
to re-enact a love scene from a movie he had just seen. Sindy was immediately banned.

One Halloween, Connie bought Quentin his own G.I Joe fancy dress
outfit and he went out trick-or-treating. But, as he didn't have many
friends locally, it was a lonely task and he came home less than an hour
later with few candies and a sad look on his face. He had already decided
he preferred hanging out with grown-ups.

By this time, Connie had filled the house with men. There was Curt,
her kid brother Roger, and Curt's brother Cliff. Quentin was in his element. He got so used to having one or other of the grown-ups to play
with that he would get very demanding if none of the three men was
around.

One Saturday morning, Connie and her three male residents overslept. At about ten, her brother Roger came rushing into the bedroom.

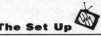
'Quentin has gone! I can't find him anywhere.'

Connie shot out of bed, aware that they lived on a very busy street and fearful that her little boy might have wandered out amongst the roaring traffic. As she ran up and down the road frantically looking for her son. Curt and Roger searched the house from top to bottom. But there was absolutely no sign of Quentin.

A distraught Connie came back into the house and headed towards the phone to call the police.

Suddenly a small figure in a Spiderman outfit leapt out of a clothes hamper in the hall giggling hysterically. The clothes hamper was Quentin's changing room. Superman had his phone box; Quentin had his clothes hamper.

Quentin felt he had gained just the right level of attention with his stunt. That would teach them to sleep late on a Saturday morning and not play with him.

Connie was furious. For the first time she hit her child. Neither of them ever forgot the incident, but for entirely different reasons. Connie believed it was the first step in building his sense of self-discipline. She believes that Quentin saw it as a classic example of injustice.

Connie has never regretted hitting Quentin occasionally as a child. She even used to pretend to have a worse temper than she really had in order to intimidate him whenever she believed he was up to no good.

'For a while, Quentin was convinced I was insane. He could not quite trust what I was going to do to him if he misbehaved. He felt as if he walked a tightrope with me,' she explains. Sometimes Connie would scream and yell at Quentin to drive home a point. There was a lot of hysteria and it certainly disturbed Quentin at times. But the only consistent characteristic of his upbringing was its unpredictability.

Despite occasional bust-ups, Quentin and his mother remained very close throughout his childhood. There was a remarkable bond between them. They were like two children growing up together.

Connie was too young to impose the usual restrictions on her son.

For instance, when Quentin was aged six or seven, she would take him to see movies that most parents would never have considered suitable for their children. One of the first adult films Quentin saw was *Carnal Knowledge*, starring Ann-Margret and Jack Nicholson.

The movie centres around a college student who embarks on an enthusiastic and varied sex life and then becomes bored and disillusioned after reaching middle age. When it was first released, some of the more lurid scenes caused quite an outcry in the press. Young Quentin conveniently got up from his seat and headed for the popcorn stand every time a sex scene came on the screen.

Twenty years later, as Quentin toiled over his script for *Natural Born Killers*, he came up with a scene that reflected the way he had been affected by seeing explicit sex at an early age.

In the original screenplay – much of which was altered drastically by director Oliver Stone after he purchased the script – Quentin tells a story through serial killer Mickey (played in the movie by Woody Harrelson) about how a little boy goes to see an adult-rated movie with his big sister and her boyfriend. The boy's mother asks the little boy what he saw in the movie theatre and the child plays out every sexual act, from kissing and 'feeling her up' to oral sex and masturbation.

It is a crude scene, which was changed by Oliver Stone, but it provides a fascinating insight into the way Quentin's mind works. He never forgot his reaction to being taken to see such adult films. Undoubtedly he gained a vast amount of knowledge, but at the same time he recognizes the harm that may have been done.

Not long after seeing *Carnal Knowledge*, Quentin once more found himself with his mother in a movie theatre – the Tarzana 6 in Harbor City – watching *The Wild Bunch*. It was a double bill with *Deliverance*, about a group of men from the city who go on a canoe trip. The expedition turns to horror when the local hillbillies decide to try and kill them.

Connie had been determined to see *Deliverance* because it starred Burt Reynolds, the actor whose character, Quint, in *Gunsmoke*, had provided the inspiration for Quentin's name. She expected a romantic adventure movie, but was stunned by one particularly disturbing scene which has also remained with Quentin ever since. It involved the homo-sexual rape of one of the canoeists, played in the movie by Ned Beatty.

'That scared the living shit out of me. Did I understand Ned Beatty being sodomized? No. But I knew he wasn't having any fun,' recalled Quentin many years later.

In *Pulp Fiction*, he recreated the scene by having two rednecks rape a man in the basement of their gunshop. The similarities are clear, with the rednecks even denied the ultimate pleasure of killing their victim. It was almost as if Quentin was trying to rewrite that gruesome scene in *Deliverance*.

Today, Connie insists that she does not feel at all guilty about tak-ing her young son to see such mature films. 'I honestly do not think it harmed him in any way.'

Intriguingly, she also took Quentin to see *Bambi*, but he was so dis-tressed when Bambi's mother died that he made Connie take him out of the cinema after the first twenty minutes.

At home, Quentin became equally emotional about seemingly harm-less cartoons like an episode of *The Flintstones* in which Bam Bam disappeared and Barney became suicidal as a result. Now that was heavy stuff... Back at the local movie theatre, the ultra-violent film *Joe* was han-dled with the greatest of ease.

As well as developing his interest in movies, Connie also encouraged Quentin to read from an early age. This gave him a genuine curiosity about the written word. He soon appreciated that television and movie drama was scripted and carefully planned before it was filmed.

At just seven years old, Quentin even understood the importance of structure in the stories he avidly read in comic books and novels. He would read and re-read whole sections to try and work out what was coming next in a particular storyline.

Quentin had the same attitude towards movies. He loved to see them at least four or five times if possible. When Curt took him to see *It's a*

Mad, Mad, Mad, Mad World they arrived fifteen minutes after the film had started so they stayed to see the first fifteen minutes of the next show. Quentin was amazed to discover that for the same admission price he could sit and watch a movie over and over again. 'When I'm an adult and I go to the movies, I'm gonna watch it *four* times,' he promised himself.

One bizarre result of this self-education was that in 1972, when he was still just nine, he wrote a moving story dedicated to his mother to celebrate Mother's Day. Connie was understandably touched as she began to read the two-page essay which featured an adult Quentin reminiscing about his childhood; how strict his mother had been; how much she had nagged him and run the house with a rod of iron. Connie was concerned but understood that it was good for her son to get his feelings off his chest and it was all so well constructed. Connie proudly read on, even though the piece was littered with spelling mistakes.

Then she got to the last section of the story. Quentin revealed that his mother had died. He wrote that he felt very bad about her death but...

Connie was stunned. She sat and read the final passage over and over again just to make sure she had read it correctly. But there was no doubting it. She looked up at her nine-year-old son who was looking sideways at her, almost as if he wanted a reaction.

'You don't really mean it, do you, Quentin?'

Quentin shrugged his shoulders. 'Of course not, Mom. I feel real bad about it, but that's just the way the story turned out. You're still the greatest mom, even if you had to die.'

The following year, on Mother's Day, Quentin wrote an even more superbly constructed essay; and guess who had to die in the final sentence...

Throughout his childhood, Quentin had an aversion to being in school photos. He would somehow go missing on the day that such pictures were scheduled and Connie does not have a single school photo of her son.

By all accounts he did not enjoy most aspects of his education. However, life at home in those early years after his mother married Curt Zastoupil, was very different and Quentin was delighted to have his picture taken with grown-ups. When posing with other children, he seemed only mildly interested in them. But when posing in a shot with adults, he literally came alive.

Quentin developed an obsession with passport photo booths and was forever nagging Connie to let him have his picture taken with uncle Roger or father Curt. A whole series of photos taken over a period of a couple of years show a happy, confident Quentin – very different from the diffident, solitary child he was at school.

These photo booth pictures show Quentin relaxed and clearly hamming it up for the camera. He was intrigued by the fact that a machine, rather than his own mother, was taking the photos.

Connie didn't like the pictures because her son's hair looked so terrible. Quentin actually cut his own hair from the age of five. On the first few occasions, Connie tried to convince her son to go to a barber's shop. But in the end she gave up. She just wasn't prepared to stifle a free spirit.

'I want to be alone'

Greta Garbo, in *Grand Hotel*, 1932

Problem Child

TARZANA 6 MOVIE THEATRE, HARBOR CITY,
SUMMER 1971

Q uentin's movie consumption as a small child continued to be rather unusual. By the age of eight he had developed a liking for grisly horror flicks. He adored *Frankenstein Meets the Wolf Man*, which was shown regularly at the one-dollar Saturday morning matinées and starred Lon Chaney Junior and Bela Lugosi (as the monster).

Quentin liked it even better when his horror heroes appeared with madcap comics in mixed genre movies. Years later, he reflected on his early taste in typically Tarantino terms. 'My first understanding of genre distinction in films came when I got real attached to *Abbott and Costello Meet Frankenstein*. I loved that movie,' he explains. 'It's not like the way they do comedy films now. The fact is that the monster in that movie actually killed people.'

One particular scene, when the monster picked up an innocent nurse and killed her by throwing her out of the window, has stayed with Quentin his entire life. Seconds earlier he had been laughing helplessly at the antics of Abbott and Costello, then suddenly a murder was committed.

'I remember thinking *wow*, because the scary parts are scary and the funny parts are really funny,' he recalls.

Meanwhile Connie's appetite for superhero comics was still outstripping her young son's. She had grown particularly fond of the *X-Men* and. as Quentin grew up, their love of comics formed a useful bond between mother and son. They would spend hours discussing the relative virtues of the superheroes.

Connie often found herself playing with Quentin's toys rather than clearing them up in the evenings. Her son was contributing to her life in every way. She was still very much the child mother.

When Quentin was seven or eight years old, Connie regularly took him to nearby Disneyland and Knottsberry Farm for days out. But the solitary child would wander amongst the crowds, not particularly interested in any of the rides, apart from Disneyland's Pirates of the Caribbean and Captain Nemo's Submarines. These fantasy rides appealed more to the young Quentin than roller coasters or river rapids.

The first time Connie took her young son on the Pirates, he seemed mesmerized from the moment they got into the tiny boat and it skimmed over the first steep waterfall down into the murky depths. Throughout the ten-minute pitch black ride, Quentin did not utter a word but when they emerged back into the glaring sunlight at the end Connie noticed that the little boy had wet himself with fear. 'But he loved it and pleaded with me to take him back on it almost immediately,' recalls Connie.

However, after a few more trips to the theme parks, Quentin abruptly asked Connie to stop taking him. He told her he was more interested in seeing the latest movies and eating fast food at the nearest McDonald's or, if Connie felt like splashing out, at Denny's.

This was a little odd but Connie was more concerned by Quentin's performance at school. He showed little or no enthusiasm in the classroom. and he was extremely hyperactive. He was always rushing around waving his arms and shouting in class. Some of his teachers recognized this as a sign of superior intelligence, whilst others just found him tedious to deal with. These teachers tended to give up on him very quickly because he did not conform to the normal standards of behaviour.

Today, Connie explains this hyperactivity by saying, 'We are both pacers who tangle up the cords when we are on the phone. I was very hyper as a child and so was Quentin.'

But there were some very worrying reactions to Quentin's hyperactivity at school. At first, his teachers questioned Connie closely about her son's home life because they were convinced that something was happening there to make him behave so strangely. Once they were satisfied that this was not the case, Connie was advised at that time to get a doctor to put her son on a course of tranquillizers to 'calm him down', as some believed he was about to reach some kind of mental boiling point.

'I refused point blank. How dare they suggest doping Quentin just because he was too damn intelligent for them to handle,' is how Connie remembers her response.

At around this time, Quentin even took an IQ test and scored an exceptionally high mark of 160. The school examiners insisted that he take the test again because they could not believe the result. He scored another 160.

Quentin had major problems at school as he would not put any effort into anything he wasn't totally interested in. His spelling was appalling because he could not see why it was important. As long as the words were down on the page as they sounded, that was all that mattered.

However one subject he excelled at was history. For, besides taking him to see explicit adult movies, Connie had also made Quentin see a lot of historical dramas, like *Nicholas and Alexandra*, and the young boy was able to use that knowledge in school. Quentin had an extraordinary appetite for any movie that contained a good story. So he was getting A grades in history and reading and failing miserably at everything else.

Connie frequently, though unintentionally, encouraged her young son's independence. She would often come home and announce to the young Quentin that she needed to be alone and would he please go to a separate part of the house so she could enjoy some solitude.

'I don't want to be bothered tonight, Quentin,' was about all she would say and that would be a signal for him to disappear to his room where he would soak up the adventures of one of his superheroes, or perhaps direct a mock battle between G.I. Joe and Spiderman.

Because he spent so much time in a fantasy world, Quentin began creating new identities for himself. His own surname had already changed from Tarantino to Zastoupil at Connie's insistence. Now he would announce to Connie that he wanted to be known for the following week by a completely different name. It seemed to help him escape from reality. New identities meant new adventures and a chance to recreate the past.

Quentin's favourite new name was Quint Jerome. 'Forget the Zastoupil bit,' he insisted. He was forever asking Connie if she thought it was a cool name. She did.

On other occasions, Quentin would imagine himself to be one of the characters in his favourite TV cartoon show at the time, *Clutch Cargo*.

Quentin became particularly wrapped up in certain TV shows because, unlike children from larger families, he had no distractions. He would sit up close to the small screen for hours on end, losing himself in whatever he was watching. Sometimes he wished he could climb inside that TV set and join his favourite characters.

Twenty-five years later, Quentin perfectly reconstructed this scene in *Pulp Fiction*. The sequence opens with boxer Butch, aged five, sitting up close to the television in a world of his own watching *Clutch Cargo* cartoons. *That was Quentin.*

At this time, Curt – with his cool goatee beard – and his brother Cliff tended to pick Quentin up from school as Connie had started working hard as a health industry executive.

Quentin's schoolfriend Joe Carabello recalls, 'Curt and his brother looked kinda interesting with long hair and dressed in hipster jeans, T-shirts and vests.'

Curt was most definitely a vest-and-ruffled-shirt-kind-of-guy and he drove a very cool Volkswagen Karmen Ghia coupe with a tiny backseat area where Quentin would crouch after being picked up from school.

Quentin even emulated his trendy stepfather by insisting on wearing rugged biker boots to school. The little boy would noticeably change character the moment he got in the back of Curt's car. Joe recalled one occasion when they shot right past him as he walked along the sidewalk. Quentin either didn't see or didn't acknowledge his friend. He was too busy acting like a cool dude.

The young Quentin rarely invited any of his schoolfriends back to his house. He did not explain why. Some of his classmates later theorized that he was in some way ashamed of his oddball home, whilst others reckoned he simply did not wish to have any other children on his territory.

Occasionally, on her days off, Connie would be seen at the school collecting Quentin. Former pupils only recall one thing about her – her long black hair. 'It was almost down to her butt,' remarks Joe Carabello.

Movies were all Quentin talked about. Father Curt contributed to his film education by taking young Quint to a cinema every Monday evening. It didn't matter what was on. Quentin demanded to be taken each week, like clockwork.

Curt liked the classic Californian biker movies of the late sixties that starred renegades like Jack Nicholson and Peter Fonda, so Quentin's tastes started to broaden out.

One of his particular favourites was the 1968 film *The Savage Seven*, directed by Richard Rush and starring Adam Roarke and Larry Bishop. The young Quentin was so intrigued by this movie that he has watched it at least a dozen times since.

More than twenty years later he explained 'What's cool about it is that you can't figure out what or who the bad guys are. The Adam Roarke character is good in one scene, bad in another. It makes him complex.'

Schoolfriend Joe Carabello remembers being shocked that Quentin was allowed to see movies that most other kids' parents deemed highly unsuitable. 'We all thought he was a lucky son of a gun because we wouldn't have dared even ask our folks to let us see such movies.'

Quentin's young friends at the time were particularly envious of him when he told them with great relish that he had been allowed to watch *Death Wish*, starring Charles Bronson. But they were all a little confused because here was a kid who didn't even learn how to ride a bicycle until the fifth grade.

Not surprisingly, Quentin decided he wanted to try his hand at creating his own films. He soon got Joe Carabello, plus two other friends called Dave Strom and Mike Gallo, to make some home movies together using an old camera that belonged to one of the other boy's fathers.

'They were about goofy things like annoying people's sisters,' explained Joe Carabello. Although he didn't have any brothers or sisters of his own, Quentin was clearly fascinated by other people's families. He always made sure he starred in and directed each of the movies they made.

When Quentin was nine years old, his life was turned upside down by two traumatic events.

First of all, Curt and Connie split up following six seemingly happy years together soon after the family had moved to a rented house in the South Bay beachside community of El Segunda. Quentin never got a full explanation of what went wrong between the couple and Connie is not prepared to discuss the details to this day.

The youngster just came home from school one afternoon to find that his father had left the house. Connie didn't want to talk about it and Quentin didn't want to ask. They both retreated into separate corners of the house and buried themselves in their favourite fantasy worlds of television and comic books.

Connie explains, 'Curt and I just went off in different directions. I was very career-orientated at the time and I just did not want to be married any more.'

After their divorce, Curt – who had been the nearest thing Quentin ever had to a father – moved up to an isolated farming community in northern California and rarely visited the South Bay area. 'Curt remarried and his new wife did not want any reminders of me and Quentin around,' adds Connie, who gradually got back on speaking terms with Curt and is still in contact with him. She even refers to Curt's new partner as her 'wife-in-law'.

Within a few months of Connie's marriage break-up, she started suffering from appalling stomach pains and sought medical advice. The diagnosis was grim. Doctors said they suspected Hodgkin's disease and warned Connie she might only have a few months to live.

Connie was understandably panicked. She was told to get her life in order and prepare for the worst. A long and painful course of treatment was recommended. The doctors warned that the after-effects would be very debilitating and it might prove very difficult to look after her young son.

Connie was especially worried because she had nowhere for her child to go. In desperation, she contacted her mother, back in Tennessee. (A number of relatives had already assured Connie that her mother was no longer boozing at the same rate as she had been a few years previously.)

Reluctantly, but with nowhere else to turn, Connie sent Quentin to her mother. 'I wasn't real thrilled about it, but it seemed as if I was about to die so you do what you have to do,' is how Connie explains it today.

She decided not to tell her son what was happening. Quentin just thought he was going on an extended vacation to his grandmother's mobile home in hicksville.

But that five-month stay was to be the most disturbing period in Quentin's entire childhood. Connie's mother was off the booze when the young boy showed up alone at Nashville Airport, but she was hiding a multitude of other problems: she was in severe debt; ex-boyfriends were still circling the trailer park with alarming regularity and her previous involvement in the manufacture of illicit home brew had exposed her to just about every lowlife character in Knox County.

Quentin's stay at the flea pit trailer that Connie's mother called home soon degenerated into something that would haunt him for the rest of his life. He was a sharp observer, even at that young age, and it struck him that his grandmother was living the sort of life he had presumed only existed in cops and robbers TV shows. One of his favourites, *Dukes of Hazzard* was based on life in a hick town just like the one he was living in with his grandma.

More than twenty years later, Quentin made a guest appearance on the *Tonight* TV show, hosted by Jay Leno, in Los Angeles, and referred to how his granny regularly beat him up. The issue only came up because Quentin found himself sitting next to another Tennessee resident, country music star Naomi Judd. She was trying to be nostalgic about her old home state, but Quentin did not exactly share her sentiments.

In fact, Quentin's grandmother started drinking with a vengeance shortly after he showed up, and he spent much of his time sitting in her rusty truck while she hopped around liquor stores in eastern Tennessee. To start with, he would get a swift right hander whenever he complained about the endless hours he spent in her clapped-out automobile.

But, as the weeks turned into months and Quentin's grandmother's consumption of alcohol escalated, so did her violence towards her grandson. Soon she began using a switch on him. Quentin was confused, lonely and very scared. He could not understand why his mother had left him with his awful grandmother for so long. What had he done to deserve this?

Back in California, Connie was too preoccupied with her apparent death sentence to realize what was happening in Tennessee. Whenever she managed to speak to Quentin on the phone he sounded OK. Quentin never actually picked up on the fact that there was something wrong with his mother, but for some reason he did not tell Connie about his grandmother's behaviour.

One of the few happy times that Quentin had during that nightmare stay was when his great-grandmother – deeply concerned by her daughter's drinking – took him off her hands for a few days. Quentin's great-grandmother was a full-blooded, golden-hearted Irish lady. His few days with her were filled with good memories, including his first experience of falling in love – with beautiful movie star Claudia Cardinale.

'We went to see this John Wayne movie called *Circus World*. There's a scene where she's smooching with some guy in the hay. I actually remember thinking, I wish that was me,' he recalls. The movies often provided his only escape from that strange environment.

Five months after the original diagnosis, Connie demanded that her doctor have her blood samples re-examined by a specialist in another part of the country. When the results came back, doctors told her it had all been a false alarm. She was not suffering from Hodgkin's disease.

Quentin was understandably relieved when he heard he was going back to California. If he had stayed much longer with his grandmother he would probably have suffered further harm.

When Connie later found out what had happened in Tennessee she swore never to speak to her mother again and has not uttered a word to her since.

'A boy's best friend is his mother'

Anthony Perkins, *Psycho*, 1960

To Protect and Serve . . .

TORRANCE, SOUTH BAY, CALIFORNIA,
SUMMER 1973

To a certain extent, the story of Torrance's post World War Two boom is the story of America during that period. Soldiers returned from Europe and Asia and settled down in suburban houses with lawns to tend and cars, appliances and furniture to buy. Then came exciting new devices called televisions; and three children – and a dog – to raise.

But away from the suburbs, in the built up districts of the South Bay, blacks, Mexicans and white trash thrived in low rent, mixed race areas. The area had more than its fair share of the infamous Southern California bike gangs, and out by the ocean was a nether world of massive oil refineries belching flames and smoke into a sooty sky. Yet just along the coastline were some of the world's finest beaches. It was full of contradictions.

When Connie arrived in one of Torrance's better neighbourhoods she had the dog, but only one child and little besides a television. Neighbours were initially inquisitive, but soon dismissive. Some were even horrified when they realized that Connie was not living with her son's father.

Quentin had just arrived back in the Los Angeles area from Tennessee, only vaguely hinting at the horrors he had suffered at the hands of his grandmother. Probably out of concern for his mother, with her health and divorce problems, he did not make a fuss. But then disaster struck when his beloved dog Baron died after being hit by a car.

Quentin was more than just heartbroken, he was devastated. Baron had become his friend, brother and pet all rolled into one. He cried for days afterwards. Connie tried to console him and hoped that he would eventually get over it, but little Quentin just couldn't understand why Baron had abandoned him for ever.

Apart from Baron, the only other consistent character in his life was G.I. Joe. Quentin began inventing more and more sophisticated scenarios for his small army. Having seen new movies that caught his imagination, his ambition was still firm – he wanted to be an actor and he was honing his skills through those dolls.

Not long afterwards, Connie bought Quentin an Old English Sheepdog which was immediately christened Condé Azul (Spanish for 'Count Blue', according to Connie).

The name was dreamt up by Connie's latest boyfriend, 'a dishy Guatemalan'. While Quentin was delighted with the dog, he made it absolutely clear that Condé Azul could never be considered a replacement for Baron.

Condé's appearance on the scene and Connie's return to good health coincided with a marked improvement in the family's living standards. Connie was rising fast through the managerial ranks of the healthcare company and her salary was going up in leaps and bounds.

Meanwhile, Quentin's growing obsession with movies led him to try his hand at writing scripts as early as the sixth grade. One particularly moving piece was constructed specifically as a tribute to the only girl of his age that he was remotely interested in – child actress Tatum O'Neal.

Quentin got quite emotional when watching Tatum's Oscar-winning performance in *Paper Moon* co-starring her real father, Ryan.

In his locker at school, he had press photos of the young actress covering every inch of the inside of the door. Connie noticed that each time he caught a glimpse of her on television, he would go weak at the knees. It took months, and a lot of ribbing from his classmates, before he accepted that he would never actually get to meet Tatum, let alone go on a date with her. After this, he rapidly retreated into his role as school geek.

Quentin never once formed an equivalent attachment to any of the girls at school. He had hidden his true emotions by doting on Tatum because he knew he could not possibly get near her in real life. Like Connie, he had already discovered that it was much easier to form attachments to celluloid fantasy figures.

Connie's decision to splash out on a sumptuous split level rented house in the Palo del Amo Woods area of Torrance certainly improved the standard of life for both mother and son. It was a palace compared to what they had been used to. Besides a huge den, where Quentin could indulge his superhero fantasies, there was a vast living room, with an incredibly kitsch rock fireplace and a large kitchen and dining area. But best of all, there was a ten foot deep swimming pool complete with diving board. The only problem was that Quentin couldn't swim. A few weeks of private tuition followed and he finally got the hang of it – just.

But thanks to that pool, Quentin went from being the nerd nobody wanted to know to one of the most popular kids in class. Most afternoons after school, at least three or four of his new best friends would herd into the pool. Condé Azul would go crazy every time the kids dived under the water for fear that they would drown.

When temperatures topped the nineties, Connie had the dog's shaggy coat shaved off to make him more comfortable.

'But the result was that he looked a kinda weird dog,' she explains. 'His face was still hairy but the rest of him looked like a greyhound.'

Quentin's mother was also surprised to discover the dog's sensitive nature. 'I sat by the side of the pool as Quentin and his friends jumped in and just couldn't stop laughing at Condé Azul. He looked ridiculous. Suddenly I looked at his face and realized he was mortified. Quentin later told me off about that. "Dogs have feelings too, Mom," he told me.'

With Quentin's new-found popularity came a fresh awareness of race and class. He was now twelve years old. He would often bring back a mixed group of friends and he knew that some of his classmates had less money than others.

Later criticism of his attitude towards blacks in his movies brought this response from Connie: 'Quentin understands racial minorities more than anyone else in Hollywood. He films it as he sees it and he saw it all while growing up.'

But one aspect of life that Quentin could never come to terms with was sport. He was too awkward and gangly to be good at most school sports and, although he had started swimming regularly, he tended to flop and splash all over the place.

Connie even bought season tickets for the LA Lakers basketball games and the Rams football games in a last ditch attempt to get her son more interested in such activities. But Quentin refused point blank to attend any of the games. Instead, he tried to persuade his mother to give him the cost of a ticket so he could buy himself a hamburger or hot dog and then go to a movie theatre.

Connie often ended up taking her son's friends to the Lakers and Rams games simply because she couldn't bear to see such valuable seats going to waste.

Quentin insisted that sport was stupid, boring and brutal. His own theory was that nobody really liked sport. He actually believed that men felt they should adore sport, so they pretended to do so.

Quentin was equally dismissive about some of his mother's friends who were forever holding forth about how marvellous The Who rock group were.

'I don't think anyone really likes that band,' he later recalled. 'Everyone thinks they are supposed to like The Who, so they just pretend. They're afraid to say the emperor has no clothes.'

When Quentin reached his early teens, the by now relatively wealthy and successful Connie decided it was time to travel and see something of the world. Unfortunately she never encouraged her young son to accompany her. Today, Connie insists she had no idea that Quentin was even remotely interested in travelling with her. 'I would have taken him all over the world with me if I had known.'

Instead, schoolboy Quentin Zastoupil was left alone at the family home in Torrance with a housekeeper, as Connie tried to forget her two disastrous marriages by escaping to exotic places.

While she was away, Quentin would slip out to a nearby movie theatre and watch the latest releases. He actually preferred going on his own because there were fewer distractions and he could really concentrate, memorizing the lines and even the credits at the end of each film.

Quentin spent a lot of time in the rougher neighbourhood of Carson where the Carson Twin Cinema showed kung fu movies as well as Allied International low budget specials like *The Van*, one of the first films ever made by Danny De Vito. Quentin also liked sneaking out to see naughty late-night Roger Corman double bills like *The Student Teachers* and *Night Call Nurses*.

At other times he went to the Del Amo Mall Theatre to see the latest Hollywood blockbusters. When he was thirteen he fell in love with the horror classic *Carrie*, directed by Brian de Palma (who later became his directorial hero) and starring John Travolta. A few days after seeing it for the second time in a week, he walked into a Miller's Outpost with Connie and spotted a redneck puffy vest and a red flannel shirt just like the one worn by Travolta in the movie. Connie reluctantly bought her son the outfit and he wore it for weeks afterwards.

Quentin's childhood centred around going to those grind houses and the art houses and he loved them both equally. The less commercial movies showed him a world he had never experienced and that he was anxious to learn about, while the Hollywood films proved just how brilliant some blockbusters could be.

Quentin began to list all the movies he had seen, although he would only count the ones he'd watched in a movie theatre, rather than on television. He'd circle the ones he thought were good and eventually built up the list to more than 200.

Meanwhile, between long hours at work and regular trips abroad, Connie finally found time to tell her son about the birds and bees.

Years later, she explains her actions in intriguingly businesslike terms, 'I have been in management since my early twenties and I don't have any trouble coping with such issues. I was determined that there should be some measure of control. I was genuinely worried about what effect being a single mother would have on a child in such matters.'

So, one day after school, Connie announced that she had something very important to tell Quentin and would he please join her in the living room. Quentin was mystified. He wondered what on earth he had done wrong this time. He had also got used to running his own life and couldn't quite cope with the prospect of actually sitting down with his mother and talking to her.

'It's time we had a talk,' muttered Connie.

That was all Quentin needed to hear to know exactly what was coming next. He had been to enough movies to recognize that classic line. He tried to move out of his chair. But Connie would not let him get up.

Five minutes later, Quentin was allowed to leave the room after he had heard his mother describe male and female anatomy in such direct terms that it threatened to put him off sex for life.

In fact Quentin already knew all about sex from some of the racier movies he had seen. However, hearing his mother explain it in such graphic detail was enough to dampen his interest for many years to come. At that time, his only love affair was with the cinema and it was proving a time-consuming and expensive mistress.

Then, out of the blue, Quentin found religion – thanks to his best friend at the time, Kevin Minky. The two boys met at the Hawthorne Christian School on the borders between Torrance and Harbor City. Connie, a strictly non-practising Catholic, had sent twelve-year-old Quentin to this private school in preference to the local junior high school where drugs and crime were prevalent, even in a suburban community such as Torrance.

Young Kevin proved a very significant influence on Quentin and the two boys began attending a local Protestant church every Sunday. Connie felt she could not stop Quentin since he was so firm in his own opinions and beliefs. She also tended to go through bouts of guilt about her efforts as a single parent. Quentin was entitled to experiment with different aspects of his life. Why shouldn't that include going to church, which was hardly in the same league as drinking or taking drugs.

Quentin became hooked on God after spending hours discussing the church with his friend Kevin, who lived in nearby Palos Verdes. He was intrigued by religion because it was something that had never really been tackled throughout his childhood. Quentin believed he had missed out badly and he began to theorize about God, almost as much as the movies.

For the next two years, Quentin became an avid churchgoer, even though his mother would never go near a house of God. Quentin was undoubtedly intrigued by the mystical elements of religion and he felt much more secure now that he had discovered God. Christianity was a substitute for certain basic ingredients missing from his home life. At this stage, the church seemed much more real than television or films. However, he eventually started to question the wisdom of God's words and became less interested in it all in his mid-teens.

Quentin left the Hawthorne Christian School when he was fourteen, having nagged Connie to let him go to the local high school because he was intrigued by the multicultural American free school system. Connie, despite her wide racial mix of friends, was anxious. She didn't mind him knocking around with kids from all sorts of backgrounds, just as long as she knew precisely who they were.

In the end, they both compromised and Quentin attended a more middle-of-the-road state supported school called the Norbonne, on the edge of Torrance. He had difficulties from the beginning and soon started playing truant, often watching films at the two-dollar afternoon matinée performances at local movie theatres. Connie, frequently preoccupied by her high powered job, was often the last person to realize her son was skipping classes.

When she did eventually find out, she was furious, but concluded that Quentin just wasn't cut out for school. Connie decided to deal with the situation before he got himself into big trouble wandering the streets of Torrance. She preferred him to get a job rather than continue to play truant. So Quentin quit school before he had completed the tenth grade. He had, in effect, dropped out at just fifteen years of age.

By this time, Quentin was well over six feet tall and extremely mature for his age. He had taught himself how to survive on the mean streets of Los Angeles, and the few friends he had tended to be a couple of years older. He had even developed a taste for beer, but could barely afford the bus ride to meet his pals, let alone a round of drinks in one of their favourite dives.

Quentin started to get reckless. There were lots of things he wanted but couldn't afford. He had read every book and comic in his room at least twice and he felt increasingly bitter about his lack of income. Connie still paid him an allowance, but she made it crystal clear that she would not support him for much longer.

So, one day when he was out browsing in a local K-Mart near the family home in Torrance, he found himself tempted into committing a crime. The Elmore Leonard novel *The Switch* caught his eye. It was the writer's latest work and Quentin – a keen fan since the age of twelve – could not resist the urge to take it. He snatched the brightly coloured paperback and stuffed it into his jacket pocket.

But, unlike the heroes of his films fifteen years later, Quentin did not get very far. A store detective collared him just as he stepped outside into the bright Californian sunshine.

Thirty minutes later, a black and white Torrance City police cruiser – motto 'To Protect and Serve' – rolled up outside Connie's house. Neighbours peeked from behind their drapes as the gangly youth was escorted to the front door in handcuffs.

Quentin developed an early obsession with photo booths and demanded to have his picture taken at every opportunity.

Left from top: Aged two and a half, with Uncle Cliff.
Aged three with Uncle Roger.
Aged five, with stepfather Curt.

Below: Aged five with Connie.
From the age of five, Quentin decided to cut his own hair.
(All courtesy of Connie Zastoupil)

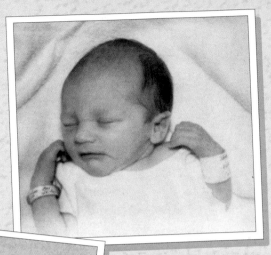

Above: Just a few hours old and spot that famous chin. (Courtesy of Connie Zastoupil)

Left: Behind bars at twelve months old. (Courtesy of Connie Zastoupil)

Above: Quint with Connie and Curt just after their marriage in 1966. (Courtesy of Connie Zastoupil)

Left: Christmas, aged two and three-quarters. (Courtesy of Connie Zastoupil)

Right: Butter wouldn't melt ... May 1967, aged four. (Courtesy of Connie Zastoupil)

Below: All I want for Christmas is a GI Joe. (Courtesy of Connie Zastoupil)

Left: Aged six, in his first *Reservoir Dogs* suit. The shades came later. (Courtesy of Connie Zastoupil)

Above: Aged eight with Curt, who legally adopted Quentin and was the only father he ever knew. (Courtesy of Connie Zastoupil)

Right: With his first best friend, Todd, in Alhambra, California, aged six.

Above: Quentin preferred the company of adults even at the age of eight. Seen here with cousin Sherry, Uncle Laurence, Connie and Curtis.

Right: Quentin's seven-year-old cousin Michael was one of the few children Quentin did play with.

Right: Natural Born Killer : Quentin in his GI Joe uniform with *(left to right)* Uncle Cliff, Connie and Curt.
(All Courtesy of Connie Zastoupil)

Right: More like brother and sister – aged thirteen, with Connie, then only twenty-nine. (Courtesy of Connie Zastoupil)

Below: Condé Azul was Quentin's second favourite dog, after the death of his beloved Baron. (Courtesy of Connie Zastoupil)

Quent & Connie ugh! (Quentin...

Right: Aged fifteen, with Connie's friend, Lilian, and Condé Azul. (Courtesy of Connie Zastoupil)

Below: Quentin and Connie at her third disastrous wedding. (Courtesy of Connie Zastoupil)

Most Unique Home In Palo del Amo Woods

Above and right: **On the up and up. This impressive house with a pool in the South Bay area of LA turned Quentin into one of the most popular kids in his class.**

Above: **Mom and son – kids together.**

Right: **Connie's image today – redhead and go-ahead!**
(All Courtesy of Connie Zastoupil)

The chameleon in his teens: cool, supercool, intellectual, laid-back.
(Courtesy of Connie Zastoupil)

Quentin Tarantino

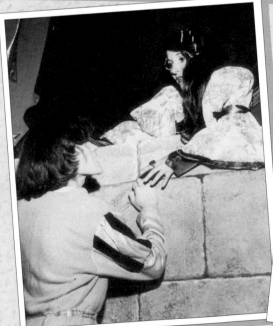

Connie was infuriated because she had always been incredibly generous about allowing Quentin any books and records he wanted. And she was doubly annoyed when she found a five-dollar bill in his room that he could have used to buy the book.

To Quentin it was just one of those things... 'I think I'll do it. I'm here and I want to do it. I don't have the money on me so I'll just take it.'

The police officers were very understanding and informed Connie that her son had been so nervous after his arrest that he had burst into tears, and they'd decided to give him a warning rather than charge him. The policemen were concerned when they heard there was no father at home, but as soon as they met Connie they decided she more than made up for the missing parent.

Connie was so angry she grounded Quentin for the entire summer of 1979. She would only allow him out for specific activities, like attending the Torrance Community Theatre Workshop he had only just enrolled in. He also said he had been offered a part-time job as an usher at a local theatre. Connie was relieved. Quentin's arrest seemed to have shaken some sense into him.

At the workshop, Quentin got one of the lead roles in the progressive play, *Two and Two Makes Sex*. No one actually realized that he was only fifteen at the time. Quentin played the husband in a twenties couple who swapped partners with a couple in their forties. Connie attended the first night and was impressed by her son's performance. 'He was very believable as an actor and I forgot he was my son within minutes of seeing him up there on the stage,' she explains.

There was also the obligatory interpretation of *Romeo and Juliet* during which Quentin made a less than comfortable attempt at the male lead role.

At this point, Quentin went to the trouble of renaming himself Quentin Tarantino after his teacher at the Torrance Community Theatre Workshop said it sounded 'really cool'. Quentin told Connie that he did it because he was seriously planning a career as an actor. His mother was just pleased that he wasn't getting into any more trouble. As far as she was concerned, Quentin could call himself Jack the Ripper as long as he kept himself on the straight and narrow.

As Quentin later wrote, in a *Pulp Fiction* scene between boxer Butch and the dishy Columbian cabbie Esmarelda, who helps him flee from a fixed fight, 'In America, honey, names don't mean shit.'

'Crime is only a left-handed form of human endeavour'

Louis Calhern in *The Asphalt Jungle*, 1950

The Good, the Bad and the Ugly

THE PUSSYCAT PORNO THEATRE, TORRANCE, SUMMER 1979

Looking considerably older than his sixteen years, Quentin had managed to land a job as an usher in Torrance's only surviving theatre, which had been converted into a porno palace. Surrounded by the cinema's motley patrons, Quentin's already dampened interest in sex now took a complete tumble when he became exposed to non-stop celluloid orgies.

Back home, Connie had absolutely no idea that her son was working in such an establishment until she found a book of matches on the kitchen counter.

'Where's this come from, Quint? The Pussycat Theatre?'

'That's my job, Mom. I told you I work at a theatre.'

Connie was flabbergasted by his matter-of-fact tone. It was as if Quentin was saying, 'It's only a place of work. No way am I interested in all that seedy stuff.'

Quentin later insisted to his mother that the sight of all that celluloid flesh put him off porn for life, but at least it was a regular kind of job which involved working normal hours.

In a strange way, Connie completely understood what her son meant. And she was relieved that he was no longer wandering the streets penniless and being tempted to break any more laws.

Working in the Pussycat Porno Theatre was tough on Quentin because it challenged his ability to cut himself off from the degrading movies on show, as well as the theatre's extremely sleazy and aggressive clientele.

Most customers presumed Quentin was older than he was and treated him accordingly. Fights would regularly break out in the auditorium and Quentin was expected to sort out every disturbance. At six feet two inches, the management saw him as a big guy who knew how to look after himself. But Quentin was not exactly fit. He regularly drank beer, adored eating vast quantities of fast food, and had grown quite a belly in the process.

Connie was actually more worried about what her son was getting up to when he wasn't at work. She knew he was a self-sufficient kid, but she worried about who he was hanging out with and whether he was involved with drugs.

Quentin would regularly brush off his mother's concern, telling her not to worry. But his demeanour was becoming increasingly laid back and that bothered Connie enormously. She had been told that kids with drugs problems were lethargic and sleepy. While Quentin was still able to transfix anyone with a dose of hyperactive machine gun conversation, the rest of the time he certainly seemed to be living in another world. He did not even wear a watch, even though he had finally bothered to learn how to tell the time when he was in fifth grade at school. And he was always oversleeping.

Connie tried to guard against any possible involvement with drugs by keeping Quentin to a fairly strict schedule. She knew there was more temptation during the evening hours so she made Quentin stick to a tight curfew.

Today, Connie believes that Quentin was a pretty good kid and not really the rebel with a cause he has been painted as since finding fame.

All the same, Connie did occasionally go through her teenage son's room just to make sure he was not hiding any alcohol or illegal substances. One time, Quentin arrived home early from his job at the porno theatre to find her searching his drawers. A classic Californian parent-child conversation followed:

'I cannot believe you are doing this, Mom. You are invading my privacy.'

'I know, Quint, and I feel terrible about it. It violates all the principles I have about privacy, but you are a minor and I have to know what is going on. I know I am breaching my own rules, but that is the way it is,' came Connie's guilt-riddled reply.

'What are you looking for, anyhow?'

'I'm just looking.'

'What makes you think that if I did have anything I would have it here?'

'Well, if you lose control then you would not have the control not to have it here. It is my responsibility to make sure you never get to the position where you lose control,' replied Connie, verging on the psychobabble.

In Connie's view, she was carrying out controlled parenting. To Quentin, it was a brazen attempt to remove what little privacy he retained living at home. He decided there and then that he would split and find himself an apartment sooner rather than later. He needed some space.

If Connie had looked more closely as she searched his room she would have noticed a scrappy collection of notes hung together by a paper clip. It was Quentin's first proper attempt to write a screenplay and was entitled, *Captain Peachfuzz and the Anchovy Bandit*. Quentin had been carefully working on the project away from the watchful eyes of his few friends. He had spent hours alone in his room trying to create a workable script. It was to be the first of many fruitless attempts over the following twelve years.

Connie admits, 'To this day, I still don't know what he really did in that room.'

Quentin also had a television in his room which encouraged him to hibernate even further. Sometimes – on his days off from the Pussycat Theatre – he would stay in there for days on end, zapping the remote controls until he found something that caught his interest.

One day he was flicking through one of the hundreds of movie magazines he collected when he noticed a small advertisement for the James Best Acting School, in Toluca Lake. The ad caught his eye because Best played the long-suffering Sheriff Roscoe Tanner in the TV series, *Dukes of Hazzard*, the show that reminded Quentin of his five-month stay with his grandmother in Tennessee.

Quentin was particularly interested in the school because it was offering three classes a week for the low price of seventy-five dollars a month. The only problem was that Toluca Lake was about thirty miles away and Quentin's weekly salary of seventy dollars would hardly cover his bus fares, once he had paid his fees and other living expenses.

But Quentin still decided to give it a shot. He was convinced that the James Best Acting School might provide a leg up in the acting world. He reckoned if he got off work by 5.30pm on Mondays, Tuesdays and Thursdays he could just about make it in time for the 7pm classes.

Quentin had already outgrown the Torrance Community Theatre Workshop, which he found to be filled with amateurs whose only interest in acting was appearing in local shows and discussing the merits of Olivier's performance in *Hamlet*. The James Best Acting School was far more professional, and run by one of his heroes.

Quentin found himself being taught by actor Jack Lucarelli. The school itself turned out to be a room above a honey-baked ham store on busy Riverside Drive, Toluca Lake, close to the Ventura Freeway in the baking hot San Fernando Valley.

Quentin found the lessons very fulfilling because he was anxious to learn. The school specialised in training would-be actors how to deal with the camera. Lucarelli's lectures were based on the premise that most actors in Hollywood would be doing bit parts in TV series. Quentin was so happy to be amongst real actors that he threw himself into every practical exercise with great enthusiasm.

Fellow student Rich Turner became one of Quentin's first friends at the school because he lived in the South Bay area near Quentin's home in Torrance. He often used to give the teenager rides home after class and had no idea that Quentin was just sixteen at the time. Everyone in the class presumed he was about nineteen or twenty. But Turner did find it a little strange that on the way home, Quentin would always insist on being dropped by an exit off the busy 405 freeway, rather than outside his actual house.

'He'd just disappear down the side of the freeway. It was weird but it was his business, I guess,' recalls Rich Turner. 'I never once got to see his house.'

The James Best Acting School encouraged students to write their own mini-plays to be performed in front of the entire class. Quentin would often appear with his own scripts written on at least three different types of paper in terrible handwriting. The other actors would have difficulty deciphering them. But when he got up and acted out his own screenplays they were well above average for the class.

Quietly spoken Rich Turner and young Quentin soon began to hang out together in the South Bay area where they were neighbours. Often at weekends they would go and see a movie and afterwards enjoy a burger and talk endlessly about music. Quentin was Turner's only buddy who was into rockabilly and they spent hours discussing their favourite artistes. Turner even turned Quentin on to surf music king Dick Dale, as well as Robert Gordon.

Dale provided Californians with early sixties music to drive to, that included 'Let's go Trippin', 'Surf Beat' and 'The Victor'. Playing his

prototype Fender Stratocaster left-handed, Dale's bass-heavy twanging
and reverberated speed spawned a host of imitators from the Beach Boys
to just about every speed-punk band since the Ramones.

The two also shared a particular passion for Buster Keaton movies
(although they were such movie buffs they would go and see anything at
the local movie theatres just so long as it looked vaguely interesting).

In Toluca Lake, Turner, Quentin and some of the other James Best
Acting school students would gather at the River Bottom Inn, just across
the street from the James Best Acting School, drink beers and eat the free
taco chips that were on offer. 'That saved any of us from having to pay
for a meal,' explains Turner.

Quentin frequently got embroiled in colourful arguments with
Turner and others about movies. His obsession at that time was the
recently released *Blow Out* with John Travolta, helmed by one of directorial heroes, Brian de Palma. No one else even remotely rated the movie,
but Quentin described it as a masterpiece.

Often, at the River Bottom Inn, Quentin ran out of cash and would
switch to iced water because he simply enjoyed hanging out with other
actors. Despite his youth, Quentin was far from shy. When he wasn't
defending the sex scenes in *Blow Out* he would be busy insisting that
Elvis was the king. (This passion had been passed down from his mother
Connie, who had filled their home with all sorts of Elvis memorabilia
over the years).

Rich Turner tried to turn Quentin on to Eddie Cochran but Elvis
always won out in the end. Quentin confessed to his fellow actors that he
had posters of Elvis hanging in his bedroom back home in Torrance, as
well as a particularly gaudy poster of the movie, *Viva Las Vegas*, one of
Connie's all time favourite films.

Quentin also admitted to Rich Turner that he had a particular fond-
ness for Westerns and at that time his favourites were the John Wayne
classics, *The Searchers* and *Red River*.

Those nights at the River Bottom Inn were particularly important to
Quentin because they represented the first time he got close to actors on

a personal level. The bar also happened to be across the street from the main Warner Brothers lot and sometimes groups of stuntmen would wander in for a drink and start swapping stories that had the young Quentin riveted. This was the world he wanted to be a part of.

If he'd had any doubts about seeking a career in Hollywood then just listening to those showbiz tales would have been enough to get rid of them for ever. He knew he would not give up until he had made it.

'Nobody loses all the time'

Warren Oates, in *Bring Me the Head of Alfredo Garcia*, 1974

Escape From the South Bay

BANK OF AMERICA, TOLUCA LAKE, CALIFORNIA,
DECEMBER 1980

C raig Hamann – small, dark, shy bank teller – had always wanted to act, but the cost of simply surviving in Los Angeles made it impossible for him to do anything about it. He had taken a 'normal' job in order to pay for rent and food. Then into the bank walked attractive Jena Lucarelli, wife of the drama coach at the James Best Acting School. She had exchanged pleasantries with Craig on a number of occasions and knew he was interested in acting. 'Why not join the school?' she said. 'We'd love to have you.'

So it was that three days later, Craig Hamann, then the wrong side of twenty-five, but looking considerably younger, walked into the life of Quentin Tarantino.

Hamann was an altogether different proposition from Quentin's other friends at the school, like Rich Turner. Here was a man on the edge, constantly losing his temper, always willing to argue a point. Quentin was immediately attracted to Hamann. This guy is wild, he told himself, within minutes of being introduced to moody Hamann.

Quentin rapidly joined forces with Hamann and another rebel, Rick Squery, and the threesome fast managed to cause as much controversy as is possible in a sedate place like the James Best Acting School.

They began borrowing scenes from controversial movies and reworking them during performances in front of their class.

'We were always coming up with ideas. We wanted to do our own stunts. everything. Nothing fazed us,' explains Hamann.

To Quentin these two guys were like a breath of fresh air. One day, he and his two friends decided it would be a gas to recreate a scene from John Carpenter's *Escape From New York*. Quentin, Hamann and Squery had first been turned on to Carpenter thanks to his highly acclaimed but extremely low budget *Assault on Precinct 13* and so it seemed only natural to perform what they considered to be a tribute to a master director.

Hamann decided that, for the sake of authenticity, he would bring in his own awesome collection of real guns to use as props. They included an M16 assault rifle, a .41 Magnum, a pump action shotgun and a whole selection of knives.

'That really bothered people,' admits Craig Hamann now. 'They got kinda freaked out, I guess.'

The person it bothered most was acting teacher Jack Lucarelli. He stopped the threesome's performance in mid-sentence and insisted on inspecting the weapons just to make sure there were no stray bullets still in them.

Hamann was so determined to retain the authenticity that from then on he insisted on bringing in the guns each time there was a relevant scene to act out. Tension grew between him and coach Lucarelli. While others in the class were rewriting scenes from dramas like Tennessee Williams' *Cat on a Hot Tin Roof*, the threesome would be putting their own spin on the grisly shoot out from Jimmy Cagney's *White Heat*.

Quentin and Hamann were quickly acknowledged by the other students as fine writers even though their choice of material was seen as rather too gory at times. They were often secretly asked to write scenes for other people to perform. Quentin didn't mind because he believed that practice made perfect and the more writing he did the better.

However, when he and his friends acted out their own crime-riddled mini-plays some of their classmates found the content quite disturbing.

'Craig, especially, would have a mad glint in his eye and it was pretty weird stuff at times,' recalls one student. 'Killings, maimings, decapitation. You name it and they did it.'

Quentin would go out of his way to be as politically incorrect as possible, stoutly defending Sylvester Stallone in fierce arguments with teacher Jack Lucarelli, who tended to look down his nose at such macho performers.

Quentin and his friends did not really consider themselves rebels. They simply had a passion for gangster movies and those bleak, film *noirs* of the fifties.

Despite being so much younger than his two friends, Quentin could more than hold his own when it came to talking about movies. At the time, he was particularly nuts about Jim McBride's *Breathless*, starring Richard Gere. The others were not so keen and took some persuading to even agree to see the movie.

Quentin had first seen *Breathless* at a cinema in a shopping mall near his Torrance home. He literally fell in love with the film because *Breathless* incorporated all his obsessions – comic books, popular music, rockabilly. In particular, Richard Gere's character was completely rockabilly. Quentin loved the way the movie was shot as if Los Angeles had been turned into a back-lot.

Later, Quentin told his friends at his favourite comic book store all about *Breathless* and they couldn't get over how he seemed to know virtually all the dialogue word-for-word. The scenes Quentin liked best were the ones where the characters read comic books as a test of true love.

Back at the acting school, Quentin eventually managed to get Craig

Hamann to see *Breathless*. Having been virtually dragged into a cinema, Hamann also fell in love with the film and realized that Quentin had incredibly good taste in movies. It also became increasingly clear to him that Quentin had educated himself through film.

Curiously, throughout Quentin's first year at the James Best Acting School, he never once admitted he was working in the daytime job at the Pussycat Porno Theatre in Torrance. All his fellow students just presumed he was paying for his acting tuition by doing some part time job or other and they still had no idea how young he was.

Quentin constantly lectured his friends Hamann, Squery and Turner about his love for so-called blaxploitation movies, which all started with *Shaft* in 1971 and led to at least a dozen poor imitations. Quentin seemed completely enamoured with the language and the music in those movies, even though the storylines were often far from satisfactory.

The big difference between Craig Hamann and Quentin's other friends in and out of acting school was that Hamann seemed to be on a knife-edge virtually the whole time. He was the kind of guy who would lose his rag with anyone for the smallest of reasons. Quentin seemed to understand this, although there were occasions when even Quentin pushed his friend too far.

During one incident at the James Best Acting School, Quentin and Hamann were acting out a scene in which Hamann – armed with his own real M16 assault rifle – was supposed to do a stick-up on Quentin, who was to instantly drop his gun: Hamann's real .41 Magnum.

'Drop it!' barked Hamann at Quentin in front of the entire class.

'Nope,' replied Quentin, much to everyone's amusement because this dialogue was definitely NOT in the script.

Then Quentin turned to their teacher Lucarelli and said, 'Jack, he has to command me much stronger than that.'

Hamann was incensed that his friend Quentin should humiliate him in front of the other students. He paused for breath, then screamed the command again and this time Quentin dropped his weapon with a told-you-so expression on his face.

An hour later, Quentin walked into the bathroom at the school and found Hamann alone. He was still fuming about what had happened earlier.

'Just fuck off, Quentin. Fuck you.'

Quentin looked mortified and walked straight out of the bathroom. Thirty seconds later, he returned obviously close to tears.

'Craig, I know you got a bad temper but you save your "fuck yous" for somebody who doesn't love you.'

When Quentin said that, Hamann was overcome with remorse. He hugged his friend and apologized for his outburst. Hamann never forgot that incident because he felt it bonded the two friends together for ever.

Quentin and the others made a number of video dramas at the school, the most memorable of which featured them being locked in solitary confinement during a biological war and then stumbling out into a world where everyone else appeared to have died.

Quentin, Hamann and Rick Squery wore punk-type army uniforms for their roles and Craig Hamann later described the video as, 'a piece of shit', saying 'It didn't work.'

He explained, 'We find out there is an antidote and supposedly there is only enough for two people and three of us are infected. The whole thing was a waste of time.'

Back in Torrance, Quentin was finding his job at the Pussycat Porno Theatre more and more unsavoury. He seemed to be manhandling perverts out of the auditorium almost every day. Sometimes they would still have their flies open when he kicked them into the gutter outside the deco-style theatre. He was starting to resent the entire place.

It wasn't made any easier by the fact that he was living a virtual Jekyll and Hyde existence; porno theatre usher by day and serious actor by night.

One evening at the school, Quentin found himself broke and without the usual ride home from Rich Turner. He was filled with dread at the prospect of the two-hour bus trip back to Torrance. Then teacher Jack Lucarelli offered to let Quentin sleep the night at the school and join in some of the earlier classes next day. Quentin knew he was risking losing his job, but he was far more interested in getting some free acting classes.

The teenager climbed into a sleeping bag loaned by one of the other students and decided that anything was preferable to going back to Torrance and working another day in the Pussycat. Perhaps not surprisingly, he was sacked by the theatre the following week, but Quentin looked on his dismissal as a blessing in disguise.

Eventually he got a dead-end job earning just a few bucks a week plus commission doing market research at a shopping mall near his home in Torrance. Quentin rarely made more than forty dollars a week, but at least it didn't matter if he failed to show up some days and he must have been relieved he would never have to watch seedy porn films again.

Quentin frequently slept over at the acting school and in many ways he became part of the furniture. Teachers and students looked on the awkward teenager as an eccentric, if somewhat erratic personality. All he ever talked about was the movies.

At sixteen, Quentin was the same age as his mother was when she'd had him. He had quit school, virtually left home and seemed to be living a Walter Mitty life. It was all remarkably similar to what Connie Zastoupil had gone through, except that there was no baby on the way.

Quentin's shyness with women was noted by some individuals at the James Best School, although he did became good friends on a brother/sister level, with a number of the female students. One of his best pals was Brenda Hillhouse, who went on to get a role in *Pulp Fiction*. There was also Brenda Peters and Jack Lucarelli's wife Jena. But once class ended, Quentin only tended to hang out with Craig Hamann, Rick Squery and, when he wanted a quieter evening, Rich Turner.

Hamann took Quentin on all sorts of eye-opening adventures. One time they decided to visit the so-called 'Boy's Town' district on Santa Monica Boulevard, in West Hollywood, where many of the gay bars served very cheap drinks and featured big screen TVs. Quentin had just had both ears pierced and tended to alternate the ear he wore a ring in. At that time, it was believed by many that gay men used a ring in the right ear as opposed to the left. (Current fashion has since completely ruled this out.) Quentin made a point of wearing his earring in the heterosexual left ear.

Quentin was terrified when he first got to the edge of 'Boy's Town'. Craig had one or two gay friends and they had taken him to the bars before, so he talked him through what it would be like.

Both Hamann and Quentin are devout heterosexuals, but at such establishments they could sip cut-price booze and watch continuous MTV music videos, featuring innovative camera techniques that fascinated both would-be film makers.

The two friends wandered into one hostelry called Revolver, settled down with a beer each and started watching the big screen TV hanging from the ceiling. Inevitably, a group of men began hustling them and Quentin 'got a bit freaked out'.

Hamann and Quentin then headed out towards Rage, on the corner of San Vincente and Santa Monica. Rage was an even more sexually heated establishment where another group of guys came on so strong that the two friends abandoned their plans to have a beer and headed east on Santa Monica Boulevard for one of the straighter hostelries. But Quentin was never angry about having been taken to Boy's Town. He simply stored a vivid picture of it in his memory, knowing that one day he might use the experience as the basis for a scene in a movie. Everything that happened to him could one day be used in his movies.

Some nights, Quentin and Hamann would go to the tatty World Movie Theatre on the gritty, far eastern end of Hollywood Boulevard, near where it crossed Gower. The two friends saw Jack Nicholson in the Tony Richardson directed movie, *The Border*, an interesting film about an LA cop who joins the border patrol in El Paso and gets caught up in squalor, violence and double dealing. Quentin was particularly impressed by one of the supporting cast, Harvey Keitel. Less than ten years later, the actor would play a very significant role in getting Quentin's career on the road.

The World Movie Theatre was a bit like a home from home for Quentin because many of the patrons were either drunk or high on drugs, just as they had been at the Pussycat. In the back three rows, at least a dozen noisy black pimps would be discussing the previous evening's takings.

On one occasion, Quentin – by now infected with Hamann's short temper – brazenly turned around to tell one of the noisier clientele, 'Would you please keep it down.'

The reply was somewhat predictable. 'Fuck you, asshole.'

Quentin exploded and leapt over the rickety seat and was about to take a swing at the man when a voice backed down.

'Sorry man. No problem.'

All that training at the Pussycat Porno Theatre was at last coming in useful.

Hamann and Quentin were continuing to build up reputations as troublemaking know-alls at the James Best Acting School. They both felt they knew more than their teachers. But it was Hamann who regularly got up and told people like Jack Lucarelli exactly what he thought of them. Meanwhile Quentin, more than eleven years younger than his friend. would smile and nod his head in agreement. But he was too bright to stand up and be counted.

*'Fasten your seatbelts. It's going to be a
bumpy night'*

Bette Davis in *All About Eve*, 1950

A Movie Geek's Paradise

ELDERGLEN LANE, HARBOR CITY, LOS ANGELES,
SUMMER 1981

A s Quentin's eyes panned around the tiny one-bedroomed apartment, a vast jumbo jet thundered just a few hundred feet
overhead. He turned to the sweaty, smelly, fat, balding landlord
and said, 'It's perfect. I'll take it.' At last, he had broken the umbilical
cord. All those stop and search operations in his bedroom in Torrance
had taken their toll.

Quentin had assured Connie he would not move a long way. He had
settled for the rougher, tougher area of Harbor City, just a few miles from
her home and even closer to the main runway at LA Airport.

Within days of moving into the one-bedroomed studio, Quentin
installed his own telephone – the ultimate evidence of his coming of age.
He was so proud of his new found-independence he even insisted on
having his full name printed in the local phone directory.

'Quint Tarantino. 1138, Elderglen Lane, Harbor City. 530 1063,' read the 1981 South Bay phone book. At that time, everyone knew him as Quint and he was trying to drop Zastoupil as his last name, even though he never actually took any legal steps to revert to Tarantino.

Quentin grew bored with the James Best Acting School and quit after two years, although he made a point of keeping in touch with all his acting friends. Then he landed a job which threatened to interfere with his long-term acting ambitions.

He needed something with a decent rate of pay, especially since Connie was nagging him to get a good job and 'start living in the real world'.

Somehow Quentin landed himself a $1,200-a-month job as a headhunter for a company which had numerous clients in the aerospace industry. When Connie heard the news she didn't know whether to laugh or cry.

'He knew nothing whatsoever about the aerospace industry yet he had got this job picking prospective employees. It was ridiculous,' she recalls.

In fairness to Quentin, he was equally bemused to find himself having to go to work every day in a suit and tie. He even managed to adopt a corporate air which he impressively maintained at his office each morning.

'What d'you know about the aerospace industry, Quint?' Connie asked him when he told her about his new, serious job.

'Not a lot, Mom. But it's cool. I thought you'd be pleased.'

Quentin's slick new job did nothing to water down his enthusiasm for movies. Indeed, he could now afford to buy himself a VCR machine, something he considered more important than anything else in his apartment besides a phone. It would have been difficult for girlfriends to enter the equation at this time.

With a VCR Quentin could greatly increase his consumption of movies. Instead of seeing five or six films a week at local movie theatres, he could easily watch double that amount.

This new obsession with videos led him to investigate the local video

stores with great interest. The video boom was slow in coming to the
United States and the number of outlets was still very limited in the early
eighties. While Britain already had the highest per capita proportion of
VCR users in the world, Americans somehow managed to resist the
temptation to watch big screen epics in the comfort of their own homes.
Going to the local drive-in or movie theatre had been a part of the
American way of life for more than forty years and there was a certain
reluctance to embrace the new technology.

However, self-confessed movie addicts like Quentin Tarantino were
not interested in tradition. His only priority was to see as many movies
as possible in any one week and the VCR was a godsend in that respect.

But Quentin faced a problem when it came to finding a well-stocked
video store in Harbor City, a community made up of small mini-suburbs
on the edge of the Los Angeles port area (which consisted of vast ware-
houses and expanses of wasteland).

Eventually he heard about a specialist store called Video Archives,
on Sepulveda Boulevard, in the nearby community of Hermosa Beach.
By this time the proud owner of a battered Honda hatchback, Quentin
was more than happy to make the twenty-minute drive from his apartment to Video Archives if they really stocked a good selection of videos.
He was not disappointed.

When Quentin walked into the store, located in a sixties built mini-
shopping mall close to a busy intersection, he found the place stacked
high with obscure movies from all over the world. Quentin knew the only
way he was going to learn about film-making was through watching
movies. The good, the bad, the ugly – it didn't matter what movies he
watched. Each one would be a learning experience. This store was like a
dream come true.

Over the next few months, Quentin became one of Video Archives'
most regular customers. He got to know the owners and the clerks. They
were all such cool people. They didn't hassle you if you were a day or two
late returning a video and they actually seemed to know something about
the films they were renting out. Some nights Quentin would hang out at

the store for two or three hours, caught up in discussions about movies. He started burying himself in so many videos that he rarely left the apartment apart from going to work.

At Video Archives, Quentin became particularly friendly with an equally knowledgeable film geek called Roger Avary, although they seemed to be approaching the art of film-making from entirely different directions. By now dressed entirely in black, driving his clapped out Honda Civic and dining mainly at fast food emporiums like Pollo Loco and Jack in the Box, Quentin fitted the role of movie nerd to perfection.

In fact, Avary and Quentin did not hit it off that well to start with because they were constantly trying to compete with each other in the movie knowledge stakes. However, Avary eventually conceded that Quentin's encyclopedic memory had him beat. Then they became very good friends. Avary was a friendly, sincere person who had spent a bit of time in Europe and seemed very worldly to Quentin, who found that arguing with Avary about certain movies was in many ways more enjoyable than actually watching them.

Over the following few months they built up a strong rapport and Quentin would often stay in the store to watch whatever movie they were showing on the big screen monitor hanging from the ceiling. Eventually, when one of the clerks left, Avary persuaded owners Lance Lawson and Dennis Humbert to offer Quentin a job at Archives. Quentin was delighted, even though he was taking a vast cut in wages, as he knew it would provide him with endless free movie rentals.

His only concern was Connie. He knew she would be bitterly disappointed that he had quit his safe, responsible position as a headhunter.

'But, Mom, that job wasn't me and you know it,' he later told Connie when trying to break the news gently that he had swapped a twelve hundred dollar-a-month job for one worth four dollars an hour, plus unlimited free video rentals.

Connie was naturally concerned. She couldn't really understand why Quentin was leaving his job. But then she had always encouraged him to be a free spirit. Now she was paying the price.

Quentin saw the job at Video Archives as a golden opportunity. Most people would have gone into it half-heartedly, planning to work there for a few months and then quit. But to Quentin this was a chance to work as an unofficial movie critic, get to see as many movies as was humanly possible and be paid in the process. What more could he ask? He had always kept his outgoings low because he had been nursing a secret ambition to try and make his own movie some day. Now that very attitude was going to enable him to take a job at Video Archives, a job he would relish and use to further his own knowledge and understanding of films. Other, richer, more academic kids might be heading for film school, but Quentin had found his own version on his doorstep.

Not surprisingly, Quentin soon got into his stride at Video Archives. He and the other clerks, including Roger Avary, started running thematic selections of certain films each week in the store. The first collaboration between Quentin and Avary was a package of videos called 'Feed Your Head', a homage to drug pictures. Another week it would be a Sam Fuller season, swashbucklers the next, then screwball comedies. The movies of Hong Kong director John Woo began to spark more interest than the latest Disney or Bond adventure, and work by New Wave masters like Jean-Luc Godard and Eric Rohmer were heavily promoted by Quentin and Avary. Quentin's favourite selection was 'Women in Prison'. At one point he mistakenly thought film maker Akira Kurosawa had died and offered a package of his movies for a week.

When the Archives clerks ran a 'Heist' week, one of the movies was *The Killing*, directed by Stanley Kubrick. Quentin loved it. He saw it as a young man's movie and was impressed by the way it broke all the usual rules. The fractured story-line took each of the criminal's roles in a race track heist up to a certain stage of the raid, then turned the clock back and hooked the audience into the fortunes and misfortunes of another hoodlum. The memory of that movie would one day inspire him to write *Reservoir Dogs*, the film that launched his career.

The atmosphere in the store, according to customers and staff alike, was unique. Instead of a place where people quietly browsed through the shelves looking for something that took their fancy, there would be constant yells of 'Got any Italian exploitation movies?' or 'Can you recommend a pre-1950 horror flick with a lot of sex in it?' or 'What's the name of that movie where Kirk Douglas plays a submarine commander?'

Gradually, owners Lawson and Humbert spent less and less time in the store.Instead they would appoint one of the clerks as manager-of-the-week and make them responsible for opening and closing the premises each day.

Although he enjoyed discussing the finer points of French New Wave Quentin still occasionally found himself having to bust a head or two when customers got to be a pain. He developed a routine that preceded each melée. Before any punches were thrown, he'd ask his foe to wait a few seconds while he removed his dangling earring, afraid it could be ripped clean off his ear. (This was the sort of deft touch that would be reflected in his movies years later).

One time a customer came into Video Archives with a tape which was more than three months late. A few days were OK, but this was pushing it. Quentin informed the man how much it was going to cost in late fees and he retorted, 'Oh, that's a lot of money. I'm just going to keep the tape.'

He then started to walk out. Quentin followed. Just as the man turned round, Quentin went – *boom!* – into his chest and then pushed him outside the front door of the store. All the other staff watched boggled-eyed.

On the sidewalk, Quentin swung into him again and then pushed him all the way up the road.

On another occasion, Quentin grabbed a customer by the back of the head and – *bam!* – slammed his head into the corner of the counter. There was blood everywhere.

Recalls Roger Avary, 'It was like a Quentin movie device. The blood came out of the forehead area and sort of collected in the eye socket.'

Quentin did not get into fights at the drop of a hat, but he knew how far he would go if he got into a punch-up although he really did not want to go too far.

If someone challenged him physically, he would not hesitate to retaliate. Yet there were other occasions when he would be having a massive argument and he never even considered crossing that line. It was all a matter of how he felt at that particular moment.

Despite such occurrences, working at Video Archives was for the most part a highly pleasurable experience.

'It was like my Village Voice,' Quentin later explained referring to the New York newspaper that has become a virtual bible for hundreds of thousands of young Americans. In other words, he got to review any film he liked. He adored putting a video in a customer's hands and then explaining to them why the movie was good or bad. It was all part of his movie self-education.

Avary – who was a couple of years older than Quentin – seemed to have far more purist views on films. At one stage, he became very concerned that he and Quentin were becoming completely dominated by home entertainment movies rather than going to cinemas. He therefore made a point of going with Quentin to see one art house movie every fortnight so they could soak up the atmosphere and enjoy a coffee afterwards with the art house brigade.

Whenever they could afford it, the two friends would attend the retrospectives of famous directors that were regularly shown at various movie theatres in LA. It was at one such event that Quentin discovered the films of Jean-Luc Godard. Typically, Quentin was objective about the Frenchman's material until he saw it for himself. He decided he would go and see Godard's movies and then make up his own mind whether or not he liked them. If he didn't respond to them, that would be that.

The first Godard movie Quentin saw was *Little Soldier*. It knocked him out. He went back the following night to see Godard's original version of *Breathless* and immediately proclaimed it one of the finest movies ever made. Quentin was hooked. He went to the Godard retrospective every night for a week and the Frenchman became one of his biggest directorial and screenwriting influences. To Quentin, the best thing about Godard's movies was that he managed to get across the idea that if you just love movies enough, you can make great films. You don't have to go to school and you don't have to know a lens from a bag of sand, but if you get your hands on a camera you could make one just like Godard.

Back at Video Archives, various important customers were starting to sit up and take notice of Quentin. Film and TV producer John Langley – who created the phenomenally successful American real-life series *Cops* – was regularly treated to doses of Quentin and Roger Avary.

'They had a purist appreciation for the medium,' remembers Langley. 'Sometimes you would have to wait to get service while they quizzed you about a movie you had done a rewrite on, but these guys knew the whole canon.'

Langley would often find himself eating popcorn – they sold it in Video Archives – and chatting with Quentin who he now says was 'so opinionated about everything under the sun it was brilliant'.

For Quentin and Avary, and a host of other young film makers who came of age in the video era, VCRs had a huge impact on their movie education. Videos allowed this new wave of auteurs to absorb vintage films without going to film school. In the dark days before VCRs, top film directors like Francis Ford Coppola, Martin Scorsese and Steven Spielberg had to undertake formal film training, partly because that's where the old films were.

Interestingly, as Quentin and Avary continued working at Video Archives, more and more film geek types gravitated towards the store. They were people who loved films passionately, but did not have the contacts. or know how, to break into the movie business.

Soon after he started work at Archives, it became apparent that, while Quentin might have an encyclopedic knowledge of movies, he was virtually illiterate when it came to ordinary paperwork. He would print everything, rather than write it longhand, and his spelling was still appalling. But he could out-talk anyone when it came to describing the camera angles in all Sergio Leone's films.

Quentin also became friends with Video Archives customer Jerry Martinez, another movie geek who found it extremely difficult to relate to anything if it did not have a film connection. Tall, gangly Quentin and short, fat Martinez initially got embroiled in a row about *Gremlins*.

'I hated it. He liked it,' explains Martinez. 'I had been a little hard on the film because I had been expecting something else. You have to remember, we are talking heavy film geek speak here and we were referring to it as a genre of movie and whether it actually worked.'

Quentin was obsessed by the in-jokes in *Gremlins* and he was a big champion of the movie's director, Joe Dante. Martinez joked that this had something to do with the fact that Quentin and Dante shared Italian origins. The movie was a classic example of Dante's style. Littered with cinematic allusions – to Capra and 1950s sci-fi – it used tension and expectation to comic and thrilling effect.

Quentin would frequently go to movie theatres with Martinez and his brother Chris and try to see every new movie on the first day it was released. More often than not, they would get in for the cheaper matinée performance of one movie and then pay out for an evening showing of another new film. Sometimes they would stay for the late evening screening as well.

Back at Video Archives, Quentin helped Martinez get a job in just the same way Roger Avary had helped him, and the family atmosphere grew even stronger.

The staff at Archives were beginning to get quite a reputation throughout the South Bay area of Los Angeles for their knowledge and stock of obscure films. They even started to get phone calls from customers in different parts of the country armed with bizarre descriptions of little-known movies. Quentin, Martinez or Avary would try and work out what they were referring to.

'The difference with us was that we felt it was our duty to turn them on to as many of those less famous films as possible and expand their horizons in the process,' explains Martinez.

Quentin and his new friend also had a particular penchant for the Japanese TV action series *Kage No Gundo*, starring martial arts legend Sonny Chiba. In *True Romance*, Clarence (Christian Slater) attends a Chiba triple bill on his birthday.

And Quentin showed just how deeply affected he was by certain movies when he turned up at Archives wearing a long coat and dark glasses and walked around with a toothpick in his mouth after watching Chow Yun-Fat in John Woo's *A Better Tomorrow Part II*.

The store was open from 10am to 10pm and staff worked two shifts, although Quentin and his friends would often hang out at the shop and come early and leave late. They all congregated around one big screen TV that hung from the ceiling, dominating the entire store. The staff would watch whatever movie took their fancy, regardless of the taste or sensibilities of their customers. If that movie caught the attention of customers and they looked vaguely interesting, Quentin, Avary or Martinez would start up a debate about some point or other in order to test out that customer's knowledge. If they turned out to be fellow movie geeks then they would be offered a job at the store, after consultation with one of the owners.

Martinez got into trouble with some of the customers by holding his own private German season during which he screened some highly erotic movies in the middle of the day, sparking complaints from outraged parents of young children.

Nevertheless the Video Archives staff continued their system of having a separate shelf to place at least half a dozen movies centred around specific subjects. However, they got increasingly esoteric, as Jerry Martinez's brother Chris explains.

'One time we ran a theme week that revolved around movies connected to water. They included *The Poseidon Adventure*, *Water* with Billy Connolly and Michael Caine and *The Titanic*.'

But on other occasions the subjects were far more intriguing. For instance, the staff once managed to get away with filling the shelf with films that only featured women beating men. 'They went down very well with local neglected housewives,' adds Martinez.

Sometimes customers would come in and suggest other movies that might qualify for that week's particular theme. It all added to the unique atmosphere inside the store. The owners never really enforced any restrictions on their staff because they were rarely there, although Lance Lawson did manage to rival Quentin in his knowledge of certain types of movies. Lawson believed that as long as his staff were enthusiastic and interested in movies then anything went, within reason.

However, customers were up in arms when one staff member devised a Charles Manson section to coincide with the anniversary of the death of Sharon Tate. The films featured included *Helter Skelter* and a selection of cheesy Sharon Tate films. A number of regulars got upset and told Video Archives staff.

Owner Lawson did get a bit peeved on that occasion, but both Quentin and Martinez insisted that the idea was so interesting that this outweighed the fact it might offend some customers.

Lawson was secretly very impressed by Quentin because 'he could tell you who the DP was, who wrote the screenplay and probably do a couple of scenes including verbatim dialogue'.

Quentin was also responsible for tripling the number of 'women in prison' movies that were rented. One customer he made a convert out of was Gene Moore, whom he introduced to the likes of *Caged Heat* and *The Big Bird Cage*. Moore even got into a discussion one evening with Quentin about tipping in restaurants and Quentin eventually used it in the opening scene of *Reservoir Dogs*.

Quentin and his pals at Archives genuinely believed that their customers wanted to be told what was good. It was very much like an extension of the Hollywood executive's traditional stance on new scripts. They wanted reassurance from others before they would consider watching or reading something new.

Quentin was a talented observer of other people and he grew to love and hate certain customers at Video Archives. One of his biggest irritations was listening to parents getting mad with their children because they wanted to watch a movie they had already seen before. Quentin sometimes took on the physchology of the child at this point because he appreciated that what they were thinking was, 'Why should I try something that I might not like? I *know* I'm gonna like *that*.' It actually made him wish he could be a child again because then he could watch the same movie on at least a dozen occasions and still laugh through it every time.

Video Archives was undoubtedly the single most important influence on Quentin's eventual success because it was one of the few places where he could be a regular guy and get a regular job and still do what he enjoyed most. But, despite his outer contentment, there was still a killer lurking within. He wanted to get out there and prove he could do it. But first he needed to write something that would make people sit up and take notice.

*'I'm from the gutter and don't you ever
forget it, because I won't'*

Gary Oldman in *Prick Up Your Ears*, 1987

Black Russians
and Vice

CRAIG HAMANN'S SHOEBOX APARTMENT, SAN
FERNANDO VALLEY, SUMMER 1984

Quentin, slouched on a crumpled couch, grabbed the bottle of Absolut from the table in front of him and splashed it into a half tumbler of Kahlua. Then he passed the bottle to his acting school buddy, Craig Hamann. They were both close to tears.

'It's just not fair, man. How could they waste him?' sobbed Quentin.

'Don't die, Sonny. For God sake don't die,' mumbled an equally emotional Craig Hamann.

The two friends were watching their favourite episode of *Miami Vice*. during which hero cop Sonny Crockett, played so brilliantly by Don Johnson, was shot and almost killed.

They had decided to spend a TV booze-fest evening at Craig's place drinking their own lethal home-made Black Russians and watching re-runs of *Vice*. Quentin immensely enjoyed his job at Video Archives, but his film education was making him increasingly frustrated and opinion-ated about directors and actors. He actually reckoned he could do a better job than most of them, given the chance.

Meanwhile, Craig had his own problems. He had been kicked out of the James Best Acting School and was drifting from job to job, occasion-ally getting a poorly paid acting gig to supplement his ego more than his bank balance. He had become very depressed over the previous year and had started drinking heavily.

But that evening at Craig's apartment they did nothing but swap opinions on *Miami Vice*. Tear-jerking scenes like the shooting of Crockett certainly had the desired effect when washed down with plentiful supplies of booze.

'You gotta pull through, Sonny. You gotta,' pleaded Quentin.

'You can make it, man. I know you can,' urged Craig, knocking back another mouthful of Black Russian.

Eventually Sonny Crockett pulled through, which was more than could be said for the two drinking partners. They continued boozing and stayed up half the night watching back-to-back episodes of *Vice*, includ-ing another classic featuring guest star Helena Bonham Carter as a drug addict.

'Wow!' exclaimed Craig, seeing the British actress's name in the credits at the start of the programme, 'how did they get her on the show?'

A few minutes later, Hamann and Quentin were back in full flow as they examined and re-examined every sequence.

'Geez, look at that wide shot, man,' exclaimed Quentin.

'But they go and ruin it with a cheesy cut-away...' And so it went on.

However their intense discussion set Quentin off thinking about his own directorial aspirations once again.

'Hey, Craig. We gotta try and shoot our own movie, man.'

'That's cool, Quint. But how we gonna pay for it?'

'I'll find a way,' promised Quentin. Craig knew that, despite the booze, his friend was being deadly serious.

Quentin and Craig Hamann never actually saw the final *Vice* episode all the way through because they both passed out, thanks to the vast numbers of Black Russians.

Next day, Hamann felt so ill he swore he would give up drinking alcohol for good and has never touched a drop since. Quentin did not seem so badly affected. He also had a perfect recollection of the previous evening's conversation and called Craig up.

'We gotta do this movie, Craig. You got any ideas?'

'Well, there is one,' replied Hamann.

'What is it? Shoot, man,' said an anxious Quentin.

'Well...' hesitated Hamann.

'Come on, pitch it.'

'It's about a guy who hires a hooker for his best pal's birthday. But it all goes wrong.'

'Hey, sounds cool.'

'You think so?' said an uncertain Hamann.

'Write it man. Then we can shoot it.'

'You got a deal.'

And so Quentin's directorial debut, entitled *My Best Friend's Birthday*, was born.

Quentin had actually been nursing the idea of making his own movie for many years. Some customers at Video Archives had told him the only way to break through as a director in Hollywood was to make your own film. Initially, Quentin presumed he would never be able to afford to do it.

So when he was in his early twenties, he had seriously considered becoming a movie business journalist in order to gain some all-important Hollywood contacts. He already had a large collection of film books, which he tended to buy at secondhand bookstores and he believed he had more genuine movie knowledge than most film journalists.

He had also maintained his list of his all time favourite movies, which he'd started when he was just twelve years old. From this list Quentin culled the names of his thirty favourite directors and decided to try and interview them. He knew he couldn't just call them up and ask them to have lunch with him, so he decided to bill himself as a journalist writing the definitive book on 'B' movies and their influence on larger Hollywood films.

The subject was irresistible to many directors and Quentin managed to interview more than a dozen before he got diverted by his first movie project, *My Best Friend's Birthday*. He found the experience enthralling and the fact that he did not even have a book deal was never actually uncovered. Only Quentin and those directors know who they were, but one of them was his hero Brian de Palma, director of *Blow Out*, *Dressed to Kill* and *Carrie*, to name but a few.

The book was a movie geek's dream come true. Often, Quentin would get embroiled in three- or four-hour interviews in which he and the directors swapped opinions. But when the interviews were over Quentin felt empty and disappointed because he had wanted each of them to go on for days, if not weeks. He made a point of asking each director what advice they would give a first time director.

Virtually all of them admitted they had started off by making their own low-budget productions. Begging, stealing and borrowing was in fact a prerequisite when it came to launching a career as a director. Scorsese made his first feature on a next-to-nothing budget, so why the hell couldn't Quentin Tarantino? It dawned on Quentin that the only person who was going to give him a movie to direct was himself. He had to get out there and do it by hook or by crook.

Another important influence on Quentin at this time was Hollywood personal manager Cathryn Jaymes. She had been introduced to Quentin on his twenty-first birthday in 1984 by Craig Hamann as they sat drinking Margueritas at the Via Taxaco Mexican restaurant on Sunset Boulevard.

Cathryn told Quentin and Hamann that there were only two routes into Hollywood for two young guys with very few contacts – put together your own low-budget movie and/or write at least three strong scripts as samples of your work.

As far as Quentin was concerned, he wanted to be more than just a writer, he wanted to be a movie star *and* director. He had been through all the acting school stuff, but he had done nothing so far to further his directorial aspirations.

Cathryn Jaymes urged Quentin and Craig to go ahead and make a movie on virtually no budget because it could end up being their entrée to Hollywood. She was impressed by Quentin's surefire attitude and felt that he was undoubtedly going to make it eventually. But it was only after Quentin had interviewed all those Hollywood directors for that imaginary book that he realized she was absolutely correct.

Quentin and Cathryn shook hands on a business partnership back in 1984 when she agreed to manage his career. She was going to be his professional mother figure and agent all in one and she would not charge him a cent unless he actually got paid for movie work. In other words, Cathryn was taking as much a risk as Quentin.

Quentin liked Cathryn because she genuinely cared about him and his career and she gave him a sense of security. At this point his mother Connie had her own increasingly successful career in the healthcare industry to worry about and, in any case, she did not understand the movie business like Cathryn.

Cathryn – an attractive, slender blonde lady – was used to playing the mother figure manager to numerous actors, writers and directors. She knew precisely how to soothe their egos and when to play hard ball. Quentin was obviously talented, but only time would tell if he really had what it took.

Initially, Cathryn Jaymes started to nurture Quentin's career by organizing getting-to-know-you meetings with some movie executives whom she believed might be interested in some of his offbeat ideas.

One time, Quentin met Cathryn at her then office in Beverly Hills before they went together to a meeting with a development executive at a television production company. It sounded impressive for the inexperienced Quentin to be going to such a meeting, but the reality is that every movie executive in Hollywood will agree to a meeting with any hopeful for one simple reason – meetings don't cost money. Usually they take about fifteen minutes and movie execs work on the premise that very occasionally they'll come across a goldmine; the rest of the Hollywood hopefuls they meet usually disappear without trace.

Cathryn Jaymes naturally wanted to get Quentin's name circulated and she felt that such meetings were also good for his morale. Meanwhile he found it bizarre that he was a mere video store clerk yet able to get in to heavyweight meetings with movie execs.

That particular day, Quentin – as always – was late getting to Cathryn's office. Suddenly, she heard an almighty rumbling from the car-width alleyway that ran along the back of her Beverly Hills office.

'There was this huge rolling noise like a tornado coming down the alley, with all this garbage and dust flying in all directions. Then there were what sounded like gunshots. It was actually backfiring,' explains Cathryn Jaymes. As the dust settled, Quentin emerged from a brown Chevy Caprice, that had once resembled a New York taxi.

But worse was to come. Cathryn was without her own car and so agreed to be driven to the meeting by Quentin. It was an experience she would never forget.

'I thought we'd never make it. His driving was appalling. He just kept taking his hand off the steering wheel to make a point with his hands and everyone kept looking at us because of the state of the car.'

Cathryn doesn't recall who the meeting was with or how it went. But the state of that car and his driving is imprinted on her mind for ever.

Meanwhile, a couple of weeks after Quentin had urged his friend Hamann to write up his movie idea, the young actor delivered a first draft of something entitled *My Best Friend's Birthday* to Quentin at a coffee shop, on Ventura Boulevard, near Craig's home in the San Fernando Valley.

For almost thirty minutes, Quentin studied the script in silence. Then he turned over the last page.

'It's great, man,' said Quentin. 'Mind if I take it home and add a few scenes and things?'

'Go ahead,' said Hamann. 'But do you think it'll work?'

'It'll work. I've thought it all through. We'll shoot it on 16mm in black and white. It's gonna be a gas.'

'Really?' said a slightly unbelieving Hamann.

'Yeah. And you and I are gonna play the leads as rockabillies.'

'Cool...'

Over the next few weeks, Quentin swiftly and very skilfully pumped up much of the dialogue in the script and added extra scenes to flesh out the relatively short screenplay. At this stage Quentin was extremely taken by a recently released movie called *Fandango*.

Fandango was the directorial debut of Kevin Reynolds and the lead acting debut of Kevin Costner. It centred around a group of college friends driving across Texas for a final weekend of fun before graduation and army service in Vietnam in the early seventies.

Quentin was so impressed by the movie that he saw it five times in one week. Costner was so supremely cool in *Fandango* that Quentin even adopted his speech for a few weeks. 'Costner made a filthy tuxedo look like the coolest thing to wear,' explained Quentin years later.

Quentin thought long and hard about *Fandango* and tried to reflect the dialogue in his re-write of *My Best Friend's Birthday*. And then he locked onto a method of using TV culture as a means of expressing one's self in movie dialogue. A classic example was the following piece of dialogue from Quentin's character Clarence, which gives a hint of what was to come in Quentin's writing:

'I felt like committing suicide, slicing open my brains. Then *The Partridge Family* saved me. I thought, I'll watch *The Partridge Family* – then I'll kill myself.'

Quentin and Craig also got some of their inspiration for *Birthday* from the fifties and sixties French farces that Quentin had borrowed from Video Archives. When they were satisfied that *Birthday* was a workable project, they started on the difficult part – trying to raise some cash.

Quentin managed to persuade his mother, Connie, to cough up a few hundred bucks. Craig – who was in his early thirties by this time – promised to use his credit cards if necessary. And Quentin reckoned he could scrounge some help from various sources.

Until that point, he had not mentioned anything about the project to his friends at Video Archives because he wanted to be sure he was actually going to make the movie before shooting his mouth off. They had all discussed trying to finance their own films many times, but none of them had ever managed to get it together.

Once Quentin was confident that he was actually going to pull this movie off, he decided the time had come to reveal all to his Archives cronies – and perhaps do a little recruiting in the process.

Quentin's best friend at the store, Roger Avary, was delighted to hear about the *Birthday* project. He and Quentin seemed to share the same determination to move on to bigger and better things eventually. And Roger realized that making a movie was the ideal ticket out of the video rental business and into real Hollywood.

Avary immediately promised to help Quentin and Hamann by working as a crew member in any capacity they required. Next, Quentin tracked down an aspiring young cinematographer called Scott McGill. He in turn brought a slightly older and wiser character called Rand Vossler on board. Vossler described himself as a producer/director. He instantly recognized Quentin's potential and quietly started to take over the production side of the project. On sound was Dave Schwartz, who managed to borrow a Nagra recording machine from an electrical store where he worked.

However, there were some basic logistical problems primarily caused by the lack of funds. After all, Quentin was proposing to start shooting the movie with a budget of just a few hundred dollars. His beloved *Miami Vice* cost in the region of two million dollars per episode..

One of the first obstacles was the lack of a camera. Craig Hamann eventually came to the rescue by borrowing an old 16mm Bolex camera from a low-budget horror movie director he knew called Fred.

The camera only held a hundred feet of film which meant that the can had to be changed every two and half minutes, which was a major pain. The other problem was that the camera was so old and heavy that it sounded like an army tank when it was turning over. In the end, one of their friends built a cardboard blimp to put over the main body of the rusty old Bolex, which cut out some of the noise.

Quentin and his friends artfully managed to borrow a reasonable package of lights for free by walking into a small, private film school in the South Bay and pretending they were students. They also saved cash by scrounging short ends of film stock from film laboratories.

Birthday turned out to be a very episodic movie and Craig Hamann summarizes the story as follows: 'My character Micky is about to turn thirty when his pal Clarence decides to have a big party for him at a local bar. But Mickey just wants to go home and forget about his birthday. He's tired, depressed and they have both just lost their jobs. Mickey has also just split with his girlfriend. But Clarence will not give up so he hires a prostitute for Mickey. However, when she shows up at the bar, it emerges that she has never done a trick before. Then her big, black pimp turns up. Mickey and the pimp get into a big fight, but then the prostitute runs off with Clarence and falls in love with him. Mickey shows up at Clarence's house at the same time as the girlfriend who's just dumped him. She thinks he's slept with a prostitute, but he hasn't. In the end, Clarence has managed to make it the worst night in Mickey's life.'

Casting actually turned out to be the easiest part of the entire project. Quentin cast himself as Clarence, the guy who hires the hooker for his pal Mickey, to be played by Hamann. The prostitute was played by Hamann's ex-girlfriend Crystal Shaw. The part of her pimp was played by another ex-Best acting school student Al Harrell. All the other parts were relatively small and people like Quentin's other old acting school pal Rich Turner were more than willing to help out.

The first week's shooting of *Birthday* was on location at Connie's house in Torrance, the same property where Quentin's dog Condé Azul used to freak whenever Quentin and his schoolfriends dived below the surface of the pool.

It was chaos.

The young, inexperienced cast and crew hit a whole range of difficulties, from electric cables that were not long enough, to actors not showing up on time. Despite all this, Quentin kept reasonably calm throughout. He recognized the entire process as part of a learning curve that he had to experience if he was ever to go on to bigger and better things.

Connie – who had now remarried, this time a man called Jan – tried not to interfere with her son's pet project. But she found it difficult not to blow a fuse when she came home one night to find that every piece of her living room furniture had been dumped unceremoniously in her kitchen.

One of the key locations for *My Best Friend's Birthday* was the real estate office where Jan worked. Quentin persuaded his new stepfather to let him shoot in the office in the early hours of the morning when no one else would be around. The problem was that none of the actors showed up that day. But Quentin proved that, even at twenty-two, he had the ability to shoot guerilla-style by moving the schedule around and only filming scenes featuring himself and Hamann instead.

'That was a stroke of genius on Quentin's part. It kinda showed what he was made of,' explained Craig Hamann years later. 'Nothing bothered him. He knew he had to be adaptable.'

But wherever Quentin went, trouble was sure to follow. During the making of *Birthday*, it came in the shape of a 'macho jock asshole' who was one of the actors in the movie.

'The problem was that this jock kept suggesting ways of beefing up his part by changing the script,' recalls Craig Hamann. 'Then he refused to act his role as stated in the screenplay. The guy was an egomaniac and he was trying to wreck our shoot'.

Not surprisingly, tension grew between Quentin and the jock actor and eventually Hamann had to play the unenviable role of peacemaker.

'I am going to beat this guy to shit when this shoot is over. I am going to beat him up,' muttered Quentin after yet another blow-up between himself and the actor. 'I am going to stick my fingers in his eye, bite his nose off and beat the crap outta him, so help me.'

To make matters worse, the egomaniac jock's girlfriend was also

playing a role in *Birthday* and the two of them were constantly ganging up on Quentin and Hamann. Hamann only just managed to prevent the six foot two inch Quentin from hammering the couple into the ground.

Quentin and Hamann rewrote and added new scenes as they went along. Rarely did they work on the picture for more than a week before it had to be wrapped for a month or two until further funds became available, usually thanks to Connie's injections of cash and Hamann's credit card.

Some nights, Quentin and Hamann would flop in front of Hamann's TV and watch re-runs of the TV tec show *Crime Story*, with Dennis Farino. It proved a further inspiration for *Birthday*, because some of the characters had a definite rockabilly feel to them. One of Quentin's heroes, stand-up king Andrew Dice Clay, was a regular guest and Quentin was rapidly learning the art of learning from others. For instance, he borrowed the idea of wearing a cool black suit and skinny tie from Mickey Rourke *in The Pope of Greenwich Village*. In fact Quentin had fallen so head over heels in love with that particular movie that he wore an identical outfit both on and off the set of *Birthday* for a month. 'He would even go into McDonald's for a burger in that get-up,' explains Craig Hamann.

Although the shooting of *Birthday* was extremely gruelling at times, there was a plentiful supply of booze, and occasionally grass, for those who wanted it.

On one occasion a sequence was shot between 4.30 and 6.30 in the morning at a bar in Torrance. The cast and crew continually drank draught beer to keep up their stamina and for some there was a stash of weed on constant standby.

As the shooting of the film progressed, so did Quentin's writing abilities. There were only about thirty scenes in total in the script (there are usually many more than that in a fully fledged feature film), but the quality of those scenes was improved with every polish Quentin gave them. He liked to keep the scenes long, which gave the actors a chance to do some real acting and also helped cut down on the number of expensive locations.

Much of the material from *Birthday* later turned up in sequences on *True Romance*, as well as smaller elements in *Natural Born Killers*. This is an inevitable consequence of Hollywood movie-making.

One scene that was eventually used almost verbatim in *Romance* was a sequence in which the two leads discussed the merits of 'fucking Elvis.' This conversation also has a similar feel to the 'Madonna, dick, dick, dick' opening sequence in the coffee shop in *Reservoir Dogs*. The characters did not, as is the case in most movies, speak in order to push the plot forward. They talked about subjects that did not directly relate to the action, but Quentin still made them entertaining and watchable and the conversation told us something about how the characters' minds worked.

Around this time, Hamann and Quentin completed a treatment for a project entitled *Criminal Mind*, which centred around a serial killer who stops killing. The cops are baffled. He no longer commits murders, and thus does not leave them any clues; how are they going to catch him? That project is still floating around Hollywood to this day.

Much of *Birthday* was ad-libbed as the actors and crew went along. However the biggest obstacle was the long, cash-enforced gaps between shooting which meant that there were terrible continuity problems.

'People would get new haircuts, forget what they were wearing in the previous scenes, and sometimes even get suntans. It was a nightmare,' recalls Craig Hamann.

Interestingly, Quentin rode with it all. He actually believed at the time that *Birthday* was so well written that any continuity problems would be overshadowed by the quality of the film. (He later caused many raised eyebrows in Hollywood when he started making bigger budget movies where continuity was, sometimes, rather lacking).

At one stage, production of *Birthday* stopped for almost a year because of money problems. Rand Vossler – originally brought in as a friend of the young cinematographer – had a particularly calming influence on the more impatient, younger members of the cast and crew.

Vossler even ended up taking over the camera work and giving Quentin endless directing advice.

'Rand deserves great credit for all the help he gave Quentin,' says Craig Hamann. 'He would be forever telling Quentin if he had gone over the top in a scene or if he hadn't shot enough coverage.'

There are numerous examples in *Birthday* of what would now be described as classic Tarantinoisms. For instance, when the dialogue from Quentin's character Clarence tries to persuade his best friend to have a party he talks about it 'being in the cards that you are going to have a good time. I'm psychic about this stuff'.

That scene ends with Mickey leaving the bar to go home just as Clarence spots hooker Crystal playing pool in the corner of the bar. He then persuades her to go to Mickey's apartment.

The wardrobe adopted by Quentin in the film is especially significant because the *Pope of Greenwich Village* black zoot suit, complete with skinny black tie, white shirt and shades, would later reappear in *Reservoir Dogs*. Quentin also combed his hair back in a quiff, in the style of his favourite father, Curt Zastoupil. Craig Hamann wore a black leather jacket that didn't fit, which is not surprising since it belonged to Quentin who was at least three inches taller and forty pounds heavier than his friend.

The filming of *Birthday* coincided with the first time that Quentin seriously started dating girls, or at least trying to. Until then, he did not seem interested enough to pursue any relationships. Movies were more important to him.

But Quentin's love scenes in *Birthday* were pretty outrageous. Quentin's character Clarence was tied to a comic book stand in his bedroom while the hooker prepared to whip him. It had a special significance for Quentin, as the scene was actually shot in the bedroom of his mother's Torrance home.

'It was kinda weird, I guess, because Quint ended up lying on the floor with his hands tied to the stand as she stood over him, whip in hand,' explains Craig Hamann. Fortunately, Connie was out at work at the time.

Despite the many amateurish aspects of the movie, Hamann was deeply impressed by the way Quentin handled the actors. 'He seemed to know precisely what they needed all the time. He was always helping them in an empathetic manner, even though he subtly let everyone know he was very much in charge on the set.'

Quentin has since used the same directorial techniques with the Hollywood stars who have appeared in *Reservoir Dogs* and *Pulp Fiction*.

The end of *Birthday* featured Craig Hamann's favourite sequence but, tragically, it will never be seen because of a lab accident that destroyed the last reel.

'Crystal the prostitute ends up trying to have sex with my character, but then her pimp turns up so I lose out yet again. We end up back at the same bar where Clarence started this whole crazy scheme,' explained Hamann.

CLARENCE

It's all my fault Mickey, I'm sorry.

CLARENCE takes something out of his top pocket.

CLARENCE

I'm going to go back in there and have a drink. What I
want you to do is have a smoke from my private stash.

He hands the joint to MICKEY. MICKEY lights it and inhales. He starts to feel a bit better.

CLARENCE

You come back in when you've finished and I'll buy you a
drink.

MICKEY sits on a wall by a car and continues smoking the cannabis joint. Just then a Black and White shows up. The cop notices that MICKEY is smoking a joint. He approaches MICKEY...

'Naturally, it was real pot,' explains Hamann. The 'cop' was played by a security guard who just happened to be on duty at the shopping mall where they shot the scene.

By the time the project faded out in 1987, *My Best Friend's Birthday* had ended up taking almost three years to shoot and cost about five thousand dollars to make. Even then a finished version could never actually be shown because the final reel of film was lost in that accident at the development laboratory. It was about sixty-five minutes in length.

The biggest disappointment for Quentin was that he had been so strapped for cash he hadn't been able to afford to process the footage as they went along. Eventually, three years after starting the project, he persuaded an editor friend to get him a cut-price deal. Everything was processed but then he ended up losing that last reel. What did come out was very disappointing, because it was nothing like he hoped. It was very amateurish and it seemed to lack all the charm of the original script. Some aspects of it had what is now recognised as the Tarantino stamp, but it was not going to get him into Hollywood.

At first, Quentin still believed he could do something with *Birthday*, even if it was not exactly perfect. For a while, he seriously considered remaking it. But Craig Hamann, exhausted by the very thought of those gruelling hours they had worked on the original movie, refused point blank to help.

Quentin was mortified to begin with. Then he took a step back and tried to be realistic. *Birthday* represented another stage in his development as a film maker. Unlike the rich and well qualified kids attending places like the USC and UCLA film schools, he had gone out and attempted to make a feature film on his own. Sure, it was a failure. In fact the whole thing sucked, but the last couple of reels at least had a hint of something in them. He had also told an interesting story.

Birthday simply represented step one in Quentin's career strategy.

Quentin actually felt so inspired by his experiences on the movie that he started writing fresher, stronger material. The idea for *True*

Romance had been germinating during the making of *Birthday*; now it was time to turn it into a reality. There was also, at the back of his mind, a project about two serial killers on the run. The seeds had been sown; it was time to start reaping the harvest.

*'It's not as easy getting laid as it
used to be'*

Jack Nicholson in *Carnal Knowledge*, 1971

Casualties of War

LA CIENEGA BOULEVARD, WEST LA, FRIDAY
EVENING RUSH HOUR, MARCH 1988

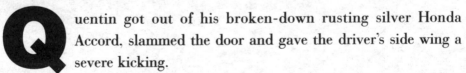uentin got out of his broken-down rusting silver Honda Accord, slammed the door and gave the driver's side wing a severe kicking.

'Fuck. Fuck. Fuck.'

This time he knew his jalopy had completely died on him. Every car journey had been a race against time since a clapping noise had started in the engine two months earlier. But that didn't make it any easier breaking down on one of the busiest intersections in Los Angeles, in bumper-to-bumper Friday night traffic.

He should have ditched the Honda months earlier, but he'd grown attached to the car because it still had Florida licence plates from the owner before the last one. The out-of-state plates were an advantage when it came to parking tickets, because it was much more difficult for the authorities to locate him.

Quentin had grown accustomed to slinging his Honda any place he fancied, on the basis that he would never be tracked down. This was a dangerous habit in a parking-obsessed society like Los Angeles where people often end up paying more than the value of their car to get a vehicle released from a police pound.

But parking was the furthest thing from Quentin's mind as he hot-footed it across the busy street towards a battered-looking payphone.

As he reached the other side of the road, a friendly Hispanic stopped and offered him a ride in the opposite direction. With his dark looks, Quentin could easily pass for a Latino and his presence on the empty sidewalk prompted numerous offers of rides. Even on busy La Cienega there were hardly any pedestrians around, apart from the occasional pan-handler. Walking anywhere in Los Angeles was considered somewhat eccentric. Even going by bus seemed to be something only Latinos and old people favoured, but then that probably had something to do with the frequently publicised crack cocaine abuse by bus drivers.

At the payphone, Quentin called at least three friends but only got through to answering machines. He started to curse after losing his third quarter. His fourth call was to Jerry Martinez, his old movie geek pal at Video Archives. At least he was in.

'You gotta help me, man. My car's died on me.'

'No problem, Quint.'

Jerry and his brother Chris were pleasant guys and didn't mind helping their old friend out, even if it involved a lengthy drive ten miles up from the South Bay. Quentin explained he did not even have enough cash for a taxi to his apartment in Manhattan Beach. Jerry was sympathetic.

Forty-five minutes later, a relieved Quentin flagged down Jerry and his brother and they pulled up behind Quentin's broken down wreck.

'Hold tight. I gotta get some stuff out the car,' yelled Quentin above the noise of the heavy rush-hour traffic.

The two brothers then watched with some surprise as Quentin proceeded to empty the car of every one of his possessions, including a pair of pants, two shirts and a battered *Thomas LA Street Guide*. He then jumped into the back of their car, flinging everything down beside him and slamming the door shut.

'OK. Let's rock and roll, guys.'

The Martinez brothers looked at each other and then at Quentin.

'You can't just leave the car there, Quentin. It's blocking the intersection.'

'Sure I can. Who cares?'

'But it's blocking a busy street. You'll get busted.'

'No way, guys. Come on, let's go.'

But the Martinez brothers would not move until Quentin had helped them push the battered Honda into the nearby parking lot of a furniture store. They were quite disturbed by Quentin's devil-may-care attitude.

Chris Martinez actually noticed Quentin's car parked in that same forecourt for months afterwards. 'Every time I drove past I thought of Quentin. He was damned lucky to get away with dumping it there.'

Quentin and his car problems seemed to be an ongoing saga during the late 1980s. One morning his old friend Craig Hamann got a call from him in the early hours of one morning pleading for a ride because he'd just got a puncture and had no money to get the tyre repaired.

Hamann had quite a temper and he laid into Quentin for waking him at such an ungodly hour. He actually had a rare acting gig the following day and had to be on set for 6am. He slammed the phone down on Quentin and the pair did not speak again for months.

Car problems, rent problems, cash problems – they all seemed to conspire against Quentin. He created an impressive acting CV by claiming to have appeared in Jean-Luc Godard's *King Lear* (on the basis that no-one in Hollywood could have heard of the director) and *Dawn of the Dead* (chosen because Quentin reckoned he looked a bit like one of the bikers). but he still got nowhere. Even so, respected movie critic Leonard Matlin ended up listing Quentin as a cast member in both films in a book he published. However, real casting sessions were rare and usually disastrous. Quentin would find himself competing with dozens of others for lowly paid single-sentence bit parts if he was lucky. No way could he quit his day job yet.

Nevertheless the guys at Archives were not that surprised by Quentin's restlessness. They had sensed his ambition; they just hadn't been sure if he really had the talent to succeed.

Following the disappointment of *Birthday*, Quentin's manager Cathryn Jaymes had already told him that the only way into Hollywood might be through clear evidence of his strong writing talent. Even if he couldn't get his projects sold, at least he could use them as samples to get commissions. Accordingly, he put his directorial and acting aspirations to one side and tried to concentrate on his writing.

The first script he wrote was *True Romance*, which started life being called *The Open Road*. That script was relatively easy for Quentin because he was inspired by some of the better aspects of *My Best Friend's Birthday*. He made Clarence the main male lead and then developed the character of the prostitute Crystal into a much stronger role, renaming her Alabama.

Badlands, the Terence Malik-directed movie starring Sissy Spacek and Martin Sheen, had an influence on *Romance*. It was even replete with the same Erik Satie theme and gauche voice-over by the female lead. The Coen brothers' *Blood Simple* also provided Quentin with part of the basic framework for *Romance*.

Quentin wrote the first draft of *Romance* with the help of his best friend at Video Archives, Roger Avary. Avary was a much more laid back character than Quentin and was able to help give the movie a romantic dimension, despite the gritty aspects of prostitution and drugs.

Romance was originally a tribute to the road movie genre which has been the staple diet of American film goers for more than forty years. Quentin and Avary were both keen fans of Jack Kerouac, who wrote that 'the open road can be as true an experience as any.' That was the key to their script, at least at the beginning. They both adored the whole idea of being on the road with two days' stubble on the chin, the heater turned up and the radio blasting. The road would take the characters towards an understanding of self that was unattainable in a traditional movie set-up. They wanted to create the kind of movie where, as Kerouac, put it, 'you know all and everything is decided for ever.'

In America, road trips are as powerful a symbol as the Empire State Building, signifying the boundlessness of the country, liberty, prosperity and the restlessness that drives successive generations of dreamers and outlaws over the next ridge or across the next river. From *Huck Finn* to Steinbeck to Kerouac to *Thelma and Louise*, the allure of the road runs through American popular culture as steadily as the purr of a well-tuned engine.

Quentin and Avary went in search of that elusive road movie and came up with *The Open Road*. Then they turned the entire script on its head and lost a lot of the road movie ingredients in the process. Eventually, some of this material influenced Quentin's next screenplay, *Natural Born Killers*.

True Romance is especially significant because Quentin's writing was extremely raw at that time and he could not help using his own real life experiences and feelings. Here are some classic examples.

Firstly, when Clarence meets his father after a gap of more than three years, he pleads for his help by saying, 'Did I ever ask you for anything?' That was how Quentin must have felt he would have responded to his own real father (or stepfather Curt Zastoupil for that matter).

Likewise, Quentin recreated the agonies he had suffered going to no-hope casting sessions for Hollywood TV series bit parts, when Clarence's buddy Dick goes to an embarrassing casting session. Clarence's job in a comic book store is the equivalent of Quentin's own job in Video Archives. And Clarence's boss is called Lance (the name of Quentin's boss in real life).

Then there is the classic story told by Clarence's father, about how all Sicilians are related to black people as he is about to be blown away by killer Christopher Walken. This story was actually told to Quentin by a guy called Don, the brother of an African American friend of his mother's.

When Clarence finds himself in a trash yard next to an airport he tells Alabama, 'It's frustrating living next to an airport when you've got shit.' Quentin, of course, lived near LAX in that dive bomb apartment in Harbor City.

When Clarence admits his idea of a perfect birthday is to go to a triple bill of Chinese martial arts movies, it is really Quentin speaking.

Years later, Quentin explained why so many of his life experiences had to be injected into his screenplays.

'I have to bring those experiences with me. I'm not there unless I bring that on with me and make that work inside my material. If I'm not, then you could send a robot out there. If I was writing *The Guns of Navarone*, all right, and then right at the beginning of writing it I break up with my girlfriend, who I'm like madly in love with and then my heart is shattered, all right, that's got to work into it. Now, the story is still about a bunch of commandos going to blow up a couple of cannons, all right. but that pain that I'm feeling has got to find its way into the story or else. what am I doing?'

Apart from his personal experiences, other influences were reflected in *True Romance*. Quentin had actually moulded much of the plot and structure around the Elmore Leonard books he had read, including *The Switch* (which had almost landed him in jail when he stole it from K-Mart at the age of sixteen).

He also developed the idea of using mundane conversations as a way of taking the plot forward by reading the novels of Charles Willeford who had mastered the technique some years previously.

When Quentin presented *Romance* to his hardworking, but ill-rewarded manager Cathryn Jaymes she was astounded. 'The script was brilliant. The best thing I had ever read,' she recalls.

Cathryn was convinced she could quickly get a deal for the movie quickly set up, but told Quentin that he might have to relinquish any

ambitions to direct the project. Quentin, sapped of energy after the years
of toiling with *Birthday*, said he just needed some cash – fast.

As his character Clarence said in *True Romance*, 'I don't have a pot
to piss in or a window to throw it out of.'

But Cathryn James' initial burst of energy and enthusiasm for
Romance was rapidly extinguished by the worse-than-cautious replies
she received from Hollywood studios and major production companies.
One particular letter stood out because of its incredibly vicious tone:

> Dear Fucking Cathryn,
>
> How dare you send me this fucking piece of shit. You must
> be out of your fucking mind. You want to know how I feel
> about it? Here's your fucking piece of shit back. Fuck You.

'Most of them were so offended by the violence and vulgarity in the
material that they couldn't see beyond it. But I was still convinced it was
brilliant,' explains Cathryn James.

At one stage, she sent *True Romance* to Madonna's movie production
company, Maverick, to see if the singer was interested in the role of prostitute, Alabama. One of her producers wrote back, pointing out that
Madonna would never appear in a movie that endorsed drugs.

'But *Romance* was completely anti-drugs, even more so than what
was eventually made,' explained Cathryn James. 'I just continued to get
more and more abuse from all directions.'

Ironically, three years later Madonna came back, wanting to be considered for any of Quentin's movies, following the phenomenal success of
Reservoir Dogs. Such is Hollywood.

But in those early days it dawned on Cathryn Jaymes that, if she
wasn't careful, *True Romance* could seriously damage her professional
standing in Hollywood. She spent entire evenings in tears because of the
frustration and abuse she was getting for staying on Quentin's side. Some
studio executives were even suggesting that whoever wrote the script had

to be sick in the head, if not mentally deranged, and that Cathryn Jaymes should disassociate herself from him immediately.

'Quentin was so obviously talented. I just didn't get it,' she explains.

Cathryn decided to have one last try with British producer/manager Stanley Margolis. She had known the London-born former accountant for many years after he moved to Los Angeles in 1976. He had become a business manager to actors, directors and writers after setting up his own highly successful company. Then, in 1980, he produced something called *Ball Bearing Boogie* which was followed, in 1984, by *The Dark is Mine*, starring Tommy Lee Jones. Neither of these masterpieces exactly set the world on fire, but they did make Margolis a legitimate producer because he had actual credits, which amounted to gold-dust in Hollywood terms.

Margolis was not impressed when he started reading *True Romance*. He almost gave up after the first four pages which at that stage featured the later (and briefer) scene with Drexl (played by a manic Gary Oldman in the actual movie) and two black dudes talking about cunnilingus. It was extremely explicit. Then, on page six, Margolis suddenly found himself hooked and couldn't put the script down until he had finished it.

'One half of me was laughing and the other half was squirming. I thought an audience would react in exactly the same way, so I followed my instincts and went for it,' he recalls.

Margolis rapidly promised to try to get a deal. Cathryn Jaymes was relieved, if only because it proved she had not gone insane, as most of her Hollywood contacts had been suggesting.

Margolis decided that the only way to get *Romance* off the ground was to raise six hundred thousand dollars for a limited partnership for the movie. He was intending to retain a percentage interest. Quentin and Roger Avary went to meet Margolis at his offices on Wilshire Boulevard and a deal was hammered out. Avary was at that time slated as a producer for the film but it should be pointed out that everything was still dependent on getting the production money in place. Neither Quentin or Avary received a penny at this stage.

Quentin was keen to show Margolis a copy of his two-thirds

completed debut movie, *My Best Friend's Birthday*, to prove he was capable of directing *Romance*. But the producer was far from impressed when he saw the film and advised Quentin never to show it again as an example of his directorial experience. Quentin took note of that advice and it served him well. Two years later when he was pitching to direct *Reservoir Dogs* he did not even mention the existence of *Birthday*.

Margolis was impressed by Quentin's confidence, but not by his table manners. Whenever they went to a restaurant together, he noticed how Quentin shovelled food into his mouth, slurped his drinks and tended to spit fragments of food in all directions, besides holding his knife and fork as if they were ballpoint pens. But Margolis was even more bemused by Quentin's verdict on certain legendary directors, particularly the highly respected John Huston.

'He described him as a hack and knocked a lot of other very well-known names. Coming from a young guy who had done squirt, I thought it was a bit much,' explains Margolis.

Stanley Margolis put his personal feelings aside and started going through the exact same routine as Cathryn Jaymes before him – sending the script out to his contacts at the major studios. The reaction was just as terrible as before. They just didn't get it.

Most of the executives who received *Romance* assigned it to be read by one of the thousands of out-of-work actors, writers and directors who earn extra money in Hollywood by reading scripts for production companies and studios, usually at a pro rata rate of fifty dollars per script. The reactions of some of these would-be filmmakers is fascinating in the light of what has happened since. One wrote:

> For me, the moment we exited the realm of comedy, the racist slurs, and violent action and language became offensive and overbearing, hitting the reader/viewer over the head with an unrelenting aggressiveness... the characters and their dialogue do come to life, although what they do once they come to life may make you want them to go back where they came from.

Another reader – remember, these are the people who recommend every unsolicited script that arrives on a Hollywood producer's desk – went even further by stating:

> This is a story that does not need to be told. It fails on every count. The action is not exciting, and the characters are under-developed and unbelievable. *True Romance* is one long hollow adventure.

One representative at the Miramax company – which later became the US distributor for *Reservoir Dogs* and then fully financed *Pulp Fiction* – did not even bother to send Margolis back a letter of rejection. Instead, the exec wrote in thick black felt-tip pen across the top of the producer's letter of introduction, 'UGH! HATED CHARACTERS.'

But the worst response to *True Romance* came from Bud Grossgroff, former CEO of Republic Pictures. In a handwritten note to the producer/manager he said:

> Stan,
> Fortunately, this is a business of opinions. Who is to say yours might be more valid than ours.
> Ours would be very strong – stay with management! The script is without any redeeming virtues.
> We always ask:
> 1/ Who will go to see this?
> 2/ Why?
> 3/ Can we get a director and cast that will get the financial backing?
> This script fails these three basic questions – it equals, who cares about these people, their story? They're both shit, to quote the characters.

Stanley Margolis was clearly facing an uphill struggle with *True Romance*.

A year after he first took the project on, Margolis was tearing his hair out with frustration. He called Quentin up, only to discover that he was temporarily staying at his mother's new house in Glendale. He also did not have a car and told Margolis he couldn't afford to travel to his Beverly Hills offices for any more meetings.

'I'll come to your place,' responded Margolis.

The following day, Hollywood producer Stanley Margolis knocked on the oak front door of the house in Greenbrier Avenue to find himself being greeted by Quentin's mother Connie.

'I'm sorry, he's not up yet,' explained Connie.

Margolis was hardly going to turn around and drive the twenty miles back to LA.

'It's OK. I'll wait.'

Margolis then made polite conversation with Connie while her son struggled under a shower. Sometimes dealing with Quentin really was like handling a child.

Thirty minutes later, a meeting was convened in Quentin's adolescent bedroom, plastered with movie posters and littered with dirty clothes, old cereal bowls and comics on the floor.

Quentin agreed to give Margolis a further year's option with no up-front cash and then insisted that the British producer stay and watch a Chinese martial arts film on the big screen TV that Connie had set up in the den.

Quentin fast-forwarded the movie to specific scenes which he wanted to show Margolis because he was hoping they could be recreated in some way in *True Romance*. Margolis was more interested in getting some backing first.

Half-way through the development of *Romance*, Quentin started to worry about being stuck in the pleasant, party atmosphere in Manhattan Beach and Video Archives. He wanted to get more focused and he reckoned the only way to do that was to move to Hollywood and get a job inside the industry – any job to start with.

He got a one-room apartment over on Western Avenue, in a gritty neighbourhood of central Hollywood and surprised his friends at Video Achives by suddenly quitting. He intended to soak up the atmosphere like some latter-day Raymond Chandler and begin writing about the LA lowlifes he found so fascinating. And his research was about to get an injection of the sort of reality he would have done better to avoid...

'What are you going to do, kill me?
Everybody dies'

John Garfield, to racketeer Lloyd Goff, in *Body and Soul*, 1947

The Animal Factory

LA COUNTY JAIL, DOWNTOWN LOS ANGELES,
FALL 1989

'**E**verything on the table. NOW!' Quentin pulled off his jacket, slapped down his wallet and keys and everything else he had in his pants pockets. The smell of disinfectant wafted across the holding room as the glassy-eyed warden continued to bark orders.

'Remove your clothes.'

This was serious. At 6am that morning, Quentin had been hauled out of bed at his rundown apartment on Western Avenue, Hollywood, and informed he was being arrested for multiple parking ticket violations. The cop who handcuffed him said something about seven thousand dollars worth of outstanding, unpaid fines.

Quentin had presumed he would be taken to the local precinct, officially charged, processed and released. It did not seem such a big price to pay for avoiding payment of so many parking tickets.

But he could not have been more wrong. The black and white that picked him up actually took him to the most notorious jail in the city, the LA County; a grim, square, white-washed, faceless building where everyone from O.J. Simpson to Charles Manson has been incarcerated. This is a jail where one inmate a month is murdered. It's the holding tank for gang members, misfits, dropouts, psychos, druggies, child molesters, wife beaters and underworld people from all over southern California – it feels like a jail that is specifically designed as a subdivision of hell on earth.

Quentin removed his pants and stood there, shivering with a weird combination of fear and genuine cold, aware he was about to undertake a voyage into the unknown depths of society.

'Spread your cheeks.'

A moment passed as the guard squinted.

'Now cough.'

The mandatory finger-printing a few minutes later, after he had changed into a regulation orange boiler suit, seemed tame in comparison with those earlier inspections.

The law had caught up with Quentin, but at least he was getting some invaluable experience to use in his writing. This was like going right into the horse's mouth.

As Quentin was escorted along the corridor of the area known as 'The Hall', on the eastern side of the jail, he saw eyes peering from between the bars, inspecting him, hissing, whistling admiringly; some even blew kisses. Fresh meat is always greatly appreciated in a place like the County.

The shackles around Quentin's ankles were removed as the door to his new home slid open and he was told that lunch was at twelve noon. The electrically operated door slammed shut the moment he stepped over the threshold into that new world.

Inside the cell were about twenty-five other bedraggled inmates, mostly Hispanics, with banderos, six or seven blacks, plus two or three whites who looked unnervingly pale in comparison.

The moment Quentin walked in, the earlier sterile smell was

replaced by a waft of puke, piss and shit. In the far corner, a fat, greasy mulatto squatted on the crapper, smiled and strained. A black guy leaning up against a wall was removing the braids from his hair. Next to him, another black, wearing a hairnet down over his forehead like a sweater cap reached into his pocket, pulled out a half-smoked cigarette, fumbled in another pocket, and retrieved a match. He struck the match on the concrete floor, lit his cigarette, and sat back coolly on the bench. His homie stood across from him near the door.

Quentin remained cool and kept his eyes down. He had read enough gritty LA prison novels like the classic *No Beast So Fierce* by ex-con Eddie Bunker, to know that a fresh, young, white man is like meat to a pitbull in the County. Keep your eyes down. Chew that gum hard. Don't smile at anyone. Then you might just survive. If you didn't stick to those house rules you were likely to end up as a sex slave to some boy-hungry monster. The very notion filled Quentin with terror.

Quentin was going to have to make his mark at the County, or else they'd piss on him in every sense of the word.

By mid-morning that day, he was lining up to make a call to his mother, Connie, to see if she could lay out some cash to help get him released. The queue for the only public phone on that wing of the LA County was twenty men long and Quentin knew he only had thirty minutes before free time was over and they would be locked back inside that stinking hellhole of a cell.

Quentin made it to the phone just in time. He asked the operator for a collect call and then waited to be connected. Seconds later, Connie was reading him the riot act. No, she was not going to help bail him out. She'd told him over and over to pay his parking fines. Quentin slammed the phone down in anger. He knew there was no one else who could help him. He'd have to grin and bear it in jail until he could find someone to bail him out. It's not going to be easy but think of the great dialogue, he told himself.

At home, Connie was feeling bad about her son's incarceration but he had to learn a lesson. She was worried about what might be happening to him inside the animal factory, as the County was known, so she called a friend in the LA County Sheriff's Department to see if they could move him into a safe cell. Unfortunately this probably had the effect of guaranteeing that he was locked up with the worst of the worst.

Quentin knew that first night in the County would be the toughest because he'd be put to the test by the other inmates. Tough or soft was all they were interested in. Quentin found a corner of the concrete floor and tried to curl up to get some shut-eye, but there were diversions every-where; along one wall a drug addict in need of a fix was puking his guts out; in another corner a white guy was sobbing like a baby; over by the toilet two guys were doing something together under one blanket. Quentin pulled his own prickly blanket over his head and tried to block it all out.

He was just beginning to nod off when suddenly the blanket was being pulled off him in a short sharp jerking motion. For a few seconds he did not dare move. Then Quentin looked up and saw a smiling Hispanic settling down with his blanket just two feet away.

'Hey, man. What's your problem?' shot Quentin, trying to sound tough.

The Hispanic looked up and smiled a toothless grin. 'I got no prob-lem, man. Why? You gotta problem?'

Quentin grated his teeth together for a couple of beats, then exploded. 'That's my blanket, motherfucker! I want it back, NOW!'

'Fuck you!'

In another corner, three black members of the notorious Crips street gang watched with interest. This was just the kind of Mexican stand-off they enjoyed. It was also the type of no-win situation that would eventu-ally mark the climax of all Quentin's movies.

'I told you, cocksucker. Gimme the fucking blanket back, NOW!' Quentin knew he might be about to provoke a vicious assault, but he was well aware that backing down was tantamount to committing suicide in a place like the County. He was terrified. But those acting classes were coming in useful.

Quentin stared straight at the blanket-snatcher and then became uncomfortably aware of two other Hispanics watching him. His eyes snapped between the three men. He got up.

Just then, two of the Crips who had been watching all this with a look of vague amusement on their faces, winked at Quentin. Quentin knew they would never support the Hispanics because they were sworn enemies inside and outside jail.

One of the Hispanics stood up. He was easily as tall as Quentin and three times as muscly. Quentin knew he could not climb down. He had to go through with it. They approached each other. Elsewhere, the inmates looked on, detached, as if they were watching a Western on TV. This clash seemed to be heading in one inevitable direction.

Suddenly two of the Crips moved between Quentin and the tall, muscly Hispanic.

'Give him the blanket, motherfucker.'

'Why?'

'Cos he's got our respect, that's why.'

Another beat of silence followed. Quentin, sweating profusely by this time, stood his ground. The man on the floor threw him the blanket, grudgingly. The stand-off had ended in a climb-down. Quentin spent a further eight days in the County without incident. He even began writing a new screenplay, called *Natural Born Killers* in his head. It was going to be about a desperate guy, just like some of the inmates in the County. He even thought about casting his friend Craig Hamann as the criminal.

When Quentin got out of jail, it was almost an anticlimax. He knew he had been lucky to survive intact, but the glare of the hot sunshine bouncing off the County's whitewashed walls made him blink as he walked through the glass swing doors. He realized that he could not make a habit of being slung in jail, but those eight days had taught him more about the real world than just about any other experience in his life.

He had felt great empathy with some of the characters he

encountered, especially those Crips who had taken him under their wing with no strings attached. His stay in jail proved a turning point in Quentin's writing. Now he could write with some authority about something he had experienced for himself, rather than seen on TV or at a movie theatre.

Not long after this, Quentin met and fell in love with his first real girlfriend, Grace Lovelace, an attractive English lecturer at the University of California at Irvine. Grace seemed to instantly understand and appreciate Quentin's slightly unorthodox approach to life.

She was nothing like the handful of wannabe actresses he had met over the previous couple of years. She was wise, well educated and very savvy. She was not impressed by Hollywood, but she appreciated Quentin's desperate ambition to succeed in the movie industry.

Grace even acknowledged openly that Quentin's affection for her would always have to take second place to the movies. He continued to see a vast number of films each week and he was trying to complete *Natural Born Killers*, a script that would eventually take quite a number of painful rewrites before he got it right.

At the same time, Quentin was taking intensive acting lessons with a drama coach called Allen Garfield in West Hollywood. The individual classes actually proved invaluable and Quentin started to get more call-ups for minor roles in TV shows. The only gig he actually got was as an Elvis impersonator on *The Golden Girls* comedy series. It was the high point of his acting career at the time. He was one of twelve Elvis impersonators – just a glorified extra. For some reason they had to sing Don Ho's *Hawaiian Love Chant*. All the other Elvises wore Vegas-style jump suits. but Quentin wore his own clothes because he was the early Sun Records Elvis. 'I was the hillbilly cat Elvis. I was the real Elvis, everyone else was Elvis after he sold out.' But at least it was a start and his role did make it through the editing process. Connie and his friends watched the episode with pride when it was screened.

But one very brief TV appearance was hardly going to pay the rent, let alone launch his career as a Hollywood star. Many casting agents

found Quentin's looks difficult to handle. He was tall, awkward and a bit strange-looking in the face. At certain angles he was almost ruggedly handsome, but from other angles he looked downright ugly, with that jutting out chin.

But Grace's entry into Quentin's life definitely seemed to mark some kind of upturn in his career. In 1990, shortly after they met, he picked up the princely sum of one thousand five hundred dollars for writing a script. Special effects man Bob Kurzman had penned a treatment based on the story of two bank robbers who flee to Mexico and end up in a top-less bar run by vampires. It was entitled *From Dusk Till Dawn*. And Kurzman hired Quentin to work it into a screenplay.

That fifteen hundred dollars was especially significant to Quentin. As he later explained, 'No one had ever before hired me and given me money to write.'

At last, Quentin was beginning to see some light at the end of the tunnel. He calculated that the fifteen hundred dollars would last him about three months if he was careful. He just hoped that something else would come along after that.

In fact, after Quentin delivered the bank robbers/vampires project to Kurzman it rapidly died. Even Quentin later admitted his writing was not very good and the project took more than five years to re-emerge as a green-lighted movie with Quentin and others involved.

Quentin also completed the first draft script for *Natural Born Killers* around this time. Cathryn Jaymes bounced it around a few people in Hollywood, although she was extremely careful not to show it to the same characters who had so despised *True Romance*.

Meanwhile, *Romance* was floating in search of finance, through pro-ducer Stanley Margolis, so Quentin was still earning next to nothing from the movie industry.

At one stage, he even decided to try and make it as a novelist. He had been particularly moved by Larry McMurtry's *All My Friends Will Be Strangers* and it had made him want to write a book about his zany, off-the-wall experiences at Video Archives. He was so serious that he wrote two chapters and then spent nearly six months re-writing those chapters in an effort to make them read absolutely perfectly. Then other concerns took over.

By this time Quentin was starting to circulate in the lower reaches of the movie business proper. In 1990, he met two young film school grads-turned-producers called Don Murphy and Jane Hamsher, who had produced an incredibly low-budget movie called *Several Dragons* and had an office on the MGM lot.

Murphy and Hamsher's partnership had been forged at the USC film school in the late eighties, where Jane, former editor of San Francisco's punk-rock fanzine *Damage*, had met Don, a six-foot-two fast-talker from a place really called Hicksville, in Long Island. (Murphy had earlier fled the 'soon to be a senator's aide' tag at Georgetown University.)

Quentin had first met Murphy in Video Archives a few months earlier when he'd picked Murphy's brains because he wanted to direct *NBK* himself on the cheap.

'Quentin seemed cool and interesting and we kinda hooked up,' explains Murphy.

Quentin told Murphy he had all but given up hope of *True Romance* ever getting made and had switched his attentions to *Natural Born Killers*. He offered it to Murphy to read, but Don never actually got around to reading it.

Some months later, Jane Hamsher's antenna immediately shot up when Quentin mentioned *NBK* again. Just then Don Murphy chipped in, 'Oh, we have a copy lying around the house.'

After Murphy and Hamsher read *NBK*, they said, 'We have to make this – it's the best script we've ever read.'

But they were unable to categorize the film easily. 'We couldn't exactly say it was a cross between *Heidi* and *Lawrence of Arabia*,' explains Murphy. But they did consider it a *Bonnie and Clyde* for the nineties.

Murphy – an alarmingly straight-talking type of guy – told Quentin that he would have a tough time directing any of his projects himself, as he had no real experience helming a picture.

A few days later, Quentin – who fully appreciated the importance of getting out and about in Hollywood – turned up at a showing of Murphy and Hamsher's low-budget movie *Several Dragons* at the Imperial Movie Theatre. Murphy told Quentin he knew someone who claimed to have the right financial connections to back *NBK* on a strictly low budget basis.

Quentin was not over-impressed, but anything was worth a try so he got Murphy to link him up with these 'financial connections' who turned out to be a couple of meaty bodybuilders living near Quentin's old stamping ground in Torrance.

The two muscle men claimed they had enough money to shell out two hundred and fifty thousand dollars for the movie to be made. Quentin was impressed. This could be the chance he was looking for. They even agreed to let him direct it and he was convinced he could get away with making it for this relatively low sum (which sounded enormous after his experiences on *My Best Friend's Birthday*).

'But, there's one condition,' the two bodybuilders informed Quentin. 'We get to be in the movie.'

Quentin hesitated for a moment, well aware that this was shaping up into a classic flaky Hollywood dodgy deal.

'You want to be in my movie?'

'It'll be no sweat, Quentin. We just want a small part each so we can get our union cards.'

Quentin sighed with relief. For a moment he had thought they wanted to play Mickey and Mallory in drag. He happily went away and a new scene featuring two bodybuilders was co-written by Quentin with his Video Archives friend Roger Avary. A few days later, Quentin held another meeting with the two keep-fit fanatics and showed them the new scene which featured two bodybuilders who have had their legs shot off by Mickey and Mallory. Despite their horrendous injuries, they tell tabloid TV journalist Wayne Gayle that they still don't hold any grudges against the serial killing couple.

But, within a few weeks, Quentin and Don Murphy came to the inevitable Hollywood conclusion that the bodybuilders had been 'full of shit˙ and the deal collapsed. Nevertheless, Quentin was so happy with the scene that he kept it in the script and it was even eventually shot by director Oliver Stone for his version of the movie.

A year later, Don Murphy was at a party when he heard that Quentin had rewritten *Natural Born Killers* and given it to Rand Vossler, the producer/director/father figure who had helped him so much during the making of *My Best Friend's Birthday*. Murphy's ears pricked up and he contacted Vossler. Within a few weeks he had persuaded Quentin and Vossler to give him a free option to try and get the movie made. Murphy argued that he could not provide any advance finance because he was almost as broke as Quentin at the time, but if it did get made they would all make hundreds of thousands of dollars.

Quentin had heard all this many times before, but he felt he had no choice. Most of Hollywood hated his material and he was just grateful to find two soulmates like Don Murphy and Jane Hamsher who seemed to have their finger on the pulse of the younger, more independent film-makers in town.

With the fifteen hundred dollars from the bank robbers/vampire project long gone, Quentin started desperately casting around for something inside the movie business – however mundane – to keep the wolf from the door. It was going to be tough.

Roger Avary had by this time also quit *Video Archives* and, in desperation, the two movie geeks decided it was time to call in some favours from the few Hollywood contacts they had made while working at the store. Surely someone could offer them both a real movie job?

Telephoning all their ex-customers proved a demoralizing task for the two video store assistants. Many of the people they contacted were confused because they could not understand why the two film buffs were cold-calling them for jobs in the movie industry. Some of them told the pair to get their jobs back at Video Archives – quick. Many of the other people they called were either not in or on the other line and never actually bothered to call them back. In the end, their bid for Hollywood fame

and fortune resulted in a single job offer which could fairly be described as the lowest of the low.

So it was that Quentin and Roger found themselves working as production assistants, for a basic rate of twenty dollars a day, on a Dolph Lundgren workout video.

As PAs, the pair were treated like serfs by everyone from the star himself downwards. For two weeks their main job was to go ahead of the cast and crew to locations all over LA to ensure they were pristine for the coming of muscle bound Dolph. (Dolph's career took off after he played Sylvester Stallone's Russian opponent in *Rocky IV* and he even grabbed a few tabloid headlines by dating Hollywood babes.) This is going to be a really classy production, mused Quentin and Avary.

By the time they got to one location – the front garden of a house near Venice Beach – their task had become what Roger Avary later aptly described as the 'shittiest job in the world.'

The front lawn of the house was covered in dog shit and one of the producers started barking orders at his two PAs.

'You two guys clean up the dog shit.'

Quentin and Roger Avary looked disdainfully at the producer and then spotted the grip's truck pulling up just by the front garden. They set off to scrounge a few shovels to do the dirty work

But one of the demarcation lines that has always existed within the movie business suddenly came into force.

'No way are you using our equipment to pick up a bunch of dog shit.' one tough-looking grip informed them.

So Quentin and Avary got a roll of paper towels and started ripping off chunks which they used to delicately pick up every piece of dog shit from the front yard.

'There must have been a hundred stools and it smelt appalling,' explained Roger afterwards. 'If anyone ever says that they had a crappy job I can always top them with that particular assignment.'

Welcome to Hollywood, boys...

Act II

The confrontation

'I wouldn't mind making the most violent movie ever made some day, but I didn't...'

Quentin Tarantino, 1991

'If you want to find an outlaw, you call an outlaw. If you want to find a Dunkin' Donuts, call a cop'

Randall 'Tex' Cobb, in *Raising Arizona*, 1987

The Rookie

RUNDOWN APARTMENT BLOCK, CORNER OF
WESTERN AND THIRD, HOLLYWOOD,
NEW YEAR'S EVE 1989

The staccato vibrations of automatic gunfire on the stroke of midnight woke Quentin from a heavy slumber. Dozens of local crazies were test firing their Uzis into the night air. It might be a tradition in the neighbourhood, but that didn't make it any easier to sleep. Welcome to nineteen fucking ninety.

Quentin lay there in his cramped crash pad, wondering what he'd done to deserve to live in such squalor. His latest daytime job, performing cold-call telephone sales on would-be video purchasers was wearing down his ambition to become a genuine Hollywood player. Was it really worth the struggle?

Here he was, twenty-six years old, with barely enough spare cash to afford a Big Mac. Then there were the hookers, pimps and drug dealers he had to battle his way past each time he entered his crummy apartment block.

Quentin believed getting known in Tinseltown was the key to realizing his dreams. That was why he had taken a lousy job at the Imperial Entertainment Film Company, even though it bore no relation to actually making movies. In some ways a telesales job was like working a phone sex line – an occupation shared by many out-of-work actors in LA. After all, Quentin had to put on his most charming voice and his best good manners in order to convince folk to buy his company's fine selection of low budget videos, which included such classics as *Operation 'Nam* starring Lee Van Cleef. Would phone sex have been easier?

At the office a couple of days later he made the acquaintance of a character called Sheldon Lettice, a writer/director who had been involved in a number of Jean Claude Van Damme movies. Quentin was impressed, especially when they got talking one lunchbreak about Lettice's great pal, fellow writer/director Scott Spiegel.

Quentin immediately enthused about Spiegel's *Thou Shalt Not Kill* movie, not to mention his work on *Evil Dead 2*, with Quentin's acting hero, Bruce Campbell. They also discussed Spiegel's directorial debut, a little known straight-to-video effort called *Intruder*, which featured a cameo by Campbell and starred Emilio Estevez's sister, Renée. The film is best summed up by a blurb for it written by Spiegel: 'They're closing Walnut Lake supermarket and it's not just the prices that are being slashed! Yep, we're in stalk 'n' slash territory once more with this tale of a mad killer haunting the deserted aisles of a late-night grocery store.'

Sheldon Lettice was also particularly impressed when Quentin described in detail the plot and casting of *Intruder* and *Thou Shalt Not Kill*. He surmised that if a guy was that interested in such obscure movies he had to have some talent.

Lettice even agreed to contact Scott Spiegel to arrange a meeting so that Quentin could bounce a few ideas off the young schlock master.

'This guy Quentin just loves *Thou Shalt Not Kill*. You mind if I give him your number?'

'Sure, that's cool,' came director/writer Scott Spiegel's reply.

A few hours later, Quentin was delivering the story of his life machine-gun style down the line to Spiegel, who hardly had a chance to get a word in edgeways.

Quentin even managed to pitch *Natural Born Killers* to Spiegel in thirty seconds flat. The writer/director – also a self confessed movie geek – felt an immediate affinity with Quentin. He invited him round for a beer some time.

Quentin – realizing that Spiegel's home was only twelve blocks away – leapt at the chance, especially since it meant he wouldn't have to find any transport.

'How about now?'

Spiegel was cool. 'Come on over.'

That night Spiegel and Quentin discussed the nuances of great Italian exploitation movies and then Spiegel got out his all-time favourite board game based on the tacky TV show, *Charlie's Angels*. Quentin was in heaven. A bond of friendship had been formed. The two movie fanatics played until dawn.

Quentin was particularly taken by Spiegel because the young film maker had just co-written *The Rookie*, which was about to be released starring Clint Eastwood, Raul Julia and Sonia Braga. *Now that was impressive.*

'Hey Scotty, mind if I crash here?' enquired Quentin, realizing the time and being slightly concerned at the prospect of walking through the most dangerous part of Hollywood at five in the morning.

'Go ahead, Quint. *Me casa, su casa.*'

Soon Scott and Quentin were inseparable. They would regularly go and see black comedian Rudy Ray Moore at a hole-in-the-wall establishment called Club Lingerie, on Sunset. Quentin frequently insisted on popping out to Tony's Burgers for some fast food in the interval.

One time, Quentin even persuaded Scott to go and try out one of Tony's specials.

'They're the coolest burgers in town, man,' insisted Quentin.

Reluctantly, Scott joined his friend at the fast food emporium. He

was astonished at how carelessly Quentin flashed his wallet around the restaurant, which was filled with drifters and street walkers. When Quentin foolishly left his wallet on the table while he went up to collect his burger, Scott decided to teach his new friend a lesson and snatched it. Quentin only realized his wallet was missing when the dynamic duo got back to Club Lingerie.

'Fuck, my wallet! Where's my wallet, man! I gotta go get it,' screamed Quentin as their hero Moore walked back on stage.

Scott chuckled. 'Get a life, Quint. Like it'll still be there! Get outta here!'

Quentin was about to fight his way through the Club Lingerie crowds when Scott smiled and handed the wallet back to his friend. Quentin had actually believed that he would find the wallet if he ran back to Tony's Burgers. That streak of naivety would stay with him for ever.

Rudy Ray Moore was a particular favourite of Quentin and Scott's. Moore's stand-up routine was brutal, black and very cynical. Quentin had also seen many of Moore's outrageous low budget blaxploitation movies, including *The Avenging Disco Godfather*, *The Devil's Son-in-Law*, *Monkey Hustle* and *The Human Tornado*. They could all be called cousins of the daddy of them all, *Shaft*, which came out in 1971.

The plot of *Human Tornado* was a classic of its genre. Moore plays his favourite character, Dolemite, an ass-kickin' mutherfucker who can kick lightning's ass and throw thunder in jail. Dolemite speaks through-out the film in rhyming rap-type speech. He was on the run from a redneck sheriff who killed his own wife because she went to bed with Dolemite, who is also trying to rescue some whores from the Mob.

Moore was, in many ways, the father of rap as it is now known. The character Dolemite kept reappearing in his movies and was a pivotal part of his stage show.

'Dolemite is my name and fuckin' up mutherfuckers is my game,' was how Moore introduced himself to the crowd at the Club Lingerie most nights.

Black humour is the only comedy in America that fully appreciates and uses sarcasm and irony. Quentin certainly found it easier to relate to than *The Brady Bunch.* His other favourite hard-hitting black comics included Pryor, Murphy and Carlin.

Years later, Moore's influence made itself felt in some of the most controversial scenes in both *Reservoir Dogs* and *Pulp Fiction.* In *Dogs,* when four of the gang are in Nice Guy Eddie's caddy they get into a conversation about black women being tougher than white women when it comes to 'taking no shit from their men'. This was one of Moore's favourite lines.

In *Pulp Fiction,* there are even more references, especially in the dialogue of the hitman played by Samuel L. Jackson.

'*Pulp* is especially like a homage to Rudy,' explains Scott Spiegel. 'It was all pretty wacky stuff.'

On the way home, one night back in 1990, Quentin astounded Scott Spiegel by reciting a long rap he had made up himself. 'It was brilliant. It captured the whole black rap thing perfectly,' explains Spiegel.

During this period, Spiegel and Quentin were particularly moved by a night of back-to-back Vincent Price movies at the Vagabond Theatre, in east Hollywood (They both had a healthy obsession with Price.) On another evening they went to see the classic *House of Wax* in 3-D and bumped straight into Price outside the movie theatre, where Quentin promptly obtained his autograph.

The two buddies then wandered back to Spiegel's bungalow at 2130, Vista Del Mar, where they analysed every scene in *House of Wax* as they munched their way through an entire packet of Spiegel's favourite cereal, Fruit Brute. They then had a three-hour marathon on the Charlie's Angels board game, plus a thirty-minute session with *The Legend of Jesse James* game.

Quentin never forgot that evening at Spiegel's, mainly because he had been introduced to Fruit Brute for the first time. This became a life-long cereal obsession which culminated in Quentin using it for Mr Orange when he is in his apartment preparing to go out on the *Reservoir Dogs* heist.

Quentin was genuinely excited for Scott Spiegel the night *The Rookie*, starring Clint Eastwood and partly penned by Spiegel, opened in Hollywood. Spiegel told his new friend the line in *The Rookie* of which he was most proud: 'There must be a hundred good reasons why I don't blow you away, but right now I can't think of one.' Spiegel and his roommate held a small party back at his house to celebrate and Quentin provided the sort of sideshow only a bunch of movie geeks could really appreciate.

He'd got hold of a rough video recording of a live show from Miami called *Super Cool Kung Foo Alley Cats* and it consisted of a very lame male stand-up comic doing dreadful impersonations of just about every famous person in America.

Quentin could hardly contain himself as he stabbed the video into Scott's well worn VCR machine. He explained that the tape had become a virtual collector's item amongst Hollywood's smaller, trendier film production companies.

'You just will not believe this guy,' enthused Quentin as he provided Scott and his friends with the full background to the video.

Within seconds of *Super Cool Kung Foo Alley Cats* coming on the small screen everyone was in hysterics and started doing copycat impersonations. Quentin's taste had once again proved impeccable.

After their sideshow, Quentin, Spiegel and associates wandered off towards the livelier end of Hollywood Boulevard to see if they could score some fast food. Quentin rapidly got embroiled in a deep and meaningful movie geek discussion about *The Adventures of Baron Munchausen*, the movie which was helmed by ex-*Monty Python* member, Terry Gilliam. No one really cared except Quentin. Ironically, a few months later, it was to be Gilliam who came to his rescue when he was severely-mauled at the Sundance Film Institute.

Quentin was also particularly impressed by Scott Spiegel's Detroit connection with director Sam Raimi, whose brilliant low budget debut, *Evil Dead*, has long been considered a classic of its genre. Scott and Raimi had been contemporaries in Detroit before finding fame (of sorts) in Hollywood. Quentin particularly admired Raimi because he had stuck to his guns and insisted on directing his own way – and he was only in his early twenties when he made his debut film.

But that night out in the seedier areas of West Hollywood almost ended in murder and mayhem for Quentin when he was waiting for a bus home on a notorious hooker-infested corner of Santa Monica Boulevard. While he was standing next to a black transvestite street walker a van suddenly pulled up. A Mexican kid jumped out with a baseball bat and rushed up behind the TV hooker.

The transvestite turned around the instant she sensed the Mexican behind her and looked down at the weapon he was brandishing.

'Don't do it. I'm Vice.' It was a terrific response under the circumstances.

However the Mexican looked as if he was going to ignore her advice and said nothing. Quentin watched the entire proceedings in horror.

'Don't fucking do it...'

BOOM! He hit her anyway. The hooker then fought back and suddenly another six men emerged from the van. Quentin and the transvestite immediately took off at high speed.

It was a brush with LA street violence that Quentin would never forget.

In May, 1990, Quentin was delighted when Spiegel invited him to a huge Memorial Day barbecue. Quentin was particularly interested because he knew the gathering would include some of Tinseltown's brightest young talents.

Quentin turned up for the lunchtime barbecue at least two hours late because he'd overslept after going to the midnight showing of a horror film. But his timing was perfect. A sprinkling of minor celebs were on show, like Michael Rooker, who'd just starred with Tom Cruise and Nicole Kidman in *Days of Thunder*, but was actually better known to this hip, young crowd, as the lead character in the infamous low budget flick, *Henry, Portrait of a Serial Killer*.

Then there was the blonde actress Tracey Arnold, who had been the

victim of all sorts of dastardly deeds in Spiegel's own directorial effort, *Intruder*, as well as at the hands of Rooker in *Portrait*. There was also a fairly interesting array of on-the-edge-of-employment technicians, producers and directors.

On the far side of the back yard, a quiet, solemn, thin man in his early thirties was explaining to a friend that he was about to jack in the movie business, and return to New York to join his family business. Nothing was moving fast enough for him in Hollywood. The industry of dreams was turning into one long nightmare.

Lawrence Bender was a bit part actor-turned-producer who had actually put together the incredibly low budget for Scott Spiegel's *Intruder*, and managed, like everyone else involved in the production, to earn virtually nothing in the process. He also took a major acting role in the movie to save the meagre budget even further.

Bender's background was varied, to say the least. He had gained a degree in civil engineering back east before enrolling in dancing classes and then winning a scholarship to *Fame* choreographer Louis Falco's New York dance academy. 'I had, like, six call-backs for *Cats* but I didn't make it,' he jokes now. Then a serious injury forced Bender to try acting, where he studied in New York, alongside names like Jessica Lange, Mickey Rourke and Christopher Reeves. 'By that time I was a triple threat,' he later explained. 'I was a dancer, singer and actor. But I was threatening nobody.'

Bender's biggest movie to date, *Intruder*, had gone straight to video and caused a reasonable ripple of interest, but it was dawning on him that it was time to get a real life. Making movies and making money did not seem to go hand in hand and Hollywood was fast becoming a place of bitter rejection for the young film maker.

Just as Bender was about to announce his early retirement from the entertainment industry, Scott tapped him on the shoulder and introduced him to Quentin.

An hour later, the two were still locked in conversation and Quentin's enthusiasm for movies was reviving Bender's flagging interest in the Hollywood film business. He loved the sound of *Natural Born Killers* and was disappointed when Quentin said he had given away an option on it to two young film school grads-turned-producers. But he sensed that Quentin had real talent and flair from the way he was selling himself and his obsessive love of anything to do with the movies.

Off the top of his head, Quentin then pitched a very vague outline of a story about a heist that goes wrong, even though he had not yet written a word of the script. Lawrence Bender told Quentin to go away and write it. He advised him that if he really wanted to direct his own project then this could be the one because it sounded relatively easy to shoot.

Quentin picked up a vein of genuine common sense from Bender. This wasn't just another film school geek producer promising him the earth and delivering nothing. This guy had a down-to-earth realistic attitude. Maybe he was right?

In any case, he had already thought up the perfect title – even if he had no idea what it meant. The name *Reservoir Dogs* had been drifting around in Quentin's head for quite a while a sort of 1990s *The Wild Bunch*. Quentin later claimed that the title came from a girlfriend who one day said to him, 'I want to go see Louis Malle's *Au Revoir les Enfants*' and Quentin said he replied, 'I don't want to see no *Reservoir Dogs*.' Who knows what the truth is? As Quentin once admitted to a close friend on the set of the movie when it was eventually made, 'They're going to try and attach so much significance to the title of the movie while in fact it means jack shit. I made it up.'

Back at the barbecue that afternoon, Quentin and Bender swapped phone numbers and drifted apart. Bender was not in the mood to party and slipped out of the back gate quietly. Quentin, newly enthused by Bender's advice. moved up a notch and found a couple of familiar faces in the crowd and started discussing the nuances of the *Indiana Jones* movies.

He was prepared to lecture anyone who would listen on why the second of the films had been such a letdown. His views had, naturally, been

fuelled by long discussions with Video Archives compatriot Roger Avary, who would defend the follow-up Indiana Jones film on the basis that 'it was its own movie'.

'You want more of the first one, then watch *Cocoon II The Return*. Better still, watch *The Last Crusade*. There's your crappy sequel,' Avary would tell Quentin.

But, with Avary out of the way, Quentin had the perfect platform at Scott Spiegel's barbecue to make his point.

'It was too much. The fucking banquet scene with the gorilla heads and eyeball soup. What the fuck was that?'

By the end of the afternoon, Quentin was comfortably oiled by a boatful of beers and talking so fast that, as Scott Spiegel recalls, 'You needed a filmgoer's companion to make sense of what he was talking about.'

Bender meanwhile put his encounter with Quentin out of his head for the moment. He had met lots of bright kids in Hollywood. Many of them could pitch their movie ideas brilliantly, but when it came to the crunch, few of them ever actually delivered. Lawrence Bender certainly wasn't going to hold his breath in anticipation of what Quentin had promised him. But he had a sneaking feeling that maybe this time something would come out of what they had discussed.

*'Never apologize and never explain. It's a
sign of weakness'*

John Wayne in *She Wore A Yellow Ribbon*, 1949

A Script is Born

IMPERIAL ENTERTAINMENT OFFICES, WEST
HOLLYWOOD, MAY 1990

The first thing Quentin did when he got to work the following
day was get hold of a copy of *Intruder* – the movie produced by
Lawrence Bender – from the Imperial video archives department. He intended to watch it at least half a dozen times to get a real feel
for the sort of movies Bender was interested in.

Scott Spiegel has no doubt that *Reservoir Dogs*, which Quentin then
sat down and hammered out in just three weeks, had similarities to
Intruder. But he considers that to be a back-handed compliment.

'They are both very simple, easy-to-make movies. He had guys in a
warehouse; so did we. There was this grotesque scene in *Intruder* that
was similar to the ear cutting in *Dogs*. He even eventually used some of
the same actors,' explains Spiegel.

Quentin appreciated the small-scale values of *Intruder*. And he was
astute enough to know that if Bender had produced a film like *Intruder*
he would be attracted by certain familiar elements. In any case, there

was absolutely no point writing a sequel to *Lawrence of Arabia* as your directorial debut because Quentin knew that whatever he wrote would have to be made on the proverbial shoestring budget.

Quentin showed remarkable determination in writing *Reservoir Dogs*. He would flop down on his broken waterbed at the dive he called home, in deepest, darkest Hollywood and write and write until the early hours each and every evening after work. Outside the building, whores were screaming at their pimps, black and whites were speeding past. sirens wailing. In the clear starry sky, helicopters whirled a few hundred feet above, spotlights snapping in all directions. In that cramped room, Quentin just cut himself off from the troublesome outside world and began creating a masterpiece.

In the back of Quentin's mind must have been the hundreds of different movies he had absorbed during his childhood and those five years working at Video Archives, not to mention the dozens of movie books he had read. One quote seemed more significant than all the others. It was from Stanley Kubrick, director of one of Quentin's favourite fifties film *noirs, The Killing.*

> In a crime film, it is almost like a bullfight: it has a ritual and a pattern which lays down that the criminal is not going to make it, so that, while you can suspend your knowledge of this for a while, sitting way back in your mind this little awareness knows and prepares you for the fact that he is not going to succeed. That type of ending is easier to accept.

Quentin had studied film in his own crazy way for long enough to know the wisdom of Kubrick's words. His intended story for *Reservoir Dogs* would be based on characteristic ideas that related closely to *The Killing*.

In both movies, the characters imagine carrying out a bold robbery with its enormous pay-off. Apart from the cop infiltrator (Mr Orange). they are all marginal men.

Again, in both movies there is a distrust of emotions, and the characters make mistakes. Though the brilliant plan succeeds, everyone dies or is caught in the end.

The journey to freedom is another theme shared by both films. Mr Orange, who's infiltrated the gang, is using the robbery as a journey to his own freedom. But circumstances block him again and again.

Finally, there is the triumph of the obsessional, dedicated hero. Mr Orange comes closest to succeeding but ultimately he, like the others, dies.

While he was writing the script, Quentin couldn't get out of his head one of the classic lines of dialogue from the character played by Sterling Hayden in *The Killing*: 'I'll slap that pretty face into hamburger meat.'

Something about that line thrilled him and seemed to capture the mood of the film he was trying to create. It had a sick sort of humour, despite the vicious threat of violence. It provoked the sort of emotions he wanted an audience to feel when they saw *Dogs*.

At weekends, Quentin barely had time to pick up a hot dog and a Sprite from the fast food joint just up the street. Even while he walked there and back, his mind was buzzing with the characters from *Dogs*.

Quentin became those characters the moment he stepped inside the front door of his apartment. He would act out every single scene in loud, varying accents. For instance, when he devised the opening scene in which the gangsters talk in lurid terms about Madonna wanting 'dick, dick. dick', he took on all the roles and cross-fertilised the conversation to make sure it worked.

Quentin's friends and mother heard nothing from him during those three weeks in the summer of 1990. He didn't return anyone's calls. He was having the time of his life being the ultimate chameleon. For the first time he felt that his writing was genuinely flowing. There were no interruptions. This was it.

The dialogue was coming out with such ease, Quentin could barely control it. 'You shoot me in a dream, you better wake up and apologize,' says Mr White in one of many memorable lines from *Dogs*. Quentin was living a real life dream and he did not want it to end.

He started to examine his own attitudes and beliefs and compressed them into his characters. He wanted them to show respect and loyalty, two elements he felt that had been missing from much of his life. He had always been intrigued by the unwritten rules between men that existed in some of those brilliant film *noirs* of the fifties. He wanted to get them right, down to the last bloody detail.

Once he had illustrated the lowlife humour through that infamous Madonna speech, he would hit the audience with a furious boiling point scene. And so it went on.

Then there were the directorial elements that he knew were essential in order to persuade anyone to let him direct the movie. He set it against a dishevelled LA backdrop and bolstered it with a super-cool seventies soundtrack.

He put everything into the script. Quentin wanted to make films and the only way he could convince anyone he was capable was by putting it all on the page. The chase scene was broken down shot by shot with phrases like, 'POV through windshield. Mr Pink offscreen.'

The message came over loud and clear – I have already directed this in my head, now give me a chance to do it for real.

Besides *Intruder* and *The Killing*, Quentin thought back to all the classic scenes and dialogue of movies like *The Taking of Pelham 123*, where the villains also give themselves code names to disguise their real identities. John Woo's *A Better Tomorrow II* was also locked in Quentin's memory bank, especially since it featured villains who dressed in black suits and skinny ties.

Then there was *Rififi*, a 1955 French movie about an elaborate raid on a jewellery store during which the thieves fall out and the caper ends in bloodshed. *Plunder Road*, *Bob Le Flambeur* and *Baretta* were also highly influential. Another influence was the Dustin Hoffman movie

Straight Time, based on a book by real-life convict Edward Bunker (later cast in *Reservoir Dogs* as Mr Blue). There was also *Kansas City Confidential*, whose crooks looked so cool in dark suits and skinny ties. Finally, ther was *Q – The Winged Serpent*, about an ex-con on the run who comes across a monstrous Aztec god.

Quentin's favourite war movie, Brian de Palma's *Casualties of War*, had a major impact. Quentin remembered being particularly moved by the scene where Sean Penn's character's best friend is shot and he takes care of him. *Dogs* reflected elements of the dialogue, but more importantly, the feeling between the two men when Mr Orange has been shot and Mr White tries to convince him that he's not going to die. Quentin even managed to put his own spin on the dialogue between the *Casualties of War* characters when he makes Mr Orange plead with Mr White to 'look into my eyes' to stop him drifting towards death.

Quentin's near photographic recollection of *Casualties of War* was helped by the fact that he had built up an obsession with the works of director Brian de Palma. He even had a scrapbook filled with press interviews with de Palma.

Quentin had always been fascinated by the way de Palma presented fear and violence in his movies and desperately wanted to emulate that in some way in his own film. Not surprisingly, he was later compared with de Palma, who was an undoubted hero to Quentin because de Palma also understood what a rich source of inspiration other people's movies could be.

Quentin's rather surprising interest at this time in the music of white rapper Vanilla Ice was also very relevant when he wrote *Reservoir Dogs*. For Quentin was fascinated by the way rap groups took samples of other tracks and integrated them in their own music. Vanilla Ice's 'interpretation' of the rock group Queen's music was a classic example. Quentin saw his own habit of borrowing scenes from other movies as a filmic version of sampling. But what he saw in the appallingly unhip music of Vanilla Ice one can only guess at.

However the biggest and most controversial influence on Quentin's

Reservoir Dogs was a little known Hong Kong gangster movie called *City on Fire*. Film junkie Quentin had absorbed literally thousands of movies during his life, but this 1987 Ringo Lam-directed action-packed picture was without doubt playing in his mind throughout the writing of *Dogs*.

City on Fire starred one of Quentin's heroes of Asian cinema, Chow Yun-Fat, as an undercover cop who's infiltrated a band of thieves as they prepared to rob a jewellery store under the tutelage of a balding, patriarchal boss. Quentin had been particularly struck by the way in which director Lam managed to spin together intricate plot lines and he decided to use the movie as the basic framework for his own action in *Dogs*.

Some time later, Quentin's old friends at Video Archives had a chuckle and put bets on the fact that Quentin lifted certain elements of *City on Fire* and used them in *Dogs*.

But in Quentin's mind there was nothing wrong with recycling stories, which he had always been told was common practice in Hollywood. In any case, his movie would end up with much better dialogue, performances and film making, even if both movies climaxed with a classic Mexican stand-off. Quentin saw the influence of *City on Fire* as the ultimate compliment to a movie he truly adored. He knew only too well how many movies stole from their predecessors.

He was determined not to show the heist in his movie. In fact, it was never in the equation. He wanted the audience to keep asking questions. When each of those guys came through the door into that warehouse they would have different perspectives. And the audience would have to try and figure out what had happened, what had gone wrong.

On the musical front, Quentin thought it would be really cool to create a Super Seventies weekend of music on an LA radio station to help merge the action. He didn't want the serious stuff like Led Zepplin and Marvin Gaye, so he decided to go for the bubblegum variety instead. There were two good reasons; it would really piss some people off and these were the tracks his mom Connie adored and used to play throughout his childhood.

Three weeks after starting to write *Dogs*, Quentin called up Lawrence Bender to tell him he had something for him to read. Bender was sharing a small apartment in West Hollywood, only a notch above the death hole where Quentin lived.

'He didn't have a car and I couldn't afford the photocopying costs,' explains Bender. 'So I drove over to his place.'

Bender did not bat an eyelid when he walked into Quentin's garbage can apartment. The script for *Reservoir Dogs* consisted mainly of scribbled notes on hundreds of pieces of paper. As Bender read the notes, Quentin bent over a rusty old manual typewriter and tried to turn them into a legible screenplay. An hour later, Bender flipped over what he considered to be the most extraordinary piece of writing he had ever seen.

But Quentin – after five years of bitter Hollywood rejection – was more used to disappointment than adulation. He had reassured himself throughout the writing of *Dogs* that this would make an ideal guerilla movie project.

'I don't want to wait for somebody to give me a shot. I'll make it myself if you're not interested. I've got it already planned – black and white on 16mm, starring a few friends,' insisted Quentin in his usual rapid-fire, high-pitched delivery. 'Fuck everybody else. I don't need permission to make a movie – I'm just gonna make one.'

However Bender had bigger, bolder plans for the project and he begged Quentin to give him six months to come up with some decent money to make the movie.

Quentin's reply astounded the young producer. 'No, no. I'll be twenty-eight in six months. I want to make a movie before I'm twenty-eight.'

But Bender continued to plead for time. He was convinced he was on to a winner even though he knew as well as anyone else that there was – and still is – no such thing as an overnight deal in Hollywood.

Quentin fired back, 'It won't work. Nobody will ever give me a chance to direct a movie. I wouldn't give me a chance to direct a movie. Why should they? I'm tired of chasing the elusive deal.'

He was almost at the end of his tether in many ways. He had heard

all these broken promises before, from more than half a dozen producers.

'I'll give you two months,' he barked.

It was an insane demand. Here were two young film makers who knew virtually no one. But Bender had so much faith in *Dogs* that he even agreed to a stipulation that, if no deal was struck, they would finance the project themselves. Bender also promised to act in the movie as Nice Guy Eddie, if they had to make it on a shoestring.

Naturally, Quentin was still in hock to the bank and behind on the rent for his crash pad in Hollywood. Lawrence Bender warned him that the next few months developing the project would be even more difficult financially, until they got the all important deal. Then, once production got under way, his feet wouldn't touch the ground for the best part of six months.

Quentin was concerned that a *True Romance* deal would come through soon. So if Bender's deal came to nothing he could still afford to shoot *Dogs* himself to prove his abilities. But that meant saving every penny.

Accordingly, he called up his mother Connie at her comfortable detached home in Glendale, twenty miles north of Los Angeles, and announced that he was moving back home.

Connie was delighted by the news. But little did she realize that Quentin was simply swapping one dingy crash pad for another much cheaper, cleaner version. Just because Quint had come home it did not mean she would see any more of him.

In fact, her prodigal son had only returned because he believed that fame and fortune were just around the corner, and he wanted to tread water for just a little longer.

Meanwhile back in LA, *True Romance* was finally beginning to get some legs. Producer Stanley Margolis brought in a director called Bill Lustig to helm the picture. He hoped that Lustig – who'd previously directed an impressive TV movie called *Relentless* – might make the picture a viable proposition for a movie production company.

Lustig insisted on changing Quentin's script. He restructured it and made it more readable (in his own and Stanley Margolis's opinion, but not Quentin's). A company called Cinetel then got very interested in *Romance*.

Quentin, Margolis and Lustig had a meeting with Cinetel in early summer 1991. Both the director Lustig and screenwriter Quentin impressed executive Catalaine Knell and she immediately hired Quentin to do a script polish on a cable movie called *After Midnight*, starring Rutger Hauer and Natasha Richardson for which he was eventually paid twenty-five thousand dollars. Cinetel also announced that they were prepared to put up 2.73 million dollars to make the movie. Margolis was incredibly relieved that after three years of slogging the project around town it was at last reaching fruition.

Then the rules of the game changed overnight. Quentin and Margolis were not invited to any more meetings to discuss the movie's development. Margolis's option on the film was about to expire and he feared that he might end up without a penny from the entire deal.

Suddenly, Geordie-born director Tony Scott came on the scene. The moment Margolis heard this he realised that the entire project had shot up in value. With a star director like Scott attached the budget would probably rocket towards the thirty million dollar mark. Scott – who had just finished the $50 million Tom Cruise flop *Days of Thunder* – was looking for something with a strong story but no major stars. He wanted to make a movie that would alter the Hollywood perception of him as a director only capable of handling huge-budget movies featuring excessive numbers of plane crashes, car crashes and all the other ingredients of such films.

Within weeks, the movie was being packaged and Stanley Margolis was assured he would get some sort of fee.

Meanwhile, Quentin was informed that he would be paid the writer's guild minimum of fifty thousand dollars for that particular script, with no ancillary fees if and when the movie was made. Quentin did not know how to react. In some ways he was delighted – and relieved – to have got a promise of some much needed cash and at least one of his movies appeared to be about to go into production. But it grated that he was not even considered to direct it and he was getting a paltry sum, considering the size of the movie's projected budget. Without his creative genius there would have been no *True Romance*, but he was not exactly being well rewarded. The producers later generously offered Quentin seven and a half per cent of the net takings of the movie. However, Quentin's manager Cathryn Jaymes pointed out that he would not see any of those royalties unless the film took more than five hundred million dollars at the box office. It took less than twenty million dollars in the US when it was released in late 1992.

As Clarence so prophetically says in the movie, 'Trouble is when I am offered a deal that is too good to be true it's a lie.'

Quentin took the money out of sheer desperation, but refused to rewrite the ending when Tony Scott had asked for a more upbeat finale. Scott didn't want the downbeat – some would say far more believable – version that Quentin had written where Clarence dies in the Mexican stand-off in the hotel and Alabama makes it to the car with the cash, a Sargeant Fury comic book and a napkin on which Clarence had written the words 'You're so cool' a few minutes earlier.

At first, Quentin was distraught about the enforced change. He even considered asking for his name to be taken off the credits. But he had a lot of faith in Tony Scott and was an especially big fan of his little known movie, *Revenge*, which has been somewhat overshadowed by Scott's bigger action flicks.

Quentin got together with Scott and tried to get him to change his mind about altering the ending. In the end, the down-to-earth Englishman came up with a solution.

'Quentin, I'm going to defer to you. I'm going to shoot both endings. Then I'm going to look at them, and then decide which one I want to go with.'

Quentin later recalled, 'As much as I didn't want my ending changed, I figured I couldn't really ask for more than that. When it came to it, he really liked the happy ending and went with it.'

Roger Avary – whose contribution to *Romance* is little known – got no story or screenplay credit. He was paid just one thousand dollars for rewriting the ending so that Tony Scott could have Clarence and Alabama living happily ever after and retiring to Cancun, Mexico, to have babies.

Two years after its release, Quentin insisted he would have shot *Romance* an entirely different way if he had been allowed to direct it. 'He [Tony Scott] always uses a lot of smoke – I like that in his films, but if ever I saw a guy show up on the set with a smoke machine I'd throw him off. I don't want any smoke whatsoever.'

Stanley Margolis is remarkably unbitter about his experience with *True Romance* and he still looks upon his dealings with Quentin as 'something I would not have missed for the world'. Despite getting an impressive-looking Executive Producer credit on the movie, he received a relatively low fee and was effectively prevented from getting involved in any way with the production. He did not even get to meet Tony Scott. Such is life in the Hollywood fast lane.

'I'll give you a dollar if you eat this collie,'

Martin Sheen's first line in *Badlands*, 1973

Enter the Godfather

LAUREL CANYON, HOLLYWOOD HILLS, OCTOBER
1990

Monte Hellman – balding, hippy-lookalike Los Angeles-born movie director, who spent years shooting final acts of films for low-budget king Roger Corman – got a call from a woman friend who knew Lawrence Bender's room-mate. She was raving about a script called *Reservoir Dogs*.

'It's the greatest thing I've ever read. You gotta see it. It would be a perfect movie for you to direct,' enthused Hellman's friend. It wasn't the first time he had heard such a hard sell.

'OK. Send me the script.'

'I'll do better than that. I'll read you the opening scene,' said Hellman's friend.

Then she proceeded to act out the entire 'Madonna dick, dick, dick' scene over the telephone. Monte Hellman was hooked.

'Get it to me, NOW!'

A few hours later Hellman put down the tatty, badly spelt, but still wonderful *Reservoir Dogs*, genuinely believing he had just read a masterpiece.

With the meticulousness of a veteran film maker, he then sat down at his desk and copied the entire eighty-nine-page script onto his computer, editing out all the spelling mistakes and literals along the way. He knew that corporate Hollywood would not even read the script unless it was cleaned up and properly punctuated.

Then Hellman called Lawrence Bender and begged him to give him a chance to direct the movie. Bender contacted Quentin and recommended that it would be worth listening to Hellman, if only because he was a guy with some genuine Hollywood experience. Quentin was reluctant, as he was still set on directing the movie himself. He had already been busy trying to recruit his old acting school pals, like Rich Turner.

Quentin had sent a copy of the script to Turner, with a note scrawled in his barely legible block-lettered writing on the first page (see p138).

The same page also featured an intriguing and highly prophetic dedication to various movie people.

Meanwhile, Monte Hellman was still pushing hard for a meeting with Quentin, who agreed, on condition it was somewhere close to Hollywood Boulevard because it was easy to reach by bus from his mother's house in Glendale. (Quentin had no car at the time.) They settled on CC Brown's – renowned for their hot fudge sundaes – on Hollywood Boulevard.

Hellman was in for a bitter blow when he sat down for that first meeting with Quentin, who announced apologetically that he had just sold *True Romance* to Tony Scott's company and he intended to use the fee to make *Dogs* himself.

'I'm sorry for having wasted your time, but I am determined to direct this movie myself,' said Quentin almost immediately.

Hellman looked at the wildly expressive, enthusiastic figure shovelling down a vast ice-cream nut sundae and somehow saw something through the fudge. Quentin was clearly being deadly serious.

Hellman picked carefully at his own sundae (minus ice-cream for

This Movie Is Dedicated To These's Following Sources Of
Inspiration:

              TIMOTHY CAREY
              ROGER CORMAN
              ANDRE DeTOTH
              CHOW YUEN FAT
              JEAN LUC GODDARD
              JEAN PIERRE MELVILLE
              LAWRENCE TIERNEY
              LIONEL WHITE

Hey Rich,
This is the scoop. I'm Mr. Pink.
My producer (who's also a very good actor)
is Nice Guy Eddie. I want you to look at
Mr. Blonde and Mr. Orange, and what the hell
Mr. White too. Now understand, I'm not promising
you one of these parts. But I will read you
for them. This gives you a jump on the other
people. And the fact I know how fuckin
good you are.

                              Q

P.S.
I hope you like it
call me. I'm real confident
about it. so you can say
what you feel.

health reasons) and engaged Quentin in his favourite subject – filmspeak. For more than an hour, Quentin imparted his detailed knowledge of the genre-bending movies Hellman had made, which included *The Shooting* (with his old friend Jack Nicholson) and *Ride in The Whirlwind* (also with Nicholson).

Then they discussed Hellman's only fully financed studio picture, *Two Lane Blacktop*, with Dennis Wilson of the Beachboys, singer James Taylor, and Warren Oates (who also starred in his rough and ready effort, *Cockfighter*).

By the end of the meeting, Hellman was mightily impressed. He no longer had aspirations to direct the picture, he simply wanted to be part of this exciting project as some sort of executive producer. With his Hollywood connections, he could probably help Quentin and Bender raise some useful production money.

'You can be our, like, Godfather. That's cool,' enthused Quentin.

Monte Hellman smiled. He knew precisely what the young wannabe director meant.

A couple of days later, Monte Hellman, Quentin and Lawrence Bender met up at Hellman's picturesque house in the Hollywood Hills and signed a simple one-page contract with a view to Hellman assisting in raising the finance for the movie. All three became equal partners in the project.

As soon as Quentin and Bender had departed, a very excited Monte Hellman hit the phones and started sounding out his friends in the industry: Dino De Laurentiis, Tony Stafford at New Line, plus a host of other players. They were all most enthusiastic about *Dogs*, except for two serious reservations.

One was that Quentin was a first-time director. That was bad news when it came to raising cash for movie-making. The other was that, in almost everyone's opinion, the violence was oppressive and gratuitous.

A handful of meetings followed with various companies, at which Quentin sat quietly and listened as movie company executives pitched their requirements if the movie was to get financed.

'We like it, but can we put a babe in it?' suggested one bright spark, who wanted to finance the movie on condition his mistress played the part of Mr Blonde.

While another pleaded, 'How 'bout we make one of these guys nicer?'

Quentin didn't know whether to laugh or cry. Instead, he kept quiet and told Bender and Hellman what he thought of these putzes after the meetings finished. Quentin was still perfectly content to go away and use his *True Romance* fee to make the movie guerilla-style himself. That gave him just the right amount of leverage to dispose of these 'creative suggestions' from potential investors.

Hellman and Bender never once tried to put pressure on Quentin to agree to these proposed changes and eventually they found two companies who were prepared to invest in *Dogs*.

The first offer came from a former producer at Cannon, who reckoned the movie could be shot for a million dollars with unknown actors. But, although the essential ingredients of the script remained untouched, Quentin was not happy with certain elements of this executive's approach. He appeared to see it as some kind of blood-fest, rather than the subtle film *noir* that Quentin visualized.

Then Richard N. Gladstein at Live Entertainment showed interest. He had first been alerted to the project by Monte Hellman, who had directed a Live movie called *Silent Night, Deadly Night Part 3 Better Watch Out for Them* (a helluva title for a fairly average film).

Hellman dropped the *Dogs* script off at Gladstein's home on Sweetzer Drive, West Hollywood. The movie executive read it immediately and called Hellman enthusiastically the next morning.

A few hours later, Quentin, Bender and Hellman showed up at Gladstein's office for a meeting. Gladstein was ready to agree in principle to a non-interference deal, but Bender and Hellman feared that he was deeply troubled by Quentin's lack of directorial experience. Things were initially made worse by Quentin's insistence that he had not directed anything before, despite the existence of *My Best Friend's Birthday*.

Quentin had actually decided not to mention *My Best Friend's Birthday*, after sitting down a few months earlier and viewing the unfinished film for the first time in more than a year. He realized it was dreadful and unscreenable and he had heeded the advice of *True Romance* producer Stanley Margolis, who had told him not to show it.

Monte Hellman believes that was one of Quentin's shrewdest moves. 'He was very astute not to show that film. I think that was the day Quentin took control of his own career.'

Quentin convinced Gladstein that he should be given a shot at directing *Dogs*. In any case, as Quentin and Bender pointed out, they would go away and shoot it on a peppercorn budget if anyone tried to remove Quentin from the helm.

At the time, Gladstein was impressed by both Quentin and Bender's commitment, although he fully appreciated what a huge risk it would be to allow Quentin to direct. Monte Hellman even chipped in with an offer to keep an eye on things, just to put Gladstein's mind at rest.

However, Hellman was supremely confident that Quentin knew precisely what he was doing. Although he kept a fatherly eye on proceedings, he did not wish to interfere in any way and he assured Quentin of that after the meeting.

Years later, Gladstein told Quentin that, after he read the script, he surmised that whoever had written it had to be an intelligent person and he was instantly prepared to let them direct the movie.

'In other words, I would have had to be a complete jerk not to have been allowed to make this movie,' explained Quentin.

But the deal was far from finalized. Next, the team had to work out how to cast it. Gladstein's Live Entertainment which then specialized in straight-to-video releases had a list of ten actors from which they insisted Quentin would have to choose one of his leads.

'If we get one from the list you'll get a million three. Two and I'll up the budget to two million,' explained Gladstein at a meeting at his office on February 4, 1991.

Amongst those on the list were Dennis Hopper and Christopher

Walken. There was also Harvey Keitel, the New York tough guy who
had first come to prominence in Scorsese's *Mean Streets* almost twenty
years earlier. He had in fact only become an actor after answering an
advert in a New York newspaper asking for actors to appear in one of
Scorsese's even earlier low-budget efforts, *Who's That Knocking on
My Door*.

Bender and Quentin left that meeting with Gladstein a little deflated
to say the least. They were far from making the movie yet and what if
none of the actors on that list wanted to appear in *Dogs*?

A few days later, Lawrence Bender's acting coach Lilly Parker read
the script, and was so impressed that she passed it on to her friend,
Harvey Keitel, who wanted in immediately. Suddenly, with Keitel
attached, Quentin and Lawrence had a lot more pull. Keitel said he was
particularly impressed by the screenplay's Hemingwayesque code which
guided the characters' lives in a world without meaning. 'There needs to
be a hero. Those are the things that are universal,' Keitel told Quentin.
'And you don't see them in many screenplays.'

Keitel assured Bender and Quentin that he could get Christopher
Walken on board to play Mr Blonde, the psychopath who cuts off the
cop's ear. The two young film makers started to dare to contemplate a
two million dollar budget for *Dogs*. In the end Walken decided not to do
the part. No one ever established why. The role of Mr Blonde eventually
went to Michael Madsen who had met Monte Hellman a couple of years
earlier when he starred in his movie *Iguana*.

It was the spring of 1991 – more than six months after Quentin had
originally penned *Dogs* during those three balmy summer weeks the previous year. All his pals in the industry were telling him this project had
legs and was moving very quickly. But it wasn't fast enough for Quentin's
bank balance. He had quit his telephone sales job at Imperial because he
wanted to throw everything behind *Dogs*, but no one seemed to appreciate that he was in dire financial trouble. The twenty-five thousand
dollars he got for a rewrite on the TV movie *Past Midnight* barely
covered his debts.

With Walken out, Bender and Quentin started to panic in case Gladstein changed his mind. They needed reassurance that the 1.3 million dollars was in place. At this stage, not one penny had changed hands and Bender and Quentin were still broke. Living on hot air can be exhilarating, until you actually begin to starve. Quentin had some of the money from *True Romance* coming but he did not want to spend it, just in case the Live Entertainment deal fell through.

Meanwhile Harvey Keitel, the lean, mean, fifty-year-old muscle machine from the Bronx, who struck terror into audiences in *Bad Lieutenant*, with his bloodshot eyes, long stringy hair and truly manic stare, was turning into the movie's unofficial casting agent. He would spend hours on the phone from his New York home advising and recommending potential actors for the parts in *Dogs*.

Bender eventually realized that it was time to expand the actor's off-screen role.

'Harvey, at this point we really think that we should make you a producer,' exclaimed Bender during a phone call to Keitel.

'Lawrence, it's about fuckin' time. I've been waiting for you to say this. What took you so long?'

Keitel's first duty as co-producer was to cough up fifteen hundred dollars for Quentin and Bender to fly to New York to hold casting sessions. There was simply no way that either of them could afford the fare without the actor's assistance.

In the Big Apple, Keitel wheeled out more than a dozen of his fellow actors for consideration. Only the not-so-well-known Steve Buscemi seemed suitable. He came with solid credentials, including roles in Scorsese's *New York Stories*, *Slaves of New York* and the Coen Brothers' *Barton Fink* and *Miller's Crossing*. Buscemi actually lobbied hard for the Mr Blonde role. This one-time New York fireman had an edge to him that impressed Quentin, who had long since worked out exactly what each actor should look like in his head. Quentin reckoned Buscemi would be ideal for the part of Mr Pink, but he wanted the role for himself. It was a bit of a dilemma.

Lawrence Bender made the point that Quentin's directing might suffer if he had too big an acting role in the movie.

After the casting session with Buscemi in a New York church hall, Buscemi was taking a leak in the bathroom when Quentin strolled in and started doing the same in the stall next to him.

'Oh, by the way, I cast you as Mr Pink.' That was it, no other words were exchanged.

Co-producer Keitel was disappointed that Quentin did not go for any of the other New York actors, but he was pragmatic enough to accept the decision. In a backhanded sort of way, Keitel was impressed by the fact that Quentin and Bender did not just accept his recommendations despite their gratitude for the airfares to get to New York in the first place.

Back in Los Angeles, Quentin and casting director Ronnie Yeskel really started to get into their stride. Michael Madsen had appeared with Keitel in *Thelma and Louise*, but it was Monte Hellman's connection that got the tall, dark-haired actor on board as the perfect Mr Blonde. British actor Tim Roth followed as Mr Orange. His roles in a number of low-budget flicks appealed to Quentin.

The script had only caught Roth's eye when his agent sent him a stack of screenplays and stuck a note on *Dogs* saying, 'Look at Orange.' Roth was puzzled at first because he did not even know what 'Orange' was.

When he was told by Quentin that he had the part of Mr Orange, Roth asked the rookie director what he should do to prepare for the role. 'Let's meet up next week and I'll bring a few tapes with me,' replied Quentin.

The following week, Roth – who has a tattoo with the letters 'P.E.R.I.S.H.' branded on his forearm – met Quentin at a friend's apartment. Quentin immediately jammed a video into the VCR machine. It was his favourite cartoon, *Clutch Cargo*.

'That's cool,' said a slightly bemused Tim Roth.

'Don't you dig it? I got *Gigantor* here as well.' That was Quentin's second favourite cartoon series. These cartoons were to be Roth's only preparation for his role as an undercover cop, besides some voice coaching for his American accent.

Roth even managed to persuade Quentin to cast his actual voice coach as the woman whose car is hijacked by Mr Orange. (He later admitted he got her the role because he wanted to pay her back for all the hell she'd put him through to ensure he got his American accent absolutely right.)

What especially attracted the actors who auditioned for *Dogs* was that each of the eight major roles required very different personalities and Quentin had managed to make each character incredibly dynamic in his own way.

As Keitel explained, 'All the characters looked like fun to play but they weren't simple. Each of them was kinda complex because half the time you were rooting for them and half the time you didn't like them – but you were always interested in what they were doing.'

Over the following few weeks, Keitel and Quentin built up a strong friendship that helped answer a lot of questions for the actor.

'I just kinda presumed that Quentin's father or brother or uncle was associated with these kind of people, or a cousin or perhaps himself. I was astonished to discover that none of this was true because he had gathered it all by watching movies,' explained Keitel.

Quentin became incredibly attached to Keitel and looked on him as a father figure throughout the pre-production and shooting of *Dogs*. To Quentin, he was the epitome of a good male parent: strong, firm, yet soft at the edges when circumstances demanded.

But Quentin's most important task was to become commander-in-chief of the *Dogs* and gain their confidence, much like the character Joe Cabot in the actual movie. Quentin's dream was beginning to take shape. But there was still a long way to go...

'Made it Ma. Top of the world!'

James Cagney, about to be blown to Hell in *White Heat*, 1949

Butch Terry and the Sundance Kid

LAW OFFICES, CENTURY CITY, LOS ANGELES,
JUNE, 1991

With most of the *Dogs'* casting in place, the deal with Live Entertainment was signed around a vast oval table in the offices of Monte Hellman's legal advisers. The movie had been given the green light in under a year, which was pretty fast by Hollywood standards. In Quentin's mind, it had taken almost seven years, because that was how long he had been toiling without reward.

A few days after the contracts had been signed, the Sundance Film Institute contacted Quentin to inform him that they were so impressed by his *Dogs* script – which had been submitted for possible funding some months earlier – that they wanted him to travel to Utah to take part in a workshop.

Godfather Monte Hellman convinced Quentin that attending the programme would provide him with an ideal opportunity to test out his ideas before actually going into production with *Dogs* in August. It would, in effect, be a test run.

Going to the Sundance Institute (started by movie star Robert Redford almost twenty years ago) would also give Quentin an opportunity to get away from LA for the first time in years. Set amongst rolling mountains and wooded hillsides, it was specifically set up by Redford to bring professional film makers and writers together with people who were trying to get into the business.

The Sundance Institute wanted Quentin to spend two weeks at their workshop, using their camera facilities and actors to recreate scenes from his screenplay. The Institute turned out to be the best and worst thing that ever happened to Quentin, who had very firm ideas on how he wanted to film the scenes.

'I wanted to experiment on my first scene by doing it in long takes. I didn't want to do coverage. I wanted to string a bunch of long takes together and see how it worked,' he explained later.

As an added bonus, New Yorker Steve Buscemi (already cast as Mr Pink) was one of the team of young actors attending the workshop. Quentin had a perfect opportunity

But there was one problem; Quentin's arrival in Sundance overlapped with that of two groups of professionals who were there to advise and encourage movie rookies like Quentin. The first group savaged the young film maker.

They attacked Quentin on all fronts. They hated the long takes he insisted on shooting. They didn't even like a vast wide shot he took of a location that had to double for the eventual warehouse setting in the real film. They complained about his camera angles and how they could see too much floor in each shot. They even attacked Quentin for daring to shoot a bathroom scene through a mirror.

Then the second group of professionals took over and they included the king of off-the-wall film making, one-time *Monty Python* Terry Gilliam.

In director Gilliam – enjoying a much-deserved renaissance,

following the release of *Fisher King* with Robin Williams and Jeff Bridges – Quentin found a genuine soulmate.

'He had this incredible enthusiasm and this outrageous script filled with amazing energy,' explained Gilliam. 'It had great dialogue and there was a sheer audacity about what he was doing.'

Gilliam was particularly impressed by exactly the things which had irritated the previous group of professionals. 'The camera literally would not keep still. He was everywhere – down people's backs and up people's noses. It was just marvellous.'

By the time Quentin returned from Sundance, the advance buzz on *Dogs* was truly phenomenal. There was still a bit more casting to be done, and Quentin and Lawrence Bender held some sessions on the wooden deck in front of Monte Hellman's Hollywood Hills home.

Hellman observed Quentin's casting technique with great interest. He was truly an actor's director. He had developed the habit of telling an artist their performance was 'great, cool' and then asking them to do it all over again. They were always happy to oblige because of Quentin's incredible enthusiasm.

Another piece of casting that probably contributed to the eventual success of the movie was the decision to dust down Lawrence Tierney for the role of gang boss Joe Cabot. A year earlier, Quentin had dedicated the original script to the actor, even though he did not know if he was still alive. Tierney – well into his seventies – had become another of Quentin's movie heroes, thanks to a variety of bleak Hollywood B movies made in the late forties and fifties. He tended towards the sort of hoodlum roles that George Raft would have rejected.

Tierney's most infamous role was in the 1947 movie *Born to Kill*, in which he played a hood on the run who has already killed two people and commits a series of murders with two sisters. In all, he had appeared in more than eighty films since making his debut in the 1943 Mark Robson-directed *The Ghost Ship*.

Quentin only found out that Tierney was available after being

introduced to the actor by fellow director Jeff Burr, an old friend of Tierney's. Burr had casually mentioned to Quentin that he knew Tierney, after reading the dedication to the actor.

'Wow! Wouldn't it be cool to cast Larry in *Dogs*?' said Quentin. A few days, later Tierney was in. In the middle of casting, Quentin even found time to polish the *Dogs* script a little more, after casting sessions had exposed a few deficiencies in the dialogue.

Another interesting piece of last-minute casting was hiring ex-convict-turned novelist Eddie Bunker as Mr Blue. Quentin was thrilled to get Bunker because he had written one of his favourite books, *No Beast So Fierce*, which had been converted to the big screen as *Straight Time*, one of Quentin's major influences during the writing of *Dogs*. Bunker – released from jail in 1975 – even acted as unofficial on-set specialist when it came to certain points concerning the *Dogs*, thanks to his previous incarnation as a robber.

At seventeen, Bunker had been the youngest prisoner in San Quentin and it was only in his late thirties that he had discovered books and begun to read and write. Besides *Beast*, he also penned *The Animal Factory* and *Little Boy Blue*. In 1985, he even co-authored the movie *Runaway Train*, a critical and commercial hit that gained Oscar nominations for its stars Jon Voight and Eric Roberts.

Casting the rest of the movie was not considered as important as getting the budget straight, and ensuring that Quentin provided a sensible shot list as far as the movie's French/American backers were concerned.

Hellman and Bender persuaded Quentin to come up to Hellman's house every day for a week, while the shot list was devised, revised and then checked again and again. There had been some apprehension about Quentin's ability to plan ahead, but it proved wholly unfounded because he had shot the movie over and over in his head.

Thanks to his extraordinary memory, Quentin was able to take the other two film makers through every shot in *Dogs* without referring to his script. Instead, they were treated to an impromptu performance of every single role in the order in which it had been written. Hellman was particularly mesmerized.

Next, Quentin's two associates had to impress upon him just how important it was to choose a good director of photography. They were surprised when Quentin reeled off a list of at least a dozen DPs whose names he had memorized after studying the credits on some of his favourite movies.

Monte Hellman was concerned about Quentin's choice of DP because the end product on the screen does not always accurately reflect the abilities of a cameraman, especially in these days of complex, sophisticated post-production film enhancement. In other words, a brilliant-looking movie was not always the result of a brilliant DP.

Hellman recommended that Quentin should view the work of a London-based Pole called Andrzej Sekula, who had come highly praised by one-time Roger Corman assistant Francis Dole. Sekula had shot a number of British television films, as well as dozens of carefully constructed TV commercials.

Initially, Quentin was torn between Sekula and two or three LA-based cameramen. But, when the Pole heard that he was competing with others for the job, he paid for his own flight to California from Europe. He went straight into a meeting with Quentin, who was so impressed by his determination he gave him the job there and then.

The 1.3 million dollars allocated to make *Dogs* was hardly a king's ransom by Hollywood standards. Even very basic made-for-TV films come with budgets of upwards of two million dollars, so it was clear to all concerned that every penny counted.

That meant hiring all the actors to work for 'scale' – the US movie unions' recommended minimum pay, plus ten per cent for their agents, which amounted to approximately eighteen hundred dollars a week. Harvey Keitel got seventy thousand dollars for the entire movie because, without his name attached, the movie would never have been made.

Even DP Sekula – whose rate on TV commercials was as much as two thousand dollars per day – settled for a weekly wage of less than two thousand dollars. The remainder of the crew were on considerably less.

Quentin might have considered this the big time, but to many of the cast and crew this was the guerilla-style on-the-run movie he had wanted to make all along. His own wages reflected that. Quentin was so happy to be directing his own movie, he accepted an all-in fee of just twenty-five thousand dollars. This was his apprenticeship and he was simply grateful to have the opportunity to make the film.

It is worth noting here that the similarities between *Dogs* and Quentin's favourite fifties film *noir*, Kubrick's *The Killing*, do not just concern the films themselves.

There is a much more poignant aspect. When Stanley Kubrick (then virtually the same age as Quentin) wrote a screenplay version of the Lionel White book *Clean Break*, and started hawking it around Hollywood as *The Killing*, nobody wanted to know. Then he got actor Sterling Hayden to agree to star and soon he had managed to raise the very modest sum of three hundred and twenty thousand dollars to make the movie. It was the first time that Kubrick had ever worked with professional actors and a fully professional crew.

Thirty-five years later, Quentin was repeating history, thanks to Harvey Keitel, an actor who has often been compared in stature to Sterling Hayden.

'If you tell people what to do, as opposed to how to do it, they will surprise you with their ingenuity'

General Patton

'All my life has prepared me for this moment'

Winston Churchill, at the start of the Second World War

Let's Get Ramblin'

RUNDOWN OFFICES, 6753, HOLLYWOOD
BOULEVARD, JULY 1991

Angelyne is a Jayne Mansfield-lookalike who first took out a billboard in Hollywood in the late eighties, advertising herself as an actress. 'Call Angelyne' is the admonition. There is no evidence she has ever had a major role. However, she has achieved fame as a traffic hazard in Hollywood, thanks to posters featuring her in pink and gold lamé, rumoured to have been paid for by her rich Arab lover.

A vast fifty feet by twenty-five feet Angelyne billboard looked down at the window of the office where Quentin was moving his hands expressively and pacing the floor in front of a group of people.

'...and then Pink says, "Get outta the car! Get the fuck outta the car!" Pink tries to rip open the driver's side door, but it's locked...' continued a breathless Quentin. '"Open the fuckin door!" Pink then SMASHES it in her face. He DRAGS the shocked woman outta the car. Just then the cops reach the street corner, guns aimed.' Quentin acted out every piece of action as it happened, sweat pouring off him on a day when the air was so hot you could have punched a hole in it.

'Using the car as a shield, Pink FIRES three shots at the cops; (a pause) BANG! BANG! BANG! Everybody hits the ground.' Quentin flung himself onto the filthy, ripped vinyl floor in front of more than a dozen senior production staff attending a pre-production meeting at the offices of Dog Eat Dog Films, the production company set up specifically to make the movie.

Then Quentin got up. 'Pink hops in the car as the cops continue firing. BANG! BANG! BANG!'

The crew all sat in silence, gobsmacked by this extraordinary virtuoso performance of the movie, shot by shot for their benefit. Usually, directors would quietly, almost shyly, go through a shot list, scene by scene. in monosyllabic tones. Sometimes they'd even leave it to their producer. Not Quentin. He wanted to live each sequence with them. He also wanted them to be a part of the process.

He continued, 'Then Pink floors it, speeding down the street.' Quentin sat on a flimsy chair which almost buckled under his heavy frame as he steered an imaginary steering wheel. 'Cops are still firing. BANG! BANG! BANG!' Quentin screeched the car round a corner as he makes his getaway.

First Assistant Director Jamie Beardsley watched the awkward-looking first-time director continue his one-man show and sensed she was in the presence of a genius.

'I'd never seen anything like it before in my entire career. He had such enthusiasm and he knew every word of dialogue off by heart. I knew I was involved in something special from that moment onwards,' she recalls.

But beneath Quentin's bravado lay some very understandable fears. There was no hiding place now. All of a sudden writing seemed an easy alternative because if that didn't work out you could always throw the script away. And if another director took on your screenplay you could always blame him if it got screwed up. But this was on the page and they were his words. If he screwed up directing his own film there'd be no one else to carry the can.

Jamie Beardsley and the rest of the production staff knew it was going to be a helluva tricky shoot. To start with, the temperatures in Los Angeles tended to push towards 100 degrees at this time of year. Jamie had also heard that the Director of Photography Andrzej Sekula had inspirationally persuaded Quentin to shoot the entire movie on 50 ASA film, despite the scorching sunlight that flooded onto the streets of LA in August and September. Beardsley feared the actors could end up looking like glowing saints rather than hardened criminals when the film was processed.

Jamie also noticed that she was one of the few females on the *Dogs* production crew. This was macho time, she rapidly concluded. The movie was a lesson in male bonding and the production staff reflected this.

Quentin later insisted the only reason for the all-male plot was because 'the entire movie takes place basically in real time'. In other words, the men don't come into contact with women because the film is focused on the robbery and its aftermath. 'I mean, is one of the guys gonna bring his girlfriend to the rendez vous? It didn't fit into the way I was telling the story.'

Jamie Beardsley had been recruited just two weeks before the first day of shooting by the movie's production manager.

'You want to make a strange little movie, Jamie?'

'Depends whether it's any good.'

'I can't honestly tell you. But I'll send you over the script and see what you think.'

As was a common place occurrence with anyone who read *Dogs*. Jamie was hooked the moment she picked it up. 'It was the best script I had ever read.'

Within seconds of meeting him, Jamie was completely hypnotized by Quentin's enthusiasm. He seemed supremely confident and had a savvy side to him that equally impressed her, considering he was a first-time director.

Quentin insisted that the final shot list for the movie should be kept secret because he did not want the movie's backers, Live Entertainment, to start breathing down his neck if he deviated in any way from the official shot list. Quentin believed he should have the freedom to alter scenes as he went along; they might work on the page in one way and then have to be rewritten to work on the day of the actual shoot.

Quentin took this very sensible course of action after reading numerous books about disastrous movie productions, like the classic *Final Cut*, which told the story of the most expensive flop in the history of Hollywood, *Heaven's Gate*.

In this way, he managed to add an entire sequence which was not in the original script, when Orange (Tim Roth) retells a lie. Originally, Quentin had written it as a simple voice-over but, timing Roth through the camera's viewfinder, he realized he was onto something much more powerful. 'I was like, Oh my God, this is it... and we can do it!' So an entire section of *Dogs* was created on the run.

As Tim Roth later noted, 'Quentin isn't a first-timer, he's been rehearsing all his life.'

First Assistant Director Jamie Beardsley was intrigued by Quentin, especially when he insisted he had never directed anything before. 'He had a wealth of knowledge about every aspect of the process. It was only later I realized he had learnt just about everything from watching movies and reading books about the business.'

As First AD, Jamie was supposed to provide the link between the director and his actors, as well as being an ear for the producers. It was a precarious line to tread. But she was so bowled over by Quentin's devil-may-care attitude that she let him do it his way entirely, even allowing him to do a vast number of takes on some of the lengthy dialogues in the movie.

The advantage from Quentin's point of view, was that he had as many as ten chances to get a good take. The disadvantage – from the producer's point of view – was that it cost a lot of money to use up so much film.

Not surprisingly, Lawrence Bender became very pissed off about this and regularly screamed at Jamie Beardsley to keep a tighter rein on Quentin. But that was easier said than done, especially as she had to be the ultimate diplomat when mediating between the director and his actors, and the rest of the crew.

'One day, Quentin got rimmed out by Lawrence about shooting too much film and he seemed real upset,' explains Jamie. 'I told him to forget it. I guess I shouldn't have said that. Lawrence wanted me to tell Quentin that was what happens when you shoot too much film, but I just wasn't prepared to. I really did believe in him that much.'

However, these relatively minor problems were completely overshadowed by a flare-up that came just a few days after the shooting of *Dogs* began.

'What's his beef, Quentin?'

Lawrence Tierney (who played Joe Cabot) was old-fashioned in more ways than one. The actor who had made a name for himself playing wise-assed tough guys in those no-nonsense forties black and whites completely blew a fuse when he had problems with his lines. He started blaming the other *Dogs*, in particular Mr Blonde, played by Michael Madsen.

'Hey, cool it, Larry. That doesn't have anything to do with it.' responded Quentin, immediately sensing the bitterness in the old timer's croaky voice.

Quentin was actually shaking in his boots as he said that because he was trying to discipline Lawrence Tierney, (the same Lawrence Tierney whom he had dedicated *Dogs* to, along with those other actors and film makers: Timothy Carey, Roger Corman, Andre DeToth, Chow Yun-Fat, Jean-Luc Godard, Jeanne Pierre Melville and Lionel White).

Tierney was one of Quentin's favourite movie heroes, but here on the sweltering set of *Reservoir Dogs* he was just another member of the gang. Admittedly he was playing Mr Big, Joe Cabot, but that didn't mean he could get away with pissing off all the other actors.

Quentin took a deep breath and continued, 'This is the deal. I want you to go practice with Michael and then we can get this just right. D'you dig?' It was pleasantly delivered. He hoped it would have the required effect of cooling things down. Unfortunately it did not.

'I don't need your advice, cocksucker,' said Tierney in his finest tow-truck winch growl. Everyone else on the set stopped what they were doing.

First AD Jamie Beardsley placed her very slight 110 pound figure between these two heavyweights who had taken a Mexican stand-off position about a foot away from each other.

Eyeball to eyeball, the young maestro and the old-time movie star tried to outburn each other with manic, air piercing stares.

'Fuck you, Larry,' said Quentin. There were a couple of gasps from the audience. He had clearly decided not to lose face amongst the other Dogs.

'Shut the fuck up, you fucking jerk.'

Suddenly, producer Lawrence Bender walked calmly onto the set and split the atmosphere in two. The two warring parties turned and headed in opposite directions as if nothing had happened.

When Tierney's character Joe Cabot tries to calm down the warring robbers and tells them, 'I need you cool. Are you cool?' it summed up Quentin's approach when handling Tierney from that moment onwards. Ultimately it earned him a great deal of respect from the old timer and the rest of the cast.

Explains Jamie Beardsley, 'I was surprised that Quentin took the approach that he did. I would have backed down and let someone else take care of it, but he wanted to show he could do it himself.'

In the end, Quentin and Tierney sorted out their difficulties by having a beer together. And some production members believe the tension caused by the incident actually helped some of the actors' performances.

To Quentin, it was more than just a matter of pride. He had

something to prove. He was a Dog along with all the other actors on the set that day. and a Dog would never allow themselves to be pushed around, even by the powerful Joe Cabot.

'It was as if Quentin was flexing his muscles. I would never normally have accepted that from such a young, inexperienced director. He wanted to show he wouldn't take any shit,' says Jamie Beardsley.

Chris Penn (who played Nice Guy Eddie) probably summed up everyone's true feelings about Lawrence Tierney when he was asked about the veteran actor after the shoot: 'He's everything you'd expect. He's mean. cranky, loving, a real pain and a great guy.'

The actor with probably the worst job in the entire movie was Tim Roth, who had to lie in a pool of blood for two weeks for his part as the cop infiltrator Mr Orange.

Temperatures inside the warehouse that had once been a funeral home on the corner of Figueroa and 59th Street – where the post-heist scenes were shot – were in excess of 110 degrees thanks to the hot weather and lighting rigs. (The two-storey structures around East LA were the perfect setting because they gave a feel of the old Los Angeles.)

The old embalming rooms were put to good use by doubling as Orange's apartment and Cabot's office for shooting purposes. The set designers also hired artists to create a new character, Kamikaze Cowboy. for both a poster and comic book used in the movie.

Meanwhile. Roth was soaked in sticky red gluey liquid each morning before positioning himself at that familiar spot on the floor, where he collapsed after being dragged in by Mr White (Harvey Keitel), following the earlier shooting. Many of the cast and crew suspected the quality of his acting was enhanced by the authentic agonies he was suffering, all in the name of art. He certainly did not have a comfortable time.,

But despite all this, Tim Roth built up a particular rapport with Michael Madsen (Mr Blonde) and on the day the infamous ear-slicing scene was shot, Roth was lying on the floor, blood-soaked as usual and desperately trying not to laugh out loud because the whole sequence seemed comical from his position. thanks to the continual humming and jiving of Madsen.

One of the most refreshing aspects of *Dogs* was that there was no room in the budget for any prima donna behaviour from the stars. Every actor made his own way to the set each morning. Steve Buscemi (Mr Pink) was so broke at the time he was sleeping on a pal's couch in West Hollywood. Even Harvey Keitel drove himself to the set. Tim Roth was hanging out with friends in Santa Monica. Most of the others were already LA-based.

Not surprisingly, the most difficult scene to shoot was the ear-cutting sequence. The actors were very reluctant to do it because they recognized it as an extremely violent scene.

There was also the problem of making Marvin Nash look as if his ear had really been sliced off. The searing heat became the biggest enemy of all because the fake remains of the ear kept melting on the side of the cop's head.

Quentin was well aware of the importance of the scene for the audience and he wanted to get it absolutely right. He actually shot it at least four different ways including one version where the audience sees the ear being sliced off. At one stage, Quentin wanted to do one of his wild and wonderful camera-angled shots through the legs of Mr Blonde (Michael Madsen), while he looked up at Mr Orange (Tim Roth), with Orange then shooting him after he has splashed petrol all over the cop. The prosthetics department were told they would have to make a fake pair of legs, but in the end Quentin abandoned the idea.

Actor Kirk Baltz, who played the luckless lawman who gets his ear so musically sliced off, understandably hated every second of being handcuffed and taped up. 'He was sweaty and he was near to tears about the whole sequence,' remembers Jamie Beardsley.

Quentin was actually piling on the pressure with take after take because he knew the scene would look more authentic if poor Baltz was suffering a degree of real-life pain.

During the same controversial scenes, Quentin proved he was more than happy to accept a certain degree of ad-libbing if it improved the script. When Michael Madsen (Mr Blonde) sliced off the cop's ear, Madsen made a quip into the severed ear as he held it in his hand.

'It was completely spur of the moment,' explains Madsen. 'I had this ear in my hand and I wondered if it could hear. I did it for myself and it was funny...which says something about me. And I didn't know if Quentin was going to leave it in.'

Quentin knew the moment Madsen did it that he was going to leave it in the final version of *Dogs* because it rounded off the scene perfectly.

But Madsen was surprised by the intensity of the adverse reaction to the ear-slicing scene when the movie was released in Los Angeles the following year. Quentin explained at the time, 'He can't believe that people are that shocked by it because he has an LA point of view – that people are going to enjoy watching a cop getting tortured.'

As White (Keitel) informs Pink (Buscemi) when the younger robber asks him if he had killed anyone during the botched stick-up, 'No real people...just cops.'

Interestingly, Steve Buscemi himself took a slightly less anti-police stance in relation to the scene. 'I feel that these guys don't have anything against cops *per se*. This is just their *job*.'

The movie's take on violence was slightly ambivalent even during the shooting of *Dogs*. Producer Bender believes that the distinction between *Dogs* and a regular action flick is that, 'It's not cool to get killed in this movie. When people get killed, it hurts. And you're there hurting with them – as opposed to some of these bigger action pictures, like *Lethal Weapon*, where people get killed and it's sort of a cool thing.'

The movie was slated to be shot over five weeks (each consisting of six days) and the cast and crew worked twelve- or thirteen-hour days before driving straight to dailies – the showing of the previous day's processed film. Then Quentin, Jamie Beardsley and some of the Dogs would gather in a bar to plan shots for the following day before collapsing for a few hours and then starting all over again.

Certain elements of *Reservoir Dogs* have taken on almost legendary status, thanks to the movie's cult following. One of the most talked about – and analysed – sequences is when Nice Guy Eddie is driving along a street and an orange balloon is seen floating through the air in the slipstream of his Caddy. Many *Dogs* fanatics believe the balloon symbolizes the fact that Orange is the rat and that's why Eddie's car runs across it.

The balloon was actually from a children's party down the street and Quentin shouted 'cut' the moment he saw it.

'It's kinda cool, Quentin. Why not leave it in?' suggested Jamie Beardsley.

'Yeah. Keep it in the shot. Movie geeks like me'll be analyzing this scene for years to come,' agreed Quentin. He was, of course, entirely correct.

It's been said many times in Hollywood that one should always avoid working with animals and children and Quentin would no doubt agree with that, after filming the brief scene in *Dogs* featuring a police dog in the toilets when Orange (Tim Roth) takes a leak.

'The dog had terrible problems barking to order, and to make matters worse, it had the longest tongue any of us had ever seen in our entire lives.' explains Jamie Beardsley. 'Every time the animal opened its mouth all the cast and crew would collapse in heaps of laughter.'

As a tribute to the police dog, Quentin freeze framed the moment when his huge tongue is hanging out in the final version of the movie. Everyone involved in the film still bursts into fits of laughter every time they see it up on the big screen.

The *Dogs* shoot was getting into its stride, but Quentin was still determined to ensure that the actors managed to hype themselves into just the right level of fury. He didn't want his Dogs belonging to the Roger Moore school of acting (i.e. walking on, switching into the character, then switching back to normal the moment they finished a scene for the day). He wanted them to be angry, evil and sensitive.

When Quentin's old acting school pal Rich Turner showed up to play one of the cops in the sequence with the dog, he got a nasty reaction. The film was still being shot in the big old warehouse in downtown LA. Turner walked straight into a bunch of very mean actors who had taken on the characters of the murderous robbers they were playing.

Turner – a quietly spoken, regular kind of guy who still lived near

Quentin's old home in Torrance – had just been fitted out as a cop by the wardrobe department when he realized that all was not well with the other actors. They would not utter a word to him.

Then Turner heard Chris Penn (Nice Guy Eddie) muttering something to Quentin. He just managed to catch the words: 'What the fuck are the cops doing here, Quint?'

Quentin shrugged his shoulders and said nothing. He was clearly enjoying the tension that had been sparked by the misconception that Turner was a real policeman.

For the remainder of that day, not one of the Dogs talked to Turner. He was mortified but later realised that Quentin had deliberately misled them because he wanted their reaction to Turner's character to be even more authentic.

'I kinda understood it in the end, but it was real scary being treated like scum by people like Harvey Keitel and Mike Madsen,' explains Turner.

The actors' ability to get into character was hardly surprising when one considers how literally some of them have taken their roles in the past. Tim Roth actually ate real paint and turpentine for his role as Van Gogh and Keitel is said to have gone to extraordinary lengths for the filming of *The Bad Lieutenant*.

Throughout the shoot, 'Godfather' Monte Hellman, the veteran movie maker who had done so much to help Quentin and Lawrence Bender get the project off the ground, discreetly kept his distance.

He only showed up about half a dozen times throughout the entire shoot and did nothing more than offer friendly advice which Quentin accepted gracefully on the whole. But there was a technical problem with the movie which has never been disclosed before, even though it is clear to anyone who watches *Dogs*. It's something that bugged Hellman enormously.

He explains, 'During the car scenes if you look closely you will see that the car itself is above the level of all the other vehicles passing by. This is because, instead of being towed as it should have been, the car was put up on the back of a trailer and then driven along. That disturbed me greatly because it was not how it should be and I felt the audience would notice it and therefore it would lessen the effect of the movie's authenticity.'

Hellman was convinced that Quentin had been sold the idea by the crew. As they were under pressure to complete the shoot on a small budget, and within a relatively short time span, he assumed they had decided it would be quicker to film those sequences using that method. Hellman was so infuriated by this technical discrepancy that he tried to get Quentin to trim all the car scenes down to virtually nothing in the final edit. But Quentin kept insisting he was not bothered about it and even told Hellman, 'Sometimes I like things to be a bit unreal. It's more interesting.'

Hellman – who was definitely from the old school of film directing – disagreed, but Quentin stuck to his guns. His view was based on the premise that he was the audience and if it didn't bother him it wouldn't bother them. The truth is that he is probably right. Next time you see *Dogs* take a look for yourself and see what you think. Most audiences wouldn't notice it unless it was pointed out beforehand.

'Godfather' Hellman's role in the shooting and post-production process of *Dogs* is interesting because he was the only one of the three principal movers who actually had experience of properly budgeted movies. In his opinion, the script had always been brilliant, but some of the film making left a little to be desired.

'There were scenes that just did not work. A lot of them were plain overkill. In other words, the audience got the message without them.' he says.

But Quentin was like a father being asked to give away his first-born child each time Hellman tried to persuade him to make harsher cuts during the editing of *Dogs*. In the end he did trim nearly fifteen minutes, although it obviously hurt him even to concede that much.

Before *Dogs* even finished shooting, the word was spreading

through Hollywood that this was going to be a really hot, funky little movie. The cast and crew members were telling anyone who would listen that Quentin was going to be a real force to be reckoned with. He had even managed to make shooting the movie a bundle of fun (albeit uncomfortable fun), which was more than could be said for ninety per cent of the productions in Tinseltown.

By the time the rap party was held in a lively, cheap Mexican restaurant on Melrose Avenue, in West Hollywood, half of Hollywood's vast population of young film makers wanted to crash the gathering. In the end, Lawrence Bender was very careful only to allow those who were involved in the actual production into the already packed out restaurant. Margaritas were flowing and photos of the party show that everyone – including Quentin – got suitably sloshed.

There was a genuine feeling of comradeship amongst cast and crew, which was summed up by Tim Roth, 'Quentin's the glue that kept us all together and it's not like corny shit that most actors say when they're asked by journalists. But it's fucking true. Never felt like that before.'

First AD Jamie Beardsley adds, 'Everyone deserved a drink at that party. We had worked damned hard and knew that we had just been involved in something very special indeed. It was a good feeling all round. All the tensions between people like Larry Tierney and Quentin were forgotten and the booze flowed just the way it should.'

The only small black cloud over the proceedings, from Jamie's point of view, was that she had a severe falling out with Lawrence Bender over her role as First AD.

Essentially, Beardsley saw herself as the protector of the cast and crew, while Bender had expected her to report directly to him. About a week before the end of the shoot she was pulled into Bender's tiny office and told she was being made unit production manager for the remainder of the production.

'But I have no hard feelings. It was a once-in-a-lifetime experience,' she explains.

Quentin even showed that beneath his confident exterior still lurked a highly insecure individual. At the time, he admitted to his manager Cathryn Jaymes that he was worried about how people might react to the movie.

'What if *Dogs* is not a big hit?'

'Then go to Europe and make your own films,' said Cathryn reassuringly. 'Listen, Quentin, you're a smart guy. You know the score. People will come around to appreciate you. If you're lucky it won't take long.'

Quentin absorbed those wise words, taking special note of Cathryn Jaymes' advice about Europe. Here he was, twenty-eight years old and he still had not once ventured outside the United States. It was pathetic how unworldly he was. He was writing Hollywood movies, yet he had not even glimpsed the rest of the world, except through movies and television. He decided there and then that if *Dogs* was the success everyone was predicting then he would use it to gain a foothold in Europe, so he could explore foreign lands.

Whatever happens, Quentin promised himself, I want a life beyond Hollywood.

Meanwhile, Quentin and his producer Lawrence Bender found themselves being courted by everyone in Hollywood following the incredible advance word-of-mouth on *Dogs*. But they decided to play it cool. What was the hurry? They had come this far on a shoestring... Why not hang back for a while and let the offers pour in.

Then, at a premiere of *Terminator 2*, in early Autumn 1991, with *Dogs* not even completed in the editing room, Quentin was introduced to a young movie executive called Stacey Sher, President of actor Danny De Vito's production company Jersey Films. Shortly after that, Sher helped Quentin secure the rights to the Steeler's Wheel classic, 'Stuck in the Middle with You', which played such an important part in the ear slicing scene.

A few weeks later, Quentin and producer Lawrence Bender signed a

development deal with Danny De Vito and Michael Shamberg at Jersey Films. Sher reckoned she could get Quentin a fee of almost a million dollars for his next project. Incredibly, she had not even seen *Dogs* at this stage. Quentin had already pitched his idea for a follow-up to *Dogs* called *Pulp Fiction*, but he had nothing more than an idea in his head.

Quentin and Bender renamed their production company A Band Apart Productions to handle that project and anything else that might come their way. The name was a tribute to Jean-Luc Godard's *Bande à Part* movie which has been one of the biggest single filmic influences in Quentin's career.

Everything was looking good on the horizon. Quentin just had to steer straight and he would get there...

'From the looks of those ears she's gonna fly before she'll walk'

Lawrence Tierney, commenting on a snapshot of a gas attendant's baby

daughter in *The Devil Thumbs a Ride*, 1947

You Gonna Bark All Day Little Doggie?

DIRECTORS' GUILD BUILDING, SUNSET
BOULEVARD, JANUARY 1992

Rich Turner was nervous. Quentin's onetime acting school buddy had been invited to the first ever screening of *Reservoir Dogs* and he'd just noticed Jack Nicholson sitting near the back of the auditorium. What the hell was he doing here?

'The buzz on this movie is incredible. Everyone wants to see it,' whispered a girl sitting next to Turner as the lights dimmed.

Quentin had been delighted when Lawrence Bender suggested screening *Dogs* at the dark brown highrise headquarters of the Directors' Guild of America, in the heart of West Hollywood. Not only was it just ten blocks east of Quentin's favourite fast food emporium, Denny's, but he also felt a kind of smug satisfaction about showing the movie in such esteemed surroundings. Quentin knew the industry was talking about

Dogs as if it was the next *Mean Streets.* Now he was about to prove them right.

In fact the movie had received such strong word-of-mouth since shooting had been completed more than three months earlier, that producer Bender had to organize six initial screenings just to satisfy the curiosity of people legitimately connected to *Dogs.*

As is traditional in any movie theatre in Los Angeles, the audience went totally quiet the moment the movie started rolling. But this was a definite hush of anticipation. The 'Madonna dick, dick, dick' opener in the coffee shop got plenty of laughs, but when the film cut to a bloodied Orange gasping for breath as White drove the getaway car, the crowd went into a stunned silence. And so it went on, as Quentin took his first ever audience through a roller coaster ride of emotions.

When comedian Steve Wright's DJ patter on the super cool sounds of the seventies radio show introduced 'Stuck in the Middle with You' and Blonde began his dance routine, the audience hummed in appreciation. Then they gasped in stunned silence as he sliced off the cop's ear. There were mutterings of discontent. A couple of women got up and walked out in disgust.

But they had misunderstood the movie. *Dogs* actually went out of its way to avoid over-the-top, slasher-style violence. The mayhem up on the screen was that much more horrifying because most of it occurred in the viewer's head. But Quentin did admit, 'The torture scene is not just gross, it's not just violent – it's disturbing.' It was also shot in real time, to add to the dramatic tension.

'It's not made easier with fast cuts. You are stuck. You can close your eyes. You can leave the theatre. But you've got to take matters into your own hands. The movie ain't helping you,' he pointed out.

In Quentin's mind, the audience became the ultimate flies on the wall as they watched the torture being played out, second by second, minute by minute. 'Before the torture starts, the cop is just a uniform – you saw a cop get shot earlier and you didn't cry.' But, as the cop pleas for mercy, the viewer can't help but become one with him.

Adding to the extremity of the scene was Blonde's perverse dance of pleasure to the nostalgic strains of that Steeler's Wheel bubblegum classic. Quentin insisted, 'You're kind of enjoying Michael's (Blonde's) performance, and then when the music comes on, instinctively you're kind of going with the beat because it's very catchy. And you can't help but get a bit of a thrill from Michael's little dance. You're kind of enjoying that aspect and then – *boom!* You can imagine what a guy like that would do with a razor in his hand when he wanted to fuck up a cop just to fuck him up.'

But at the Directors Guild that night, Quentin's friend, Rich Turner, had no such qualms about *Dogs*. The atmosphere of the movie had swept him up and he was riveted by Quentin's interpretation of the same script he had read with such awe just nine months earlier. Even the end credits made interesting reading, with notes of thanks to Terry Gilliam, who had done so much to encourage Quentin when he took the Sundance workshop by storm the previous summer; and Tony Scott, about to helm *True Romance*, who had given Quentin some fatherly advice about certain aspects of the Hollywood fame game.

When Rich Turner left the viewing theatre, he was convinced that Quentin was on the way to the very top. 'The film was outstanding and the audience knew it that night,' he explains. But there was much more adulation to come...

SUNDANCE FILM FESTIVAL, JANUARY, 1992

This really was going to be the return of the prodigal son. Quentin had very mixed feelings about his previous trip to Sundance. Then, he had been the film geeky upstart with the foul-mouthed script who wanted to shoot his camera from crazy angles.

This time, he saw snow for the first time in his life. It seemed so

bizarre to see everything covered in a white blanket. Noises were more muffled. Everyone seemed to shuffle around in a different way. Quentin was captivated.

Now he was the director of the most talked-about film of the year. Everyone wanted a piece of him. Typically, Quentin took it all in his stride. Staying in five-star hotels should have been an uncomfortable leap for a guy who was more used to tatty two-storey dive motels and a Big Mac. But Quentin rapidly developed a taste for caviar, champagne and penthouse suites.

Besides the adulation of other film makers at Sundance, there was some serious business to attend to. *Dogs* had been financed by Live Entertainment, which was primarily a video operation, and the movie needed to find a US cinema distributor. In stepped the Miramax company and its two founders, Bob and Harvey Weinstein.

The major Hollywood studios had refused to be swept up in the hype surrounding *Dogs*, and appeared to believe the movie and Quentin were one-hit wonders on the art house circuit. No one thought Quentin's movie would make any money as it was a violent, twisted tale which would cause more trouble than it was worth.

The portly Weinstein brothers from Miramax – one of the so-called mini-majors who dominate the lower budget end of the movie business in Hollywood – thought otherwise. They snapped up the US theatrical rights to *Dogs* for the bargain sum of two hundred thousand dollars. Miramax told Quentin and Bender they intended to distribute the movie later that year, city by city, in the hope that gradual word-of-mouth would ensure its success. It went on to gross approximately four million dollars in America. But Live Entertainment retained the video rights, as well as foreign cinema distribution, and went on to make an estimated fifty million dollars with the movie on worldwide video and in theatrical release outside the States.

The first screening of the ninety-three-minute *Dogs* at Sundance

Signs held in the photo: RE-ELECT Jimmy Jack ...NE SHERIFF · JACK BE NIMBLE JACK BE QUICK · JACK A-NIRO · JACK OF ALL TRADES · JUMPIN JACK · CRACKER JACK · JACK SHIT · JACK-RABBIT · JACK AND JILL · BURT JACK & RACK · JACK-ODELLI · JACK'S · JACKSON · JUMBO JACK · WOLF-MAN JACK · JACK-POT · JACK DANIELS · JACK #1 · JACK KNIFE · FLAP JACK · JACK-ASS · JACK IN THE BOX

Above: Spot the movie geek. Quentin with his acting classmates at the Jimmy Best Acting School in Toluca Lake, California. They include David Stein *(centre)*, who played a cop in *Dogs*; Brenda Hillhouse *(bottom left front)*, who played a strong supporting role in *Pulp Fiction* and Rich Turner *(far left centre)*, who also played a cop in *Dogs*.
(Copyright © Rich Turner)

Right: The Comic Book Master. Quentin's old friend Scott Spiegel in the wacky bedroom of his Hollywood Hills home. His enthusiasm for comics and strange artefacts influenced Quentin's ideas in the early days.
(Copyright © Wensley Clarkson)

Right: Quentin's directorial debut – *My Best Friend's Birthday* – a film he later denied having made because he felt it would damage his chances of being accepted as the director of *Dogs*.
(Copyright © Craig Hamann)

Above: Quentin playing Clarence in *Birthday*. Alongside him is Craig Hamann, who co-wrote the script and later briefed the cast of *Pulp Fiction* on all drugs-related scenes.
(Copyright © Craig Hamann)

Right: Quentin first developed his taste for traditional American food when working at the Pussycat Porno Theater in Torrance. Jimmy's Coffee Shop was his favourite venue for lunch.
(Copyright © Wensley Clarkson)

Left: **The Pussycat Porno Theater closed down a couple of years back, but it was recently used as a location for *Ed Wood* – Quentin's favourite film of 1994.** (Copyright © Wensley Clarkson)

Right: **The funky fifties-built Foster's Ice Cream Parlour across the street from the Pussycat Porno Theater, in Torrance, where Quentin regularly hung out.**
(Copyright © Wensley Clarkson)

Left: Movie geeks' paradise – the original site of Video Archives where Quentin worked for five years.
(Copyright © Wensley Clarkson)

Below: Rounding up the usual suspects. Quentin's producer, Lawrence Bender *(left)*, in his other 'role' as an actor in 1988, in Scott Spiegel's low budget horror flick called *Intruder*, which Bender also produced.
(Copyright © Scott Spiegel)

Above: **Talking movies. Quentin deep in discussion with *Film Threat* magazine editor, Paul Zinnerman. Later the magazine closely examined the similarities between *Reservoir Dogs* and *City of Heat.***
(Copyright © 'Mad' Malcolm)

Right: **Quentin dedicated this poster of *Dogs* to the editorial team at *Film Threat* .**
(Copyright © 'Mad' Malcolm)

The *Dogs* Hit Mob: *(left to right)* Unit Production Manager Paul Hellerman, Producer Lawrence Bender, Second Assistant Director Kelly Kiernan, First Assistant Director Jamie Beardsley, Quentin.
(Copyright © Jamie Beardsley)

Above: Actor and producer, Harvey Keitel, became Quentin's father figure on the set of *Dogs.*
(Copyright © Kobal Collection)

Right: Talking tactics. Quentin and Tim Roth during the *Dogs* shoot.
(Copyright © Jamie Beardsley)

Left: Joker in the pack. Michael 'Blonde' Madsen in *Dogs*.
(Copyright © Live Entertainment /courtesy Kobal Collection)

Below: 'Supercool'. Tim Roth getting into character as Orange in *Dogs*.
(Copyright © Live Entertainment /courtesy Kobal Collection)

Above: It's Mexican stand-off time between White (Keitel) and Pink (Buscemi) in *Dogs* .
(Copyright © Live Entertainment/courtesy Kobal Collection)

Right: The 'Dogs': team photo at the end of shooting *Reservoir Dogs.*
(Copyright © Jamie Beardsley

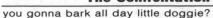
brought a mixed response from the mainly art house crowd. The final cut of the movie had actually only been completed three days before the festival began and the five screenings were amongst the hardest tickets to get. But the art house types were precisely the audience Quentin DID NOT want to see his movie.

At least half a dozen members of that first audience walked out during the ear-slicing scene. But Quentin and producer Lawrence Bender were not that perturbed. The buzz was still great and the more people talked about the movie the better.

At a post-screening conference, Quentin happily brazened out questions about the torture scene by declaring that he loved violence.

'Would you show *Reservoir Dogs* to your own eight-year-old?' asked an aggressive reporter.

Quentin shrugged. After all, he was on a roll here. 'If she reacts harshly and it gives her nightmares, so what? Part of being a kid is having nightmares.'

It all sounded so daring, even the way Quentin described the mentality of his Dogs. 'These guys aren't like the guys in *Goodfellas*. They're not wise guys or gangsters. They're like Dustin Hoffman in *Straight Time* [written by Mr Blue, Ed Bunker]: they do jobs. And a big thing in that line of work is professionalism, which is a way to bullshit themselves into thinking this is an actual job and profession, not just hooliganism.'

Those present at the conference at Sundance were amazed by the ease with which Quentin slid into the role of celebrity/director. When the predictable outrage about the ear-slicing scene continued to rumble on, he coolly replied, 'I didn't do that scene just to say, "Boy, I'm going to have a boner when this thing comes out."'

The atmosphere got even more heated when someone asked if Quentin believed that *Dogs* might incite someone to commit violence. 'I'm not going to be handcuffed by what some crazy fuck might do who sees my movie. The minute you put handcuffs on artists because of stuff like that, it's not an art form any more.'

Dogs did not win any prizes for political correctness at Sundance

because it contained aggressive dialogue about black people, some bla-
tantly macho touches, and no female speaking parts. But when Quentin
was told by one young film student, 'You know what you've done, you've
given white boys the kind of movies black kids get,' he knew it was all
worthwhile. Those blaxploitation movies of the seventies had been the
looking cool, being bad with a fuck-you-attitude-type picture that he
had hoped *Dogs* would emulate. If he had achieved nothing else, that
would be enough.

On the flight back to LA from Sundance, Bender and Quentin discussed their next move – a trip to the Cannes Film Festival with *Dogs*.

'But there's one small problem,' said an ever-enthusiastic Quentin.

'What's that, Quentin?'

'I don't have a passport.'

It was only then that it really came home to Bender and exec producer Monte Hellman that Quentin's life *was* the movies. He had never
even ventured outside the United States. His first trip abroad would fuel
his curiosity about life even more.

That evening, Quentin returned home to his mother's detached house in
Glendale and flopped onto the bed in his room, still decorated with a
Bobby Sherman lunch pail and posters of such movies as *Breathless*, *The
Evil Eye* and the French version of de Palma's *Dressed to Kill*.

The message machine was crowded with calls from agents, directors
and producers all offering him imaginary deals for movie projects they
thought he would be perfect for. Quentin's response to all of them was,
'Send it over and I'll take a look at it.'

Although he considered the scripts, he had been spoilt by his experiences with *Dogs*. No one had monkeyed around with his script. The
movie was pure and clean and no major studio could offer him that level
of control.

A few days later, Quentin got a call from his friend Jeff Burr, who
had introduced him to Lawrence Tierney the previous year. Director Burr
wanted Quentin to play a small cameo in a low-budget movie he was

making with one of Quentin's favourite actors, Bruce Campbell.

'Wow. Bruce Campbell. I'm yours, Jeff. When do we start?' responded an eager Quentin.

'Tomorrow. Be at the location at 6am,' replied Burr.

After the adulation of Sundance it was back to a dose of reality – and Quentin was delighted.

Next morning he got to the location, a deserted mental hospital in Pasadena, the same town just outside LA where his mother had first encountered his long-lost father almost thirty years earlier.

Quentin's role as a nasty hospital orderly took just one day to shoot and the movie never managed a general release. But Quentin didn't mind. He was always willing to do something if it sounded a little funky. He was determined not to be tied down by financial demands and constraints.

Meanwhile, Quentin's *Natural Born Killers* script was still being rejected by most of Hollywood, despite the efforts of his friends Jane Hamsher and Don Murphy. They genuinely believed in the project and had been hawking it around, with Quentin attached as director.

With absolutely no bites, the pair tried to persuade Quentin to let them try to get it made with another director at the helm. At first Quentin was reluctant, but he had actually grown bored with the *NBK* script after many years of reworking it over and over again. Nevertheless, he was not prepared to give the project away. If they no longer wanted him attached as director there would be a price to pay.

In the end, Quentin's lawyer called up and said a deal could be struck because Quentin had his eye on a classic red Chevy Malibu convertible that was on sale for ten thousand dollars. A deal was then hammered out so that Quentin would get the money for the car in advance (against sixty thousand dollars if the movie ever got made). Hamsher and Murphy ended up with a two-year option and Quentin got his car which he eventually used in *Pulp Fiction*.

In the spring of 1992, after years of dreaming about being in one of the transatlantic jets that had roared overhead when he lived in his

crummy apartment in Harbor City, Quentin began flying abroad. He was on the way to a new world...

So much had happened in the previous eighteen months that he sometimes wondered if it had all been a dream and he would wake up back in Video Archives arguing with Roger and Jerry about the wonders of the late fifties Italian exploitation flicks. Life had been extremely simple then. Quentin was well aware that things would get much more complex from now on.

'We didn't need dialogue. We had faces'

Silent movie star Gloria Swanson, in *Sunset Boulevard*, 1950

Foot Massages Don't Mean Shit

STUDIO CIRCUS NIGHTCLUB, CANNES, MAY, 1992

Quentin couldn't quite believe his eyes. The nightclub was virtually steaming with atmosphere. Beautiful women lined the walls. Throbbing house music shook the floor of the dance area. The constant hum of conversation, combined with the clink of bottles and glasses, dominated the dining area at the back of the club.

As Quentin tried to make his way through the crowds, every pair of female eyes within range locked on to him and his party. The movie geek really had made good. Just two years earlier, the nearest he could have got to the south of France was watching *Dirty Rotten Scoundrels* at Video Archives.

Word of the arrival of Quentin, Harvey Keitel and Tim Roth had spread through Studio Circus like wildfire. Pairs of women whispered in each other's ears as tough guy Harvey led his fellow Dogs in the direction of the bar. There were admiring glances from some, and unashamed looks of sheer lust from other bolder, brassier women with their all-over tans and gold Rolex watches.

That night, Quentin should have been a little uneasy, maybe even shy. But he must have felt as if he belonged. All those pouting lips, wiggling hips and cleavages were a sight to behold. It had been a long time coming and he was about to embark on a brilliant adventure. Quentin happily caught the eyes of various ladies that night, as the *Dogs* team settled down for a party held in their honour in one of the swishest joints in Cannes.

There was an unmistakable confidence in Quentin's swagger as he made his way behind Roth and Keitel. By the time they actually reached the bar, virtually everyone in the nightclub knew precisely who they were. Such was the power of being hailed as Cannes' latest celluloid heroes.

Suddenly the music cut. An awkward silence followed, then a gasp from the crowd. There was something vast hanging from the neon-lit ceiling of the club. It looked like a huge cake. Just then a rendition of 'Happy Birthday' boomed out over the speakers. Keitel looked down in embarrassment before anyone had a chance to utter a word.

'Happy birthday, Harvey,' said Quentin, slapping his new best friend on the back.

The vast cake gradually descended towards the crowd on the dance floor.

'Hey, Harvey, how old are you?' yelled one wise guy.

'Mind your own fucking business,' Keitel screamed back. No one knew if he was kidding or not.

The following few days in Cannes were an eye-opener for Quentin, and incredibly exhausting.

After yet another all-night party on the Miramax boat moored in Cannes harbour, he admitted he was feeling dog tired and realized it would soon be time to get away and start constructing his new project, already entitled *Pulp Fiction*.

In many ways, Quentin resembled Scorsese's *King of Comedy* character, Rupert Pumpkin, played so brilliantly by Robert de Niro. Just like Pumpkin, he had been practising for years to be famous. When it finally happened, it all seemed so natural and the travelling had only just begun.

Cannes was definitely an important stage in Quentin's development. He loved being in the heart of the film business and he adored the gorgeous topless French babes on the beach. But he did find the non-stop questions a little tedious at times. At one press conference he blew an entire room of journalists away with a memorable response to a question about film financing: 'It's not like someone just gave us some money and we masturbated with the camera.' The room went silent, then someone laughed in response and the rest followed suit.

Dogs was not even considered for the Festival's prestigious Palm d'Or award but it created a real buzz on the circuit and Quentin lapped up the tacky glamour of the event – the publicity and beautiful girls, and non-stop parties.

Quentin returned to France later that summer for the ninth annual French-American Film Workshop, in Avignon, where his presence had been requested as guest of honour.

Quentin and French director Arnaud Desplechin shared ten thousand dollars worth of Kodak film and processing as their joint prize for making the top two movies rated by the workshop. Ironically, Quentin would have found the prize invaluable a year earlier. But, with all the major studios now knocking at his door, a few thousand dollars worth of production costs was neither here nor there.

The response to *Dogs* at international film festivals seemed to create a surge of interest in all Quentin's other projects. Just a few weeks after Cannes, it was announced that the highly successful Morgan Creek Production Company had acquired US and UK movie rights to *True Romance*, and a host of stars, including Christian Slater, Gary Oldman, Brad Pitt, Patricia Arquette and Dennis Hopper, had signed up to appear under the directorship of Tony Scott.

Meanwhile, Oliver Stone's company revealed that they were intending to produce *Natural Born Killers* after finalizing a deal with young producers Don Murphy and Jane Hamsher. The word on the Hollywood

grapevine was that Stone himself wanted to direct it, as soon as he finished work on *Heaven and Earth*.

Quentin took *Dogs* to festivals and openings all over the world for the following six months. In the process he did more than four hundred interviews and travelled something approaching sixty thousand miles.

The reaction was not always entirely favourable, by any means. In Paris, where a very low-key world cinema premiere was held for *Dogs* in September 1992, Quentin was verbally attacked by an indignant French female director who said she had never been so upset as she was by the ear-slicing scene.

'What disturbs me the most is that you had such a good time making it,' she told Quentin.

'No, you had a good time watching it,' retorted Quentin.

'No, if you do a scene and if you have a feel for it, no matter how good you do it, that is apparent on the screen. If you do a scene and have fun, you capture that on screen,' came the humourless reply.

It seemed that Quentin could not win. But at least in Paris he got to a McDonalds and experienced first hand a Hamburger Royale, known as 'a quarter-pounder with cheese' in his home town. Quentin was so astonished by the French name change that he made a note to use it in his next screenplay, *Pulp Fiction*. He also enjoyed a beer with his Hamburger Royale, which was a revelation in itself.

In London, *Dogs* received glowing reviews. But, typically, Quentin turned the trip into a learning experience. One afternoon he found himself wandering through one of the sleazier streets of Soho and spotted an interesting-looking independent label record store. He spent more than three hours in the shop looking through and sampling various albums. He took a particular liking to Urge Overkill's version of the Neil Diamond classic 'Girl, You'll Be a Woman Soon'. He must have thought to himself, 'That is such a cool track, I'm gonna try and build a scene in my next movie around it'.

Quentin had made good use of music in *Dogs*. Now he was constantly thinking ahead to his next project, *Pulp Fiction*, and certain sounds inspired him. He firmly believed that music should be picked to fit a movie's plot, not written by some film score merchant after the film is shot. Two classic examples came to mind: 'Ride of the Valkyries' may have been around for a hundred years, but it would always be connected with Coppola's *Apocalypse Now*; likewise the opening bars of the Ronettes' 'Be My Baby', as Harvey Keitel hit the pillow, were *Mean Streets*. Quentin wanted to find the equivalent of those tracks to enhance *Pulp Fiction*.

While in London, Quentin even managed to date a blonde freelance reporter called Karen Krizanovich after encountering her in a pub. His relationship with girfriend Grace Lovelace back in LA had fizzled out. New friend Karen later commented, 'Keanu Reeves he is not. His face is an amalgam of huge cheekbones, lantern jaw, high forehead, low brow and a boxer's nose.'

After the interview was completed, Quentin asked Karen for a date. He phoned her that same night and the couple met at Quentin's hotel just off Oxford Street, where he managed to keep her waiting for an hour in the lobby.

'He's really very, very tall and broad. Kind of scary, actually,' thought Karen when Quentin finally appeared.

First stop on their date was a visit to a cinema showing a trailer for *Dogs* because Quentin wanted to check it out. After a ten-minute inspection in specially reserved seats they made their way off to Covent Garden and ended up in a nondescript bistro. As Quentin revealed his life story in dramatic tones, it dawned on Karen that he really did live his life through the movies.

The couple then went to a late showing of Roman Polanski's *Bitter Moon* at a little cinema just off Piccadilly Circus. Karen was quite surprised when Quentin's hands started wandering across her lap.

'Behave yourself! This film is by Polanski!' she scolded him. Karen was a little puzzled that a movie geek like Quentin should be so keen on bugging her rather than watching the film. Afterwards, the couple went back to Quentin's hotel for a coke each and then she caught a cab home.

In a rather hurtful aside, Karen concluded of her brief friendship

with Quentin. 'Did I sleep with him? That would be telling. But if I'm completely honest I have to admit the truth. He was too ugly for that!'

Another attractive female Quentin encountered during his trip to London was actress Emma Thompson, but she was only interested in his movies. She approached him at a film award gala.

'You know, I'm very intrigued by your movie but I'm a little scared to see it – I have a problem with violence,' the actress told Quentin by way of introduction.

The two then started talking movies and Quentin managed to get the quintessential English thespian to admit that amongst her favourite films were *Goodfellas* and *Henry, Portrait of a Serial Killer*.

Quentin was incredulous. 'Wait a minute! You saw those movies and you're afraid to see mine?'

Emma Thompson realized she had been snookered and decided there and then that she would go and see *Dogs* immediately. Who knows? She might even turn up one day in a Tarantino movie.

In Spain, Quentin stayed in a luxurious suite in the best hotel in the picturesque town of Sitges, half an hour from Barcelona. Some nights he would wander the main drag in Barcelona – the Ramblas – with friends, gazing in astonishment at the transvestites and street walkers.

At the Barcelona festival itself, Quentin presumed that notorious *Dogs* scenes, like the ear-slicing sequence, would be taken with a pinch of salt by Spanish audiences. (This seemed especially likely, as the movie was to be screened after an extremely gruesome effort called *Brain Dead*.) Nevertheless fifteen people walked out during the torture scene, including cult horror director Wes Craven and horror special effects artist Rick Baker.

'Wes Craven – the guy who directed *Last House on the Left*, for God's sake – walked out of *my* movie, ' recalled an astounded Quentin. 'Stuart Gordon – the guy who did *Re-Animator* – was one of the judges. and he was burying his head in his hands. It was hysterical.'

A few hours later, Quentin ran into Rick Baker, who told him:

'Quentin, I walked out of your movie, but I want you to take it as a compliment. See, we all deal in fantasy. There's no such thing as were-wolves or vampires. You're dealing with real-life violence, and I can't deal with that.'

Film festivals were becoming Quentin's staple diet. He was making up for lost time in more ways than one. He did a lot of hanging out with fans and some of them came in rather pleasant sizes, shapes and colours.

Quentin started spending much of his time leading babes to the magazine racks in airports where he would show them articles about himself – only to find that they quickly agreed to slip between the sheets. (His relationship with Grace seemed to be well and truly over.) He even seriously considered writing an article entitled, 'A Young Film Maker's Guide to Getting Laid at Film Festivals'. But there were also girls he just dated socially.

Quentin's old Video Archives friend Roger Avary had his own very apt description of what happens to a person when they attend too many festivals in a short period of time. 'It's like doing crack for a week. And that's only one festival. Quentin went to festivals for a *year*.'

By the time the US West Coast premiere of *Dogs* occurred, Quentin was in such a daze it was hard to tell whether he even realized that celebrities like Sean Penn, Jodie Foster and good ole Jack Nicholson had turned up for the show.

After the screening at the Hollywood Galaxy Theatre, the guests headed for the Roxbury Club, on Sunset, for a party hosted by Miramax and *Detour* magazine. But Quentin was fading fast. He did not hang around for his usual skinful of beers and a few hours of holding court. He even responded modestly to one writer's proclamation that he was Hollywood's brightest new director.

'I guess it's pretty cool,' was his only utterance.

At the *Dogs'* East Coast premiere in New York, a few weeks later, Quentin was back on good form after travelling to all four corners of the globe to promote the movie. At the shindig afterwards, at Robert de Niro's Tribeca Grill, he was willing to talk to anyone who would listen.

Journalist Anita Sarka attended and proclaimed that, 'Quentin Tarantino has the loudest fuckin' voice I have ever heard. He bellowed and boomed with such authority, you'd think he was trying to play to the last row of the nosebleed section, rather than work the tiny rear room at the Tribeca Grill.'

The celebrity guests that night were especially significant because Hollywood types rarely appear in New York. Shirley MacLaine and Tim Roth were spotted deep in conversation. Aidan Quinn and Harvey Keitel connected and Quentin got to ask British actress Emily Lloyd out for a date. It was a dream come true for Quentin, as Lloyd represented the next best thing to Tatum O'Neal as far as superstar babes were concerned.

But the guest of honour that night was Madonna. Everyone wondered how she would react to Quentin's 'Madonna dick, dick, dick' dialogue in the *Dogs* opening sequence. Within minutes of the start of the reception, her blonde highness waltzed over towards Quentin who was nervously sucking on a bottle of beer.

'Great movie, Quentin,' she demurred in his direction.

'Thanks,' replied an unusually shy Quentin. Then a beat of silence followed.

'But you're not right.'

Quentin looked around uneasily. 'Excuse me?'

'It's about love not dick, honey,' purred Madonna. Then Madonna revealed to Quentin that her favourite scene in *Dogs* had been the ear slicing by Blonde (Michael Madsen).

'It was sexy,' the Material Girl told Quentin.

'Cool,' came his reply.

'Oh yeah,' purred Madonna. 'Torture is sexy, read my book.'

She immediately gave him a copy with a message inscribed, 'It's about love not dick, Quentin...'

Also in New York, Quentin met French actress Maria de Medeiros. The two had a meal in a restaurant in Amsterdam Avenue and it was memorable mainly because Quentin got up halfway through to see how long the queues for *Dogs* were at the movie theatre across the street.

Quentin bumped into Maria twice more during his frequent trips round the world to various festivals. This included one great night out in Rio. during which it dawned on Quentin that he should base a *Pulp Fiction* character on Maria.

While in New York for that East Coast premiere, Quentin appeared on the cover of a magazine for the first time.

'Look, I got a cover, I got a cover,' he yelled at the top of his voice after getting on the front of the obscure *Orbit* magazine. Soon there would be so many cover photos of Quentin that he would not even have time to buy the magazines.

In LA, more and more actors were saying they wanted to work with Quentin after seeing *Dogs*. Lawrence Fishburn – whose career was back on track, following his brilliant performance in John Singleton's *Boyz in the Hood* – met with Quentin in a Hollywood diner, naturally.

'I like his style,' said Fishburn afterwards. 'We had about forty cups of espresso one day and just yammered on about *Speed Racer* and American movies where guys got to be cool and wear black suits and skinny ties. I love that line in *Reservoir Dogs* where Michael Madsen says, 'I bet you're a big Lee Marvin fan' because I *am* a big Lee Marvin fan,' added Fishburn, whom Quentin originally wanted to cast as hitman Jules in *Pulp Fiction*, ahead of Samuel L. Jackson.

Meanwhile, the interpretations of *Dogs*' so-called double meanings were multiplying almost daily. The absence of women in the movie led to predictable accusations of misogyny. But one underground magazine went even further, claiming that the scene where White comforts the dying Orange clearly indicated some kind of homosexual relationship between the two Dogs. The same publication based its conclusions on the fact that White whispered something inaudible in Orange's ear and then combed the wounded man's hair after loosening his belt. The truth was that Quentin's primary aim was to entertain rather than direct subliminal messages at his audience. His attitude after the release of *Dogs* was that if people wanted to read more into the movie than really existed then that was their problem.

Around this time, Quentin decided he wanted to resurrect *From Dusk 'Till Dawn*, the project that he was paid fifteen hundred dollars to turn into a screenplay by his friend Bob Kurzman back in 1990. The only problem was that the script belonged to Kurzman, and twenty-five actors, including Emilio Estevez, had so far turned down the lead role. There was talk of getting stand-up king Andrew Dice Clay as the lead, which would have secured a four million dollar budget, but then the alleged backer mysteriously disappeared into thin air.

Quentin and Kurzman (who was still intending to direct the project himself at this stage) even put together a four-minute filmed commercial for the movie to help sell it as a full-length film project.

'The dubbing was so bad in that commercial that it proved a bit of an embarrassment to Quentin and Bob Kurzman,' explained Hollywood movie writer Brian Williams. The project – as is so often the case in Hollywood – went back to drift mode, where it stayed for a further three years, before Quentin devised a package to actually get it made.

Reviews for *Dogs* varied enormously after the movie's release. But Vincent Canby, in the *New York Times*, picked up on something that few critics acknowledged.

He wrote: 'One of the principal reasons the film works so well is the sense of give-and-take that is possible only when two or more actors share the same image. Mr Sekula (DP) and Mr Tarantino have not been brainwashed by television movies. They don't depend on close-ups. *Reservoir Dogs* takes a longer view... Pay heed: *Reservoir Dogs* is as violent as any movie you are likely to see this year, but though it's not always easy to watch, it has a point.'

The obscure Detroit-based magazine *Orbit* published a glowing review which analyzed the film brilliantly.

'On the surface *Dogs* is a savvy updating of the classic *noir* B-movie classics of the fifties. It's about what happens when desperate men are pushed to their limits. But beneath all the sweat, blood and four-letter torrents lurks something else. Listen closely and you'll hear the rhythms of how men relate to men. Boil all the bluster and machismo down to its basics and we find the real essence of the film – it's about how men talk around other men,' wrote reviewer Paul Zimmerman, who later joined *Film Threat*.

The writer included a note at the end: 'While ostensibly a blistering black comedy, *Dogs* has gained notoriety from a brutal scene involving torture. While never gratuitous or graphic, audiences have been so repulsed that there have been walk-outs at many showings. This is merely a further testament to the power of the film, don't let it prevent you from seeing one of the best of the year.'

Quentin seemed to have created the first truly universal X-generation movie. The actors included a gaggle of X-ers, like Madsen, Buscemi, Roth and X-daddy Harvey Keitel, plus X-grand-daddy Lawrence Tierney.

In many people's eyes, *Dogs* was like a slowed-down version of doing speed for two hours. The movie was very simple visually, yet managed to be a frightening roller coaster ride at the same time. The music was an important element that helped the audience appreciate the movements in the plot. The violence was an integral part of the film, as each violent event took the story to its next stage.

In Britain, *Daily Mail* critic Shaun Usher was full of admiration for *Dogs* but feared the future effect of such a movie. He wrote, 'I applaud Quentin Tarantino's talent and boldness. But I fear he has started something we could do without.'

Even before it had been released throughout the world, a 'Who Killed Nice Guy Eddie?' controversy emerged, as audiences became concerned about certain elements of the film's ending. Tim Roth later claimed that Quentin knew full well what happened to Eddie (played by Chris Penn) and even had T-shirts printed up with 'Who Killed Nice Guy Eddie?' as a tease. On the back of the T-shirts were various theories. Most movie-goers naturally presumed it was White, but the truth is that no one actually knows for certain, and Quentin ain't saying.

Roth further increased the mystique of *Dogs* by refusing to say whether or not his character, Orange, died in that final showdown. But that was all part of the kick Quentin got from his special brand of film making. People cared so passionately about the characters that they were concerned about what happened to them after the movie ended. That was something fairly unique in celluloid history.

'There's something in the atmosphere that makes everything seem exaggerated'

David Farrar, in *Black Narcissus*, 1947

Tulips in Amsterdam

PIE IN THE SKY SMOKING CAFE,
LAURIERDWARSSTRACT, AMSTERDAM,
SUMMER 1992

A smile swept across Quentin's face as he recognized the pungent aroma of weed wafting in his direction from somewhere next to his table on the cobbled sidewalk. He sniffed the air, breathed in a lungful, took off his shades, sat back and watched the world go by this beautiful canal-corner setting.

Everyone looked so relaxed, carefree, pleasant. The whiff of danger that existed on every street corner in LA seemed a million miles away.

Quentin had caught the travelling bug while journeying round the world promoting *Dogs* at countless film festivals. When he had signed a nine hundred thousand dollar deal with TriStar, through Danny De Vito's Jersey Films, to write *Pulp Fiction*, he decided to use the first instalment of the cash to opt out of the rat-race for the first time in his life.

Amsterdam had caught his eye during his travels earlier that year because it was one of the few cities in Europe where you could see Hollywood movies with English-language soundtracks. It was also the ideal place for Quentin to just melt into the background, soak up the atmosphere and create his best screenplay yet. Some of his friends back in Hollywood were surprised when he announced that he was leaving town for a few months. They warned him that people would presume he'd quit before his career had properly taken off.

'If you leave this town you'll never get back in,' one friend told him.

But Quentin didn't give a damn. In any case, he knew he couldn't do his best work when he was being constantly hassled by phone calls from agents, studios, fans and friends. The straw that broke the camel's back was when one movie exec tried to persuade him to get 'call holding' on his phone so that people could get through to him more easily.

'Call holding,' exploded Quentin. 'What the fuck do I want call holding for?'

Quentin's manager Cathryn Jaymes was far more sympathetic.

'Amsterdam's a great idea, Quentin. Chill out, relax and get writing. I wish I was coming with you,' she told him when he announced his plans.

But there was one major problem as far as all Quentin's Hollywood associates were concerned; where exactly in Amsterdam was he going?

'Oh, I'll find a little apartment. Rent a bicycle,' came the slightly spaced-out reply.

'But where, Quentin?'

'I'll give you a call when I get there,' volunteered Quentin.

So it was that Quentin disappeared off to Europe with his nine hundred thousand dollar deal, to write *Pulp Fiction*. No one knew exactly where he was going, including Quentin himself. It was a Hollywood executive's nightmare. How could you put pressure on writers and directors to come up with the goods if you didn't know where to find them?

But Quentin was adamant that he was going and they would have to trust him to keep in touch.

The first couple of weeks were especially nerve-racking for Cathryn Jaymes, as she was Quentin's only real contact point in LA. He had merrily told various studio chiefs and execs to, 'call Cathryn if you need me. She'll know how to find me.'

However Cathryn initially had no more idea than the rest of them. As a result, she took the full force of their collective paranoia, while Quentin took in the sights, smells and sounds of his new home city.

At places like the Pie in the Sky Smoking Cafe, Quentin could sit back and think about *Pulp Fiction*, breathe in the pleasant aromas and forget all about call holding and all the other trappings of fame that were threatening to take over his life.

The 'smoking' coffee shops were easy to identify because they tended to pump out house music or hard rock, were brightly lit, featured stark modern furniture and put an accent on healthy food. It was legal to buy weed at these establishments and smoke it on the premises.

On the sidewalk outside the Pie in the Sky, Quentin sipped his espresso and relaxed. He loved looking at all the people. There was nothing more interesting to him – and they seemed so different from the folk back home. It was a bit like sitting in the biggest hotel lobby in the world and watching all the guests walk by.

Back in LA Cathryn Jaymes found herself being hauled into the office of TriStar chief Mike Medavoy to explain the current state of play on the *Pulp Fiction* script.

'Cathryn, I have really high hopes that Quentin is going to come up with a hit for us. D'you think he has it in him?' asked Medavoy with a jaded grin.

Cathryn Jaymes smiled back sweetly. 'Mike, Quentin's inspired, he's different and he is establishing a real audience out there. Don't panic.'

She didn't know for sure whether Quentin had even started on the script at that stage because he still had not called in from Amsterdam to give her a contact number.

A few days later, Cathryn actually got a collect call from Quentin. He sounded very happy with his new-found freedom in Amsterdam.

'It's so cool here, Cathryn. You gotta come over some time. I got myself a bicycle and this great little apartment right by a canal...'

'What's the number there, Quentin?'

'Number?'

'You do have a phone?'

'No one has phones here, Cathryn. It's not cool.'

'But I need to be able to contact you, Quentin.'

'No sweat. I'll keep in touch.'

The line went dead and Cathryn just shrugged her shoulders. It wasn't the first time she had experienced Quentin's irreverent free spirit.

A few minutes later she received yet another phone call from a Hollywood exec who wanted to talk to Quentin and just would not accept that he was incommunicado.

'Quentin's working hard on his script for TriStar. He doesn't want to be bothered. I speak to him regularly and I'll pass on your message,' she told the anxious caller.

Quentin was finally getting his chance to be a laid-back young hippy traveller and Cathryn Jaymes did not know whether she would ever hear from him again.

However, after his initial honeymoon period in Amsterdam, Quentin actually did get down to work. He went to a local stationery store and got himself a 250-page yellow legal notebook, three fat black felt-tip pens and three red ones.

Then Quentin wrote in his block capital scrawl at the top of page one. 'This is the notebook I'm going to write *Pulp Fiction* in.'

It was all part of the psychological ritual of getting down to business. He liked the notebook because he could use it in restaurants, houses, standing up, lying in his bed – everywhere. But *Pulp Fiction* would never actually look like a traditional script as long as it remained in that notebook.

'It actually looked more like Richard Ramirez's diary in those early days,' he later admitted. (Richard Ramirez was a notorious Californian serial killer of the mid-eighties.)

His buddies back in LA had tried during the preceding few months to persuade Quentin to get a computer. But he was adamant that he could only produce a screenplay in the strictly old-fashioned way.

'You can't write poetry on a computer,' he told one friend indignantly.

Quentin actually first had the idea for *Pulp Fiction* back in 1989. At that stage, he believed he needed to come up with three crime stories, shoot one film and take it around and see if it would get him any work. It never happened.

But just before he left for Europe he decided to revive the project. He wanted to create a low-budget crime anthology film – a series of black stories intertwined. He started to visualize the actors he wanted in the various parts he was creating and the Dogs kept coming back into view. Tim Roth (Orange) would definitely get a role and he was trying to find a way to work in both Harvey Keitel (White) and Mike Madsen (Blonde).

Quentin also felt that this time he wanted to increase the humour in the movie to give it a much wider audience appeal than *Dogs*. However he was also determined not to lose the offbeat aspects that had made Dogs such a remarkable achievement.

Quentin was particularly attracted by the idea of making the same characters move in and out of different stories. He wanted to work on a large movie canvas, using literary rules. He was particularly influenced by the writing of people like Larry McMurtry and J.D.Salinger (author of *Catcher in the Rye*) both of whom tended to have characters float in and out of their books.

Quentin also packed *No Good From a Corpse*, by Leigh Brackett, which Quentin had wanted to read since hearing that master director Howard Hawks had read the book just before shooting Brackett's *The Big Sleep*. The Anais Nin diaries were also on hand in Amsterdam for some light relief.

Quentin had always been fascinated by the way novelists could bring characters back from previous stories to appear for a moment in others. He knew this storytelling technique had rarely been used in movies, but he wanted to make *Pulp* do precisely that.

He also took with him to Amsterdam dozens of tracks he felt had orginally affected his concept of the movie. He wanted to find songs that had the same personality and rhythm as *Pulp Fiction*. They would give him an extra handle on the film.

Some days he would sit in the window of his apartment overlooking a canal and literally play around with his characters while the music blasted away. He wanted to make the movie a homage to all the *Black Mask* crime magazines he so enjoyed reading. Such publications, forerunners of the dime novel, were printed on coarse, groundwood paper. Dashiell Hammett and Raymond Chandler wrote for the pulps, as did James M. Cain and Jim Thompson. Pulp fiction was lurid, wild, sensational, cheap. Its meat was murder, and all manner of mental, emotional and physical rot.

Quentin wanted to locate his movie in the same mean streets where the pulp mags made their name in dusty trailer parks off lonely strips of asphalt. *Pulp* was non-suburban and aggressively anti-bourgeois, a combination that was irresistible to Quentin, who was also a devotee of grunge auteurs like Jack Hill. His vision of *Pulp* was going to be outrageously anti-eighties, the antithesis of the Steadicam, Louma-crane gloss of Spielberg and Lucas.

Quentin got some *Black Mask* magazines sent over to him by friends back in LA and studied them closely for inspiration. The words of the publication's most notorious editor, Captain Joseph T. Shaw, must have had an immense influence.

'Character conflict is the main theme,' maintained Shaw. 'The ensuing crime, or its threat, is incidental.'

One of the most popular stories ever published in *Black Mask* was a piece entitled 'Bodies Piled Up', written by Dashiell Hammett in 1923:

> *The inside of the clothespress door was stained with blood from the height of my shoulder to the floor, and two hats lay in the puddle of blood on the closet floor. Each of the hats fitted one of the dead men.*

> *That was all. Three dead men, a broken gin bottle, blood.*

But Raymond Chandler was the biggest hero of *Black Mask* and, although he was sometimes too much of a traditionalist for Quentin, he still wrote some stories that exerted a strong influence on the atmosphere of *Pulp Fiction*.

Eventually, Quentin decided to use the traditional situations of the rigged boxing match and the mob guy who has to take the boss's wife out for the evening, and dovetail them with a story that could have been an opener for any Joel Silver action movie – two hitmen killing some guys. And then the stories would converge at the end.

In that Amsterdam apartment, with just a bottle of beer and the occasional female for company, Quentin got increasingly attached to hitmen Jules and Vincent. He decided the last section of the movie would be even cooler if the audience hung out with them for the rest of the morning, after they'd hit those young guys in the apartment and then Vincent had accidentally shot poor Marvin in the back of their '74 Nova.

It was very important for Quentin to be able to see all his characters physically before he wrote a line of dialogue for them. The parts of Honey Bunny and Pumpkin were actually written for Amanda Plummer and Tim Roth after Quentin met both of them in real life just after the opening of *Dogs*. At the time he had been struck by their look, energy and size. They seemed a great couple and he decided to create two characters for them.

Quentin even dreamed up a minor role for his producer Lawrence Bender whom he saw as the perfect 'Long-Haired Yuppie Scum'.

The only other companions Quentin had in that tiny apartment were a VCR machine and a TV. He sniffed out the nearest video store and to his delight found that they stocked a wide range of his favourite late fifties and sixties French gangster movies. He soaked up not only the subject matter of those movies but the precise context of every memorable scene, helped by those years at Video Archives when he had earned his own PhD in cinema. All this research gave *Pulp Fiction* some interesting links with classic movies of the past.

For instance, the dance sequence featuring Mia (Uma Thurman)

and Vincent (John Travolta) in Jack Rabbit Slim's Diner was clearly influenced by Jean-Luc Godard's 1964 movie, *Bande à Part*.

Likewise, the briefcase which never gets opened is a homage to Aldrich's *Kiss Me Deadly*, made in 1955, even though Quentin later insisted he thought the idea up first and then discovered the similarity to *Kiss*.

When Butch (Bruce Willis) stops at the traffic lights and sees Marsellus (Ving Rhames) crossing the road, it is a direct take from Alfred Hitchcock's *Psycho* when Janet Leigh stops at lights and sees her boss crossing the road. In a similar way, the homosexual rape by the two red-necks came from watching John Boorman's *Deliverance* with his mother when he was just seven years old. There was also a hint of the 'Singin' in the Rain' torture scene from Kubrick's *A Clockwork Orange*, as well as quick flashes of *The Untouchables*, *The Texas Chainsaw Massacre* and various Samurai movies, thanks to the use of that sword.

The Wolf (Harvey Keitel) was created after Quentin saw Jean Reno's portrayal of a cleaner in Luc Besson's *La Femme Nikita* (a role reprised by Keitel himself in the American remake *Point of No Return*).

The bible-quoting obsession of hitman Jules came from seeing a kung fu movie where the lead character quoted the exact same version of Ezekiel 25:17. Quentin had been trying to drop it into a movie project ever since.

Ezekiel 25:17 is central to *Pulp* because it concerns the salvation of sinners who turn to the path of righteousness and the damnation of good people who stumble off the path. Eventually Jules pays so much atten-tion to those wise words, they transform his life.

As he had planned to a few months earlier in London, Quentin actu-ally constructed an entire scene featuring Vincent (Travolta) and Mia (Thurman) after listening to that Urge Overkill version of the Neil Diamond song, 'Girl, You'll Be a Woman Soon'.

Then there is the wonderful scene where Jules and Vincent show up at Jimmy's home in the Valley and keep talking about the coffee to avoid the subject of the mutilated body they happen to have brought with them. This is almost like a sketch from Monty Python, a show that Quentin watched over and over again in the mid-seventies.

In the back of Quentin's mind throughout all this was a script that his video store buddy Roger Avary had written called *Pandemonium Reigns*. Roger visited him in Amsterdam so they could work out how to fit the basic structure of that story into the middle section of Pulp. It eventually became the story that started with young Butch inheriting the gold watch.

As with *Dogs*, Quentin at no time believed that his habit of borrowing ideas from other movies was any form of plagiarism. He considered it to be the ultimate compliment and later claimed he would see it the same way if someone was accused of stealing material from his own films.

His first draft of *Pulp* came to a whopping five hundred pages, but then it was not that surprising, considering the vast amount of material floating around in his head. All the characters had come to life inside that small Amsterdam apartment but one of them, gangster's wife Mia, stood out as really special. In some ways she was a combination of Quentin, his mother and his former lover, Grace. And even though he did not have a clue about Grace's background before she became a Hollywood bit part actress, she had grown into a classic 'Pierce Them and Suck Out the Juice' kind of woman. All the male characters were basically variations on Quentin himself. They all liked eating pies, going to coffee shops and drinking coffee with lashings of cream and sugar.

One of the few Hollywood friends who heartily approved of Quentin's Amsterdam trip was screenwriter/director Scott Spiegel, who still occasionally let Quentin crash out on the sofa at his house after a night of beer and TV boardgame-playing.

'Quentin really dug it in Amsterdam. He had a dream of writing a cool script there and it was a clever move,' explains Spiegel.

In fact, if the truth be known, Quentin's stay in Europe was really every LA writer's dream. Most of them were so caught up in the watch-

your-back atmosphere that prevails in Tinseltown that they did not have the courage to cut out and disappear for a while.

When Quentin wasn't working on his script, he picked up new friends of all races, religions and nationalities. He was particularly impressed by the way people of all colours mixed openly in Amsterdam. Back in LA, despite the alleged liberalism of Californians, there were virtual ghettos for gays, blacks, Asians and the white middle class.

The inhabitants of Amsterdam also seemed far less complicated about sex. Quentin – now footloose and fancy free – decided it was time to catch up on everything he had missed during his late teens and twenties. He already had a taste for female company from his festival gigs. But, in Amsterdam, there were even a few one-night stands, including seductions of girls from Sweden and England. Quentin was particularly taken by girls in Europe because they gave him a bit of leeway when it came to personal hygiene. It wasn't as if he suffered from BO but he felt much more relaxed with a girl when she seemed happy with his smell (unlike in California where people were obsessed with hygiene). To hear a girl say she liked his smell was just about the most romantic thing in the world to Quentin.

Despite being in the so-called cultured environment of Amsterdam, Quentin could not resist the lure of American fast food. One of his favourite hang-outs was McDonalds in the centre of the city. That area was littered with drug-pushers, addicts, pimps, prostitutes and tourists who all filtered past Mickey D's. The only problem was that the french fries were not in the same league as at their branch on Sunset Strip.

Quentin could not escape his junk food past. His biggest regret about Amsterdam was that none of the shops sold twinkie cakes. He also found European cereal lacking in originality and flavour, and longed for a bowl of Fruit Brute or Capt'n Crunch.

But one of his biggest cultural shocks was when he discovered that all movies shown in Amsterdam had an intermission halfway through. In some cases he reckoned it improved them. For example, when he saw Oliver Stone's *JFK* with a break in the middle he enjoyed it more.

'The first half of the movie played and there was this big emotional moment,' explained Quentin. 'It felt like a sixties intermission. And then you go outside, and all the people that are in the theatre are drinking coffee and buying ice-cream, and you're sitting there assimilating all the information you've taken in for the first half of the movie. You have about ten minutes to do that. Then you go back in, then the rest of the drama starts. I mean, it was perfect.'

Quentin was also delighted to find that some of Amsterdam's local movie theatres ran entire retrospective weeks of films by specific directors. One of his favourites was the Howard Hawks season. Often he would go to such events alone and find a friendly face to hook up with, once he got there.

Back in LA, Quentin's long-suffering manager, Cathryn Jaymes, was trying not to panic about the fact that Quentin's deadline for delivering *Pulp Fiction* was fast approaching and he had not been in contact for weeks.

A number of bizarre postcards turned up at her home, just off Ventura Boulevard, in the San Fernando Valley. They included a classic pose of Brigitte Bardot in just a towel, Madonna hitting her own breast with a riding crop, de Niro in *Taxi Driver* armed with two meaty-looking guns, and Fred Flinstone and Barney Rubble outside a rock house (geddit?). Some of the cards even referred to a running joke between Quentin and friend Craig Hamann in which Quentin described his acting school colleague as 'the gay fag'. This was a light-hearted dig at Hamann following the expedition into the depths of LA's Boy's Town district years earlier.

Quentin's note to Hamann was at the bottom of a card addressed to Cathryn James and said, 'Hello gay fag. You should come down, the gay population is very large. You could get your dick sucked by a man every night.'

Quentin also addressed an entire postcard to Hamann via Cathryn James, pretending to be a gay rent boy, complete with a photo of a handsome, muscly, tattoed youth on the card. Unfortunately, Quentin's

trademark bad spelling and barely literate block capital scrawl gave away the identity of the author of the postcard. 'Quentin told me you were a very handsome man,' signed off the fictitious 'Tony'.

Even when writing postcards home, it seemed that Quentin couldn't help acting out a role for his adoring public...

'If I want your opinion I'll beat it out of you'

Tough cop Chuck Norris to a heckling punk, in *Code of Silence*, 1985

Uncomfortable Silences

LOS ANGELES, FALL 1992

Oliver Stone announced that he was definitely going to take the helm of *Natural Born Killers*, and he hoped to start shooting by late summer 1993 on a budget of thirty million dollars. Quentin never saw the official announcement of the green lighting of *NBK* in the Hollywood trade papers. If he had, he would have noticed a very significant reference to what was happening to his beloved script in the middle of a piece in *Variety*, headlined 'STONE GIVING BERTH TO TARANTINO "KILLERS"'.

It read, 'Quentin Tarantino – who wrote the gritty, critically acclaimed *Reservoir Dogs* – penned *Killers*, but Stone is doing "major revisions" with David Veloz and Richard Rutowski'.

'We're working as a team and changing quite a bit. We're adding character, violence and humour,' Stone told the paper. 'We love Tarantino, but he was not available to do the revisions'. Under the terms of the deal between Stone and Quentin, Stone was perfectly entitled to alter any aspect of the script.

Unfortunately Quentin did not feel the same way about Stone. Luckily thousands of miles of Atlantic Ocean had separated them during the pre-production countdown to *NBK*. Quentin was also rather preoccupied by his work on *Pulp Fiction*.

Stone had an entirely different vision of *NBK* from Quentin. He saw it as an action adventure movie that would plumb new depths of sleaze, mayhem and chaos. He believed the movie was in the same vein as the de Palma classic *Scarface* (which happens to be one of Quentin's numerous favourite films) because of its large-scale portrait of criminality.

Just for good measure, Stone intended to add a sprinkling of his own previous best movie *Salvador*, thereby giving *NBK* a road picture feel.

'It's violence in the media and the American way of debt. It's Peckinpah meets Kubrick. Not that I'm that good, but if I was, it would be somewhere in that zone,' Stone told *Variety* breathlessly. But these comments were to prove merely the tip of the iceberg.

Quentin had at one time idolized Stone as the brilliant auteur who brought one of his favourite movies, the gritty, realistic, low-budget *Salvador* to the big screen. But when he saw Stone's *Born on the Fourth of July* in 1989, he was bitterly disappointed.

'The film just became a mouthpiece for the director where the Tom Cruise character didn't seem like a character but that truck in Nashville which just goes round spouting off these political ideals.' Quentin deeply regretted giving away the option on *NBK* at a time when he was desperate. He told one reporter, 'I wish he [Stone] had just fucking ripped it off.' But even more hatred was to flow under the bridge before all sides called a truce.

Stone and his two co-writers insisted they were going to temper the *Badlands* elements of *NBK* with more romance. A typical example was the motel scene where Mallory washes Mickey's hair. At one point he realizes that she's not wearing her wedding ring and explodes. Then the camera pans over and we see that they have a hostage tied up, whom they are intending to torture and kill. In Stone's mind, this scenario was more romantic...

Meanwhile Quentin's mother Connie was quite concerned about what her son was doing in Amsterdam, even though Quentin was twenty-nine years old and more than capable of looking after himself. Connie rarely heard from Quentin and she was worried about things like AIDS and easy access to drugs. Her idea of a nightmare was a city with thousands of people on the street at any one time. The deserted streets of car-culture-capital Los Angeles suited her perfectly.

'He had not been abroad much before, so I was worried. But he needed to do it to get it out of his system,' she explains.

Quentin's mother was actually the main cause of his wanderlust because she had taken off on numerous journeys abroad and left him in the care of a housekeeper when he was a child. That had made him even more curious about the world outside the United States.

By the time Quentin finally left Amsterdam to board a plane for LA, he was already a month late delivering *Pulp Fiction* to TriStar and the studio was very apprehensive about the material. Quentin had actually got to the third draft of *Pulp Fiction* and managed to trim it to about 200 pages from its original 500 pages. (Most movie screenplays are between 110 and 130 pages in length and a page usually represents approximately one minute of screen time.) But it was still vastly over length.

Within two days of him delivering the script, TriStar asked Quentin to come in for an urgent meeting.

Minutes after he arrived at the office of TriStar chief Mike Medavoy, a number of executives rounded on Quentin because they had big problems with the scene where Vincent shoots up heroin.

'Look guys, relax, it's going to be funny,' responded Quentin in his inimitable way.

'No Quentin, heroin is not funny. A guy sticking a needle in his arm does not make for big laughs,' replied one stony-faced exec.

'You're just gonna have to trust me on this one, guys.'

No immediate response was forthcoming. By the end of the meeting TriStar informed Quentin they did not think *Pulp Fiction* was their kind of movie – whatever that meant.

TriStar publicly insisted that Quentin and Jersey Films co-chairmen Danny De Vito and Michael Shamberg shouldn't take it personally that the studio was passing on *Pulp*. It just wasn't their type of project. End of story.

Quentin's producer Lawrence Bender made a special point of saying. 'We are not upset because in the end I think we'll make the movie more in the way we see it, which has to do with the cast, the length and the tone.'

But no one in Hollywood was all that surprised when TriStar decided not to go ahead with the script. The corporate execs considered that the screenplay was far too dark and daring for a major to take on board. But having *Pulp* rejected by TriStar ended up helping Quentin to make the movie he wanted for a lean eight million dollars at Miramax – the same company who had picked up US theatrical rights to *Dogs* two years earlier.

Miramax chiefs Harvey and Bob Weinstein had absolutely no doubt that *Pulp Fiction* would be a commercial success because they had noticed the enormous earnings of *Dogs* in the lucrative markets outside the US. Harvey Weinstein actually believed he could get enough foreign pre-sales on *Pulp* to cover the movie's entire budget *before* the film even went into production. He was rapidly proved absolutely correct.

Miramax even agreed to stick to the original TriStar deal and pay Quentin the same total of nine-hundred thousand dollars for his writing and directorial efforts. It was an astonishingly high sum of money considering this was only his second movie as a director. No one seemed in the least bit bothered that Miramax had been bought by Disney the previous April and that, in effect, the ultimate family movie studio was about to invest heavily in a violent, black comedy set amongst the LA lowlife.

Quentin liked the way the Weinstein brothers did business. 'They are guys that work totally from their gut and they never lie to you. "I like it" means "I like it." "I hate it" means "I hate it." I appreciate that kind of straight talk and look forward to what they have to say. They also get my stuff, which is important.'

To Quentin, honour and honesty in Hollywood were still attainable if you played ball with the right people. As Christopher Walken's Vietnam vet character, Captain Koons, in *Pulp Fiction* explains when he's been so over zealous in delivering Butch's dead father's gold watch, 'When you're together with someone in a pit of hell, you owe something to that person.' [Butch (Bruce Willis) later finds himself in his own 'pit of hell' with his worst enemy, Marsellus, as a prisoner of the redneck rapists. Willis gets a chance to escape and leave Marsellus to suffer a slow, horrible, death. Why can't he bring himself to leave? Then the words come back to us, just as they are probably coming back to him: '...you owe something to that person.'

Meanwhile, Quentin was promising anyone who would listen that *Pulp Fiction* was going to be an even better movie than *Dogs* 'because this time I sort of know what I am doing'. He was also delighted to have the luxury of a ten-week shoot as opposed to the five weeks he was given to get *Dogs* in the can.

This time round, both Quentin and producer Lawrence Bender had actually been there and done it. They intended to have even more fun than before and produce a masterpiece to boot.

While the details of the Miramax deal for *Pulp* were being hammered out, Quentin got a call from his friend Julia Sweeney, one of the best-known stars of the U.S. cult TV show, *Saturday Night Live*, which had previously spawned such talents as John Belushi, Chevy Chase, Eddie Murphy and Dan Ackroyd.

SNL had also inspired a number of highly profitable Hollywood movies based on the various comedic characters in the series, most notably *Wayne's World*. Julia Sweeney herself was starring in a soon-to-be-shot movie featuring her most infamous character, the sweating, androgynous Pat, an apparently male character actually played by Julia.

Quentin's reputation was so hot in Hollywood at that point that the

producers of *It's Pat* (the movie), persuaded Sweeney to call up Quentin when she let slip that he was a friend.

A week later, Quentin provided a one-week polish for the script of the movie for the princely sum of one hundred thousand dollars. It seemed that wherever Quentin moved someone was willing to pay him big money to do anything. No one has ever actually calculated how much of the screenplay was influenced by Quentin but it is probably safe to say that he got in the region of one thousand dollars a word.

Unfortunately the movie was then shelved by Twentieth Century Fox who claimed the screenplay was not workable. It seemed that not everything Quentin touched actually turned to gold.

However, he was delighted to get that writing assignment because it was a chance to do some comedy. He adored the character of Pat because Pat is, as he later said, 'so fucking obnoxious'. Quentin's favourite sequence involving Pat was a sketch that Pat did with Harvey Keitel (Mr White) on *SNL*. Quentin explains, 'They're stranded on a deserted island and they have sex – and Harvey still doesn't know what Pat is. And the thing is, they kissed in it. At one point they were thinking of taking the kiss out of the sketch. But Harvey, being Harvey, demanded they keep it in. that there'd be no integrity without the kiss. Pat didn't kiss like a guy. Pat kissed like a girl.'

In early 1993, Quentin was still in demand at various functions outside the US and he turned up at an awards dinner at London's Savoy Hotel with actress Emily Lloyd once more on his arm. The two had met briefly at the time of the release of *Dogs* but the friendship fizzled out after a few weeks. In London, it was pretty much the same story.

On his return to LA, after being in Amsterdam, Quentin got out and saw dozens of new releases. The one he hated the most was *Patriot Games*, starring Harrison Ford.

He found the film's structure so obvious that he could sense the committee behind every choice the hero made. 'And then they end it in this awful way where the hero, who has been fucked in the ass for the whole first half, gets in a fight with the villain, who falls down and impales himself!' he exploded after seeing *Games*. 'Anyone who makes a movie that way should go to movie jail and not be allowed to make movies for a while. The only reason to do a revenge movie is to have the hero kill the guy at the end; otherwise, it's like watching a Zalman King movie and never seeing any sex.'

CORNER OF 84TH STREET AND BROADWAY, NEW YORK, WINTER 1992/3

Actor Eric Stoltz was minding his own business as he walked along one of the Big Apple's busiest thoroughfares when a weird-looking guy wearing a giant pink Toxic Avenger watch and black leather jacket approached him.

'Hey, man. Can I talk to you?' asked the Avenger.

Stoltz turned to cross the street to avoid the lanky creep pursuing him.

'Eric. I gotta talk to you, man,' yelled the Avenger, just as Stoltz stepped off the kerb.

'Yes?' replied a highly suspicious Stoltz.

'My name's Quentin Tarantino. I gotta screenwriter friend who's written a script for you.'

'You're kidding?'

Two minutes later, Quentin had dragged his new friend Stoltz to the nearest payphone and they were chatting to Quentin's Video Archives buddy Roger Avary about casting Stoltz in Avary's directorial debut, *Killing Zoe*.

After putting the phone down, according to the Hollywood grapevine, Stoltz made a deal with Quentin. 'I'll do *Zoe* if you come on board a little movie I'm producing and starring in called *Sleep with Me*,' said Stoltz.

Quentin accepted a goofy walk-on part in *Sleep*, on condition that Stoltz appeared in his up-and-coming *Pulp Fiction*. The rest, as they say, is history.

*'Some kind of fun lasts longer than others,
if you get what I mean'*

Betty Hutton, broaching her pregnancy to Eddie Bracken, in *The Miracle of
Morgan's Creek*, 1944

And the Beat Goes On

GREENBRIER AVENUE, GLENDALE, LOS ANGELES,
SPRING 1993

The rain started bucketing down just as Quentin and his buddy
Rich Turner managed to angle the huge ornate waterbed out of
the front door of Connie's palatial home. Seconds later, Quentin
almost lost his footing carrying the ridiculously heavy piece of furniture
down the slippery steps. Finally, they made it to Rich's early sixties
Chevy pick-up and crashed the bed onto the rusty flatbed.

'I sure appreciate your help, Rich,' said a breathless Quentin to his
old acting school friend.

'No sweat, Quentin,' replied Rich Turner, who had actually been a
little surprised when Quentin had called him a few days earlier to ask if
he would help him move into a new rented apartment in Hollywood.

With more than a million dollars in the bank, following that *Pulp
Fiction* deal and a couple of rewrites, Turner wondered why Quentin
didn't pay a removal company to do his dirty work for him. But it was

typical of only child Quentin. He didn't want anyone to touch his vast collection of records, tapes, videos, comics, cereal boxes, board games and whatever. He also didn't see any point in wasting money.

'Quentin didn't want anyone else to move his stuff and I was his only friend with a truck,' explains Turner.

Back in Glendale that wet and blustery day, Quentin agonized over whether to keep his beloved waterbed, an ornate contraption that looked like something out of a wedding suite at one of the rundown two-storey motels on Sunset Strip.

'I am kinda attached to it,' said Quentin, jumping up onto the pick-up and inspecting the drawers beneath the bed to make sure he hadn't left anything in them. His mother had already told him to get the taste-less *objet d'art* out of her house when he moved because she considered it an eyesore.

Quentin and Turner continued rapidly loading the truck with card-board boxes filled with his various collections before heading off for his new place in funky Crescent Heights, West Hollywood, twenty miles away.

En route they stopped at a very traditional-looking fifties-style diner in suburban Glendale where Quentin paid for Turner's cheeseburger and fries. Then they went into a nearby secondhand record store and Quentin bought Turner a Robert Gordon album to thank him for his help with the move. He also purchased for him an old punk album that featured a cover photo of Turner's movie idol Buster Keaton.

During the move, Quentin even told Turner that he and Roger Avary intended to use him in all their movies. Turner was touched. He had played a cop in *Dogs* and Avary had used him in a minor role in his directorial debut, *Killing Zoe*.

As the truck bounced and squeaked along the freeway towards West Hollywood, Quentin made small talk about how pleased he was with his purchase of a seven thousand dollar brand-new Geo Metro car. The choice of car surprised Turner as it was the epitome of a suburban house-wife's car – not what you'd expect of the hottest movie director in

Hollywood. But, Quentin explained, it was cheap to run and he did not like flaunting his newfound wealth. He did not mention the classic Chevy Malibu convertible, which he had decided to store in a garage a few days after buying it with the ten thousand dollars from *Natural Born Killers* because it was 'too loud' to drive around Tinseltown.

Then Quentin paused as if deep in thought. 'All this Hollywood shit is pretty fucking weird, Rich.'

'I can imagine,' replied Turner. 'But you've made it, Quentin. That must be a good feeling.'

'Maybe...' replied a thoughtful Quentin. 'Maybe...'

Rich Turner definitely noticed a change in Quentin's attitude that day. He was no longer the slightly spaced-out movie geek. 'He had an air of authority to him. He was pretty full of himself and we haven't hung out much together since then, but I guess that's pretty inevitable,' explains Turner.

He read for the role of Fred, the college kid who gets killed by Vincent and Jules in the apartment in *Pulp* but didn't get the gig. Turner has only seen Quentin once since then, when the auteur called him up at 11.30 one night to ask if he would do some sound looping on *Pulp*. Turner jumped at the chance of seeing his old buddy and rushed over to meet Quentin at a sound studio in Culver City. 'There was just Quint, the engineer and the editor and myself. He had changed. This was serious business and we never even had time to shoot the shit,' explains Turner.

Turner also dropped a rockabilly tape off at Quentin's new apartment, but he never got a call back from his old friend and hasn't heard from him since. 'What's the point in bugging him. He's busy as hell and has a lot of shit going on his life now,' is Turner's attitude these days.

Quentin rapidly introduced some Tarantino touches to the Gothic-French-style twenties apartment. The main feature of the living room became an outsized Panasonic on which friends and journalists alike have watched various flicks ever since. On one wall was a huge *True Romance* poster from Japan. Patricia Arquette and Christian Slater

peered out, some scrawl tattooed across Slater's broad forehead. A couple of stuffed animals, including a Tasmanian devil, rested on the back of the couch. In the middle of the wooden floor, there was a foot-high brown bear which looked for all the world like the state flag's mascot. There were stacks of books and videos. A fair amount of chaos reigned, though the kitsch effect was fully under control. Quentin liked the place because it reminded him of an apartment in Paris.

Shortly after moving into the apartment on Crescent Heights, Quentin managed to get his recently acquired agent at the powerful William Morris company to arrange for a meeting with John Travolta, an actor he had long admired. There was no particular reason for the get together. Quentin told them he just wanted to bounce a few ideas off Travolta.

By this stage, Quentin had finished writing *Pulp Fiction*, but was planning to cast Mike Madsen (Mr Blonde in *Dogs*) as hitman Vincent Vega. He had Travolta in mind for a role as one of the bank robbers in the horror flick he had been playing around with for years called *From Dusk Till Dawn*.

When Travolta rolled up at Quentin's new apartment he was shaken to discover it was the same place he had lived in after arriving in LA in 1974.

With this coincidence firmly established moments after meeting, the two men connected very rapidly. They sat down in Quentin's movie memorabilia-infested living room and talked, drank a glass of Californian Chardonnay, and headed off for dinner. Then they returned to the apartment and played some of Quentin's movie-buff boardgames (including his favourite which happened to be based on the show that launched Travolta, *Welcome Back, Kotter)*. Travolta won (naturally) and they headed out for a late-night coffee at Canter's Deli, on Fairfax. Then they came back to the apartment again.

Then Quentin let Travolta have it.

'What did you used to do, John?'

'What?' replied a bemused Travolta.

'Don't you remember what Pauline Kael said about you? What Truffaut said about you? What Bertolucci said about you? Don't you know what you *mean* to the American cinema? John, what did you *do?*'

Travolta was stunned and extremely hurt by this attack. But he also felt moved. He recognized that Quentin was telling him he'd had promise like no one else's. Travolta left Quentin's apartment in the early hours of the morning with his tail firmly between his legs. He was devastated. He kept thinking to himself, 'Jesus Christ, I must have been a fucking good actor.' Here he was, an actor who had been compared to Brando by movie critic Pauline Kael but his career had completely run out of steam.

A few months later, Mike Madsen pulled out of the Vincent Vega part in *Pulp* because he was already committed to three back-to-back movies. Quentin sent a copy of the screenplay to Travolta with a note scribbled on the first page, 'Look at Vincent.'

Quentin had actually already decided that Travolta would make an even better Vincent than Madsen. But he seemed to be the only guy who was thinking that way. Miramax must have been horrified when they first heard Travolta's name being bandied about. They wanted an actor with a higher profile. Travolta himself told Quentin, 'This is one of the best scripts I've ever read, one of the best roles I could ever have, but good luck 'cause I don't think you'll get me in it.' But Quentin stuck to his guns and made it clear that he would only shoot *Pulp* when Miramax agreed to accept Travolta.

Quentin also had to persuade Travolta that it really was the perfect role for him. Travolta – a member of the Church of Scientology – had certain doubts. He was concerned about what kind of role model Vincent would provide, armed with his hypodermic and machine gun.

As far as Quentin was concerned, his earlier twelve-hour meeting with Travolta was a perfectly standard casting exercise. He had developed the habit of spending at least a day with any actor being considered for a major role in one of his movies. They had to 'get' the Quentin Tarantinoisms or die. One of his classics was to ask an actor what they thought of Japanese action star Sonny Chiba.

When one actor dared to ask why he was asking, Quentin replied, 'Before he wipes anyone out, Sonny Chiba makes a speech: *"The only people who hear this speech die."*'

Quentin and Eric Stoltz had become firm buddies since that meeting on Broadway in New York, and the young actor played an important, if unintentional, role in helping Quentin decide what direction his personal life was heading.

The pair met at Quentin's apartment to discuss a possible role for Stoltz in *Pulp*. The actor settled on the couch opposite Quentin as they started discussing the part. Suddenly Stoltz's eye was caught by a small, dark oil painting hanging over the fireplace, amid all the movie memorabilia. It showed a woman sleeping on a couch.

Quentin was about to launch into the history of the apartment block when Stoltz interrupted him. 'Wait, tell me a story about this painting. What's the deal with that?'

The deal was that the painting was of Grace Lovelace, the only true love in Quentin's life. He had deeply regretted their break-up before he headed for Amsterdam and, he told Stoltz, he was desperate to win her back.

Stoltz just sat back and listened as Quentin poured his heart out to someone for the first time in months. All those meetings, conferences and interviews had not left him with time to even begin to discuss such personal matters and he desperately needed a sounding board.

Stoltz was sympathetic and offered his advice to Quentin. 'Get her back. The only thing that really matters is personal happiness. You can be the biggest player in this town but it doesn't mean jackshit if you aren't happy within yourself.'

Within a few months Quentin had won Grace back and his life took on new meaning. She became such an important part of his life that he even named the chopper that Butch escaped from those rednecks on in *Pulp*...Grace.

On April 7, 1993, Quentin made a nostalgic trip back to his old buddies at Video Archives to celebrate the US video release of *Dogs*. During a colourful two-hour session, he answered questions about the movie fielded by some of his former customers and colleagues. At the end he autographed limited edition posters being sold to benefit the UCLA Film and Television Archive.

One clerk at the store commented, 'Quentin was real nervous because he thought we'd give him a hard time.'

Being back amongst his buddies at Archives was a little strange for Quentin. They were the only guys who really understood how much time and effort he had dedicated to movies. Hollywood tended to treat him as though he was some kid who had come from nowhere and had fallen on his feet. In fact, Quentin had planned it all with the meticulous eye of an army general mapping out his campaign. He was a man on a mission...

HARVEY KEITEL'S BEACHSIDE HOUSE, MALIBU, JULY, 1993.

Keitel could have been any father as he strolled three houses up the sun-kissed beach to collect his daughter after an afternoon playing at Bruce Willis and Demi Moore's Pacific-side mansion. On arrival at the house, Keitel got talking to Willis and the subject of *Reservoir Dogs* came up. He was still raving about the movie he had helped get made and it's director, Quentin.

'You know, he's getting ready to do another film. Come over tomorrow and I'll introduce you.'

Next day, Quentin showed up for a barbecue at Keitel's home, and found himself being pulled to one side and told that Bruce Willis wanted to meet him. Even Quentin was a little awe-struck.

Within minutes of meeting Willis, it became clear that the *Die Hard* star was very interested in any of the major roles in *Pulp Fiction*. Initially, Quentin had sought out Matt Dillon for the role of Butch the boxer who is supposed to throw a fight. But, as he talked to Willis at that barbecue

he began to realize that the actor would actually make an even better Butch. A deal between the agents was struck within days.

Quentin specially chose both Travolta and Willis because he wanted them to play out of character. Travolta had never been seen as a killer before and tough guy Willis was actually going to play the most gentle and sensitive of lovers.

The next big name to come aboard *Pulp* was Uma Thurman. Her career had already been diverse. Back in the late eighties her stardom had been kickstarted by getting the female lead in Terry Gilliam's *The Adventures of Baron Munchausen*. Movies like the Robert de Niro/Bill Murray vehicle *Mad Dog and Glory* followed, plus meatier roles in *Jennifer 8, Dangerous Liaisons* and *Henry and June.*

Quentin had talked to just about every notable Hollywood actress under the age of thirty-five about the role of Mia, including Oscar-winner Holly Hunter and Alfre Woodward. He believed that when he met the one who could be Mia he would know it instantly. When he met Uma Thurman for dinner at his favourite Hollywood restaurant, Toi's, on Sunset, he knew within minutes that she was going to be Mia.

Steve Buscemi (Mr Pink) was slated to get a major role in *Pulp* but unfortunately had to cry off because of other movie commitments. However, Quentin was so determined to get him in the film that he persuaded him to go on set for one day to play the surly Buddy Holly waiter at Jack Rabbit Slims.

Actress Angela Jones was cast as Butch's cab-driver Esmeralda Villa Lobos after Quentin saw her in a low-budget short called *Curdled*, in which she played a character who cleaned up after murders.

Quentin was so impressed by *Curdled*, that he got on board as executive producer and started helping to raise money to make a full-length version of the film. It was eventually shot in Florida for a budget of just three million dollars and is to be released late in 1995.

Other members of the original *Dogs* production team also returned to work with Quentin for *Pulp*. They included director of photography Andrzej Sekula, costume designer Betsy Heimann, production designer David Wasco, set decorator Sandy Reynolds-Wasco and editor Sally Menke.

Quentin felt comfortable working with such familiar faces because he already knew their strengths and weaknesses. That made for good shorthand and meant that problems could always be worked out. In a way, Quentin was creating the family he never had.

With more than seventy sets required for *Pulp*, production designer Wasco and his set decorator wife Sandy worked incredibly hard to create the ambience of Quentin's particular vision of LA.

'There was a large amount of dialogue in the film. The trick was to keep sets as background. What we did was give actors wonderful tools to help them be their characters, we surrounded them in these rooms,' explains Wasco.

One such tool was the box in which dealer Lance (Eric Stoltz) kept his stash of drugs. Quentin was absolutely adamant that he wanted a particular style of box. That then went into research, and the set designer drew up plans to show Quentin before the actual object was made. A master carpenter constructed it and then it went to an old-time prop-maker who added the final touches, which included the scent of patchouli.

'When Eric Stoltz [Lance] opens it up, it's really this wonderful world of its own, a character in itself,' remembered David Wasco.

The most elaborate set on *Pulp* was undoubtedly Jack Rabbit Slim's. It was built inside a warehouse in the Culver City area of LA, measured more than 25,000 square feet and was inspired by Los Angeles architect John Lautner's Googie-style diners of the fifties.

Wasco said the interior of the diner was 'the fifties on heroin', in deference to Vincent's state of mind when he enters the place with Mia. It even features a raised dance floor set in the middle of the space and shaped like a tachometer. Quentin had specifically requested the tachometer as an inspiration from two movies, Howard Hawks' *Red Line 7000* (James Caan's first film) and Elvis Presley's *Speedway*, which Quentin's mother, Connie, had always adored.

Besides the six vintage convertible cars surrounding the dance floor, the walls were dotted with old AIP, Warner Brothers and Orion movie

posters, from *Machine Gun Kelly* to *Young Racers* to *Attack of the 50-Foot Woman*. The posters were actually replicas of the originals, blown up on 3-by-5 canvases. On the side wall, a set of ten video monitors played 1950s stock footage of a Los Angeles street scene shot out of a diner window.

Even the exterior shots of Jack Rabbit Slim's had an LA cultural influence. They were filmed at a bowling alley which had gone out of business.

Wardrobe-wise, the most important item to Quentin personally was the bathrobe he wore while shooting his own smallish role as Jimmy. Quentin used to tell anyone who would listen that the filthy towelling garment had been the recipient of everything imaginable. 'I did everything in that bathrobe. I ate. I drank. I masturbated in that bathrobe.'

He even spent part of one afternoon between takes comparing notes with co-star Eric Stoltz on how long you could go without changing clothes. Stoltz reckoned about five days and Quentin agreed.

Quentin surprised a lot of the cast on *Pulp* by insisting on not using a video playback monitor, a device which has become a virtually obligatory tool for most directors.(Francis Ford Coppola is even renowned for frequently hiding himself away in a trailer and directing scenes solely with the monitor, keeping direct contact with the actors to a minimum.

But Quentin did not trust video monitors. He felt that, once a monitor was on the set, *it* was doing the directing rather him. Naturally, all the actors felt far more secure dealing with Quentin rather than a machine. His attitude was that you could not see a performance on a monitor. His hero Howard Hawks never used a monitor, so why should he? Besides, he felt he had to be there, so that every actor could look to him after a scene, not with his eyes glued to a monitor on the other side of the studio. It was an old-fashioned attitude, rather like his feelings about writing on a computer.

Behind the scenes, there was a tricky dispute with Quentin's old Video Archives buddy Roger Avary over authorship of *Pulp*. This culminated in Quentin paying Avary the Writer's Guild minimum of thirty thousand dollars, after asking him to sign a waiver removing his name from any screenplay credit. Quentin had used Avary's story as the middle section of *Pulp*, starting with the young Butch inheriting a gold watch from his father and ending with the boy becoming a boxer who is asked to throw a fight. After much quibbling, Avary received a 'story by' credit at the end of *Pulp*.

'Roger wrote a script that I wanted to use for the middle story in *Pulp Fiction* so I bought it from him,' was how Quentin put it. 'Then I came up with all the other ideas and characters, and so I adapted his screenplay the way you would adapt a book. But, having said that, I don't want Roger getting credit for any of the actual monologues. I wrote the monologues.' Naturally, Avary considers that he too was influential in certain monologues.

Clearly Quentin and Roger Avary's friendship suffered as a result. Some months after their initial falling out, Avary told *Vanity Fair*, 'Quentin knows everything about pop culture. But his greatest strength is his greatest weakness. He is only interested in pop culture'.

He also told the magazine, 'The one problem people have with Quentin's work is that it speaks of other movies, instead of life. The big trick is to live a life and then make movies about that life.'

Quentin and Avary had further problems when Quentin agreed to be an executive producer on Avary's directorial debut *Killing Zoe*. He then reportedly asked for a fee of a hundred and fifty thousand dollars for lending his name to the project which seemed a vast amount of money considering the small size of the movie's budget. Quentin later distanced himself from the project because he was too busy with other things.

Subsequently, Avary said, 'I love Quentin. But I'd be lying if I said he hadn't changed. People tell you you're God's gift to film making. Can we talk to you? Can we sleep with you? It's intoxicating. You start to believe what they're telling you.'

Keeping friends in Hollywood was not going to be easy...

'Mom's the word'

Vincent Vega to Mia, *Pulp Fiction*, 1994

The Drugs Situation

TOI THAI RESTAURANT, SUNSET STRIP,
LOS ANGELES, NOVEMBER 1993

'**F**irst you'll feel a slight stinging sensation,' explained Craig Hamann. 'Then your brain will tighten like a mushroom has exploded in it. After that you'll be in so much fucking agony your head's gonna feel like it's blown apart.'

Hamann was sitting opposite a bemused-looking Uma Thurman. Quentin quietly looked on, while munching on a stick of chicken satay.

Quentin had called in his old friend Hamann as chief intravenous narcotics adviser because he had no experience of hard drugs and wanted to ensure that the drug scenes in *Pulp* were as authentic as possible. In some ways, it was like the expert Wolf (Harvey Keitel) being called in to clear up the blood and guts in *Pulp's* final act.

Hamann, Quentin's moody, yet brilliant one-time writing partner, was no junkie but he had a wealth of knowledge about the subject. He was the perfect person to explain in blow-by-blow terms exactly how it would feel for Mia to snort Vincent's heroin by accident in that remarkable sequence in the middle of *Pulp*.

Hamann continued his bizarre briefing, 'All this shit and stuff would come outta your nose. Snot, blood and then vomit. You then go out like a light. It'd be real messy.'

Uma Thurman sat demurely between the two men, completely transfixed by the details being described by Hamann. Other customers who had recognized Quentin and Uma craned their necks to listen to this extremely strange conversation.

'You gotta realise that this heroin would be high quality stuff because it's from Lance's own stash. Dealers only keep the best stuff for themselves,' explained Hamann in a deadly serious undertone.

'So?' asked Thurman between a mouthful of stir fry and eggplant pumpkin.

'So that means it'll fucking kill you when you snort it,' said Hamann, spelling out the facts bluntly as he swallowed a mouthful of fresh tofu.

After Quentin paid the bill at Toi, the threesome made their way out onto Sunset and began walking east towards La Brea as Hamann continued his drug-counselling session. Across the street, near the old Black and Blue club, a couple of young, blonde hookers hung around on a street corner. Further up the Strip, a black and white had pulled up a suspected DUI (Driving Under the Influence). But Quentin, Uma and Hamann were only interested in the plot of *Pulp*.

'It's gonna be a brilliant scene, Quentin,' asked Hamann.

'I know.'

'That's cool.'

A few months earlier, when he was putting the final touches to the *Pulp* screenplay Quentin had rung Hamann to pick his brains about drug use.

'Why would the smack make Mia OD?' asked Quentin, who wanted to be absolutely certain that this was what would happen if it occurred in real life.

'Why? Cause that much heroin – especially pure, virtually uncut heroin – should never be taken that way.'

'So how can I get Mia out of the OD situation?' asked Quentin, anxiously probing the delicacies of serious drug-taking.

'Use salt water.'

'What?'

'Shoot her full of salt water. That's what they do for ODs.'

'But that's boring, man.'

'That's the way it's done, Quentin.'

'What about an adrenaline shot in the heart? Would that work?'

'Who knows? But it would make a helluva scene.'

'You got it!'

A few days after briefing Uma Thurman on her drug-taking scenes, Hamann got another call from Quentin, asking him to repeat the exercise with John Travolta, who had to do a jacking-up sequence as heroin-addicted hitman Vincent Vega.

'I can't be there 'cause I gotta be on the set. D'you mind meeting him on your own?' Quentin asked his one-time best buddy.

'No problem.'

A few hours later, Craig Hamann found himself at a Beverly Hills hair salon where Travolta was having some long rear hair extensions fitted for his role. The two actors hit it off immediately and, while a hairdresser delicately and painstakingly attached the extensions, they talked drugs.

In all, Hamann visited five times to coach him on how to use heroin. One time, a huge bodyguard prevented him from leaving Travolta's trailer to go on the set because Bruce Willis was shooting his motel love scenes with girlfriend Fabienne (Maria de Medeiros). Willis was paranoid about the tabloids getting a snap of him making out with someone other than his real-life love Demi Moore.

The way Hamann was treated by *Pulp* stars Travolta and Thurman provides an interesting insight into their characters. 'Travolta treated me real well. Every time I'd show up on the set he'd give me a big hug,' explains Hamann.

Uma Thurman, on the other hand, appeared to ignore Hamann, following that meeting in Toi's restaurant. Hamann even asked Quentin's personal assistant why the actress had totally blanked him and she said, 'Don't take it personally. She is a very intense person. That's just the way she is.' Hamann never spoke to her again, but his words of advice about drugs were undoubtedly ringing in her ears when she acted that extraordinary overdose scene.

However the saddest aspect of all this, from Craig Hamann's point of view, was that he never heard again from his one-time best friend, Quentin. Almost as hurtful to Hamann was the fact that he did not receive any credit at the end of the movie. 'It should have been done as a matter of professional courtesy. I wanted special thanks and I ended up with nothing. Quentin said he needed help and I helped him, but he didn't remember that in the end.'

Quentin's attitude towards drugs was – and is – interesting. He gleaned a lot of his knowledge of narcotics through the so-called LSD movies of schlock master Roger Corman. He was particularly fond of *The Trip* starring Peter Fonda. Quentin also enjoyed reading novels that centred around drugs. He was intrigued by them and acknowledged them as vital props in his movies. But he did not believe he was glamorizing their use.

'I don't buy this whole idea that if you show someone shooting up, you're pro-heroin,' Quentin insists. 'That's as silly to me as the arguments I had last time round about glamorizing violence. The whole reason that the OD scene is harrowing and horrific is because I'm showing you what happens after all the thrills and spills. And, yes, there is humour lurking in even the most extreme situations. That's just a fact of life.'

And Quentin loves creating his own illusions, even when it came to particular brands of drugs. For example Lance (Eric Stoltz) refers to his quality smack as 'Babba' in the scene where Vincent scores at the

pusher's house. There is no such name. This was just an in-joke from Quentin's in-jokes – he named the drug after Italian film maker Mario Babba.

'It was totally off the wall and it sounded right so Quentin just kinda threw it in when we were shooting the scene,' explained one crew member.

He even invented a brand of cigarettes called Red Apple, in order to cut down on product placement in *Pulp*.

Quentin's prosthetic experts who had done such an authentic job for the ear-slicing scene in *Dogs* were once again in demand for *Pulp*. They provided a fake top-half-of-a-corpse for accidental shooting victim Marvin, who was blasted to death by Vincent in the back of their car. At one stage, Quentin was seriously considering showing the blown-away remnants of Marvin's body on screen, until someone pointed out that it would actually make the scene less effective (in much the same way it had worked with the ear slicing in *Dogs*). The prosthetics department also provided the blood and guts for the homosexual rape scene in the basement of the gun store.

The same team came up with all sorts of trickery to avoid Travolta and Thurman having to actually inject themselves for the camera. For his jacking-up scene at Lance's house, Travolta had a phoney syringe filled with liquid which was specially designed so that when the plunger was pushed down it looked as if it was emptying. In fact, it was all going into a tube.

For the infamous adrenaline scene after Mia's accidental overdose, Uma Thurman had a fake chest piece strapped to the front of her body, and the shot was reversed so that the needle was actually pulled out rather than plunged in. (Quentin could not resist strategically placing two of his favourite board games, *Operation* and *Life*, in Lance's living room.)

Quentin adored shooting that scene. As he later explained, 'When you watch it, the audience is broken into thirds: a third is diving under their chair, a third is laughing, and the other third is doing both at the same time.'

Quentin deliberately pushed that scene to the edge because he felt it was not only highly dramatic, but very funny. 'The comedy is coming from the real life situation of "Whadda-we-gonna-do? Whadda-we-gonna-do? Get the book. Hold the book. I'm not going to do it. You are. No, *you* are." The kicking and screaming of real life.'

Meanwhile the woman is on the brink of death and the needle looks about thirteen inches long, and Lance and Vincent are arguing about the instructions.

There are other deft touches, in-jokes and telling details in *Pulp* that only have any real significance to afficianados of the movie. But they are worth pointing out because of Quentin's sheer brilliance and audacity in planting them.

For instance, when Butch is sneaking up to his apartment to retrieve his gold watch, an advert for Jack Rabbit Slims is blasting out of a radio.

Other details refer to Quentin's own life rather than the film, as in the undercard for Butch's big fight – Vossler v Martinez. Rand Vossler was the guy who helped put together *My Best Friend's Birthday* and Jerry Martinez worked alongside Quentin at Video Archives.

The guy hiding in the bathroom of the apartment owned by Vincent and Jules' next intended victims is played by Alexis Arquette, brother of Patricia (*True Romance*) and Rosanna (*Pulp*).

When Vince is shot on the toilet he is reading *Modesty Blaise*, a pulpy novel written by Peter O'Donnell in 1965, which is very much in keeping with the film's title.

The gun Butch spotted in his apartment when Vincent was in the toilet was not Vincent's. It actually belonged to Marsellus, who was out buying coffees. That's why Vincent did not react when he heard someone in the apartment. For further evidence, note that Marsellus was carrying two cups when he walked in front of Butch at the traffic lights.

At all times, Quentin was completely positive about what he wanted in *Pulp*. He had edited the movie a thousand times in his head and knew precisely what shots he needed.

He clearly could visualize every scene and still remember scenes from his favourite movies, and he used that knowledge to direct his actors. Throughout the making of *Pulp*, Quentin's actors were given a running commentary on the movies he adored.

On one memorable occasion, he yelled to hitman Jules (Samuel L. Jackson), 'We're going to start with the opening shot of *Casablanca*, then go into something Sergio Leone did in *The Good, The Bad and The Ugly*, and then finish up with a kind of Wile E. Coyote thing.'

Quentin also motivated his cast by trying to convince them that their characters were the only stars of their own movie. When Pumpkin (Tim Roth) and Honey Bunny (Amanda Plummer) came on, it would be their movie. Then when Quentin was working with Uma Thurman, he told her, 'Pretend you're in a Mia movie. Pretend this whole movie is about Mia and this is a sequence that takes place in the Mia movie. Don't worry about explaining everything because the rest of the movie has done that.'

The relaxed atmosphere at *Pulp* locations made it seem like one big party, with cast and crew members floating about, stopping to greet Quentin and producer Lawrence Bender. Even the usually solitary Bruce Willis got into the spirit of things by raffling off four pots of fifty dollars each for the crew every week. Uma Thurman even joked, 'I can beat Bruce like that. I'll raffle off a blow job.' As Quentin later quipped, 'That would have definitely beat fifty bucks.'

The friendly atmosphere on the set of *Pulp* was further confirmed when Bruce Willis did not ask to see a rough cut of the film before any-one else. He trusted Quentin. 'It's the most creative process I've ever been involved in,' explained Willis. 'We worked on a level of focus and detail I've never experienced before.'

But handling the actors was nothing compared to the logistics of actually getting twelve Hollywood stars together to appear in one movie. Scheduling became a nightmare when one actor was offered a role in another film. Suddenly the producers had to change thirty actors' sched-ules in the middle of production.

Besides the dramatic hypodermic scene involving Mia and Vincent, the other most talked about sequence in *Pulp* is the dance scene. Quentin almost didn't pull it off because Uma Thurman got a complete attack of stage nerves and begged Quentin to change it.

She was terrified that she wouldn't be able to dance properly with the legendary Travolta. Quentin told her not to even think about the sequence until the morning it was due to be shot. Then he brought in a video copy of the dance sequence in Jean-Luc Godard's *Bande à Part* and for the first time Uma appreciated what Quentin wanted. He didn't care if the dancing was good, bad or indifferent. He just wanted Thurman and Travolta's characters to *enjoy themselves*. Then Quentin got up on the makeshift dance floor on the set and did a tight-fisted, arms-in-the-air rendition that looked like something out of Village People. Thurman and Travolta were surprised at how funky Quentin's performance was and immediately got down to work.

Even the '64 red Chevy Malibu driven by hitman Vincent had great personal significance for Quentin. It was the one he'd bought with the ten thousand dollars he'd got for the option on *Natural Born Killers*.

Quentin found the car expensive to maintain and, as it was a convertible, he feared he would be carjacked in some of the sleazier parts of town. On the set of *Pulp*, Quentin tried to persuade just about every member of the cast and crew to buy the car from him for the ten thousand dollars he had paid. But there were no takers. When the *Pulp* shoot wrapped, he had the vehicle stored back in a lock-up and continued driving his familiar, safe, economical and some would say, boring, red Geo Metro.

Quentin's attitude to the car was summed up by Vincent's conversation with drug dealer Lance, during which he complained bitterly about someone key-scratching the Malibu five days after he had bought the vehicle. That actually happened to Quentin.

The filming of *Pulp* finished on November 30, 1993, but the post-production process proved in some ways to be trickier than the shoot itself. Quentin's editor from *Dogs*, Sally Menke, got a first rough cut

together just after Christmas, but it was more than three and a half hours in length. She was very unhappy that some of the scenes were far too long, even by Quentin's excessive standards.

A classic example was the opening of the scene in Jack Rabbit Slims, which is punctuated by some awkward silences between Vincent and Mia. Quentin saw it as a moving sequence that perfectly reflected a real-life first date.

'I like the fact that you hang out with them both and you get to know them,' explained Quentin, defending the length of the scene.

Menke wanted to cut the scene down quite a bit and even take out some of the more awkward dialogue. The problem was perfectly summed up by Uma Thurman's character Mia in the scene itself, when she makes a point of mentioning the uncomfortable silences between them.

But the editor did win a few of the cutting-room battles with Quentin, including persuading him to take out a complete conversation that came later in the Jack Rabbit Slim's scene. The cut dialogue was yet another example of Quentin's brilliant TVspeak, but he accepted that it wasn't a vital part of the movie.

In March, 1994, the first reasonable cut of *Pulp* was tested at a private screening for members of the public in a small LA movie theatre. Backers Miramax wanted to get a handle on what sort of reaction the movie would get from real audiences.

Before the film was shown, Quentin got up and introduced himself and asked for a show of hands of those who liked his directorial debut, *Reservoir Dogs*. Many hands shot up. Then he asked for a show of hands to see who liked *True Romance*. More hands.

Then he asked about the latest Merchant Ivory movie, *The Remains of the Day*. When a few scattered hands shot up, he yelled, 'Get the fuck outta this theatre.' He was kidding...but only just.

The
Resolution

'The good thing
about being spoiled early
is you can't go backwards.
You can't accept less'

Quentin Tarantino

'We all go a little mad sometimes'

Anthony Perkins in *Psycho*, 1960

Someone Not to be Fucked With

LOS ANGELES, 4.31AM, MONDAY, JAN 20, 1994

The rumbling gradually grew louder and louder. Then the windows in every room flew open, as a subterranean wave of energy hit the outside walls of the building. Throughout LA, pictures flew off walls, ornaments smashed to the ground, door frames creaked, then buckled and, in certain areas, entire buildings collapsed.

Quentin awoke the instant the windows began rattling in his apartment on Crescent Heights, West Hollywood. He sat bolt upright in his futon bed as the two-storey block literally quivered. At first, he thought it was a nuclear bomb, as the crest of violent energy rumbled through the room. Moments later, the light in the hallway went off. He knew it had to be an earthquake. The movement stopped almost as quickly as it had begun. The forty-second quake had just killed sixty-one people and destroyed the livelihoods of tens of thousands of others.

Outside Quentin's apartment, there was a beat of deathly silence. Then car and house alarms started going off in all directions. Shortly afterwards, the screaming sirens and staccato din of helicopters could be heard overhead. Large areas of Los Angeles had been plunged into darkness, and wrecked electricity pylons lay bent and twisted out of shape by the 6.6 shaker. Amid the cacophony of distant sounds, a lone bus drove past Quentin's apartment, its engines seizing tightly as it braked at an empty bus stop.

Quentin glanced around his bedroom and decided there was nothing else to do but try to get back to sleep. The damage in the apartment seemed minimal, considering the force of the quake. In any case, he had a remarkable ability to get back to sleep under any circumstances. And that was precisely what he did on the most momentous day in southern Californian history this century.

Just a mile to the south, the Santa Monica Freeway had buckled, twisted and snapped in half. Eight miles to the north, beyond the Hollywood Hills and into the San Fernando Valley, fires were raging and entire apartment blocks had collapsed like packs of cards. People were buried in bricks and mortar. Water mains had burst. Electricity cables scorched roof tops as blaze after blaze erupted.

Meanwhile, Quentin simply curled up in his bed and went back to the imaginary dream world that had dominated his life since the day he was born.

Five miles north of Quentin's apartment, in the San Fernando Valley, his long-suffering manager Cathryn Jaymes was enduring a much worse fate. Her house was just three miles from the epicentre of the quake in Northridge. She, like the rest of LA, had woken with a jolt. But the damage inflicted on her wooden framed one-storey house on the corner of Laurel Canyon Boulevard was serious. Across the San Fernando Valley, the walls, gates and fences that defined this suburban sprawl, and divided neighbour from neighbour, had collapsed under their own weight.

Cathryn Jaymes picked her way through the rubble. Then she hid under a table in the kitchen, waiting for the next quake or the inevitable aftershocks that would come rumbling through everyone's homes for weeks and weeks following the quake. At first, radio stations warned that this might be the precursor to an even bigger shake. As the minutes ticked away, Cathryn trembled with cold and fear. She knew the longer it was before another quake, the more likely it was that whatever followed would be of a smaller magnitude. Radio stations revised their warnings to say that severe aftershocks were expected, but the main danger seemed to have past.

By 8am – less than four hours after the actual Northridge quake struck – more than fifty aftershocks had occurred. Each one was like another mini-earthquake and the effect on people's nerves was appalling.

Cathryn Jaymes started to clear the broken china, glass and furniture scattered throughout her house, unaware that this fateful day was about to get even worse.

Most businesses did not even attempt to operate on that chaotic Monday. Many buildings had no services, traffic signals were not working, and the collapse of numerous freeway intersections made it virtually impossible to travel to certain points in the city and surrounding areas.

But some people still managed to struggle into work. It was officially a public holiday, although most of Hollywood tended to ignore such celebrations. Amongst those who did make it to work was the business management company that at Catherine's suggestion had taken over certain aspects of the day-to-day running of Quentin's affairs. At mid-morning that day, Cathryn's phone started ringing amid the rubble. She had not even realized the phone lines were back on.

Quentin's management company had rung to inform Cathryn that her services as Quentin's personal manager were no longer required. After almost ten years of loyalty and unofficial mothering, she was being dispensed with. Cathryn stood in stunned silence after putting the phone back on the receiver. She couldn't quite believe that all her efforts and friendship over the years amounted to nothing. The worst thing of all was that Quentin had not called her himself. She looked around at her quake-ravaged house and threw herself into trying to clear a path through the debris.

By early afternoon, she had cleared up much of the mess and come to the obvious conclusion that Quentin was a heartless son-of-a-bitch for getting his managers to fire her so unceremoniously on the day of LA's most devastating natural disaster.

Cathryn then left a message with Quentin's answering service, asking him to call her urgently. She was not going to just let him walk away without at least giving her a personal explanation of what the hell was going on.

An hour later, Quentin called back.

'Hi, Cathryn. Were you returning my call?'

'No,' replied Cathryn Jaymes, knowing full well that Quentin was lying.

'Oh,' he said (sounding surprised). 'Did you leave me a message?'

'Yes I did, Quentin,' responded Cathryn in an impatient manner. But before she had a chance to continue he interrupted.

'Could you do me a favour, Cathryn?'

Cathryn was astounded. 'A favour? That really takes the cake, Quentin. You have me fired by your business managers and then you call me afterwards for a favour?'

'You're not upset about my leaving are you, Cathryn?'

'Yes, I am.'

'But, Cathryn, I truly think you are the best manager in the world. Your job was to launch my career and now that my career is launched I don't need you any more.'

That was it. End of story. Cathryn Jaymes put the phone down and realized there was absolutely no point in continuing her friendship with Quentin. He was a brilliant film maker and an extremely talented guy. In some ways it was inevitable that the Hollywood system would swallow him up and turn him on his head. But she felt very sad that it had ended that way.

Motormouth Quentin in full flow at Scott Spiegel's barbecue in 1990, where he met Lawrence Bender who was to produce *Dogs.*

(Copyright © Scott Spiegel)

Right: Patricia Arquette as
Alabama in *True Romance*.
(Copyright © 1993 Morgan Creek
International/Ron Phillips/courtesy Kobal
Collection)

Below: Brad Pitt as Floyd in
True Romance.
(Copyright © 1993 Morgan Creek
International/Ron Phillips/courtesy Kobal
Collection)

Above: Quentin took a back seat
when it came to the making of *True Romance*.
(Courtesy Connie Zastoupil)

Right: Video
Archives
moved to
these new
premises in
Manhattan
Beach, then
promptly shut
down. It is
rumoured that
Quentin bought
up most of the
stock.
(Copyright ©
Wensley Clarkson)

Above: The coolest hit men in Town. John Travolta as Vincent
Vega and Samuel L. Jackson as Jules Winnfield in *Pulp Fiction*.
(Copyright © 1994 Miramax Buena Vista/courtesy Kobal Collection)

Above: I want to be a star. Quentin in front of the camera, talking linen with Wolf (Keitel) in *Pulp Fiction.*
(Copyright © Miramax Buena Vista/courtesy Kobal)

Left: Rich Turner, one of Quentin's pals, played a cop in *Dogs.* Posing here in his classic '63 Ford Galaxy. He introduced Quentin to surf music, which was put to such devastating use in *Pulp Fiction.*

(Copyright © Wensley Clarkson)

Above: An uncomfortable silence? Uma Thurman as Mia in *Pulp Fiction.*

Right: Saturday Night Fever. Mia (Thurman) and Vince (Travolta) take to the dance floor at Jack Rabbit Slim's. (Both Pictures Copyright © Miramax Buena Vista/courtesy Kobal Collection)

Above: **Quentin administers a dose of hyperactive directing to the cast of the TV series *E.R.***
(Copyright © Foto Blitz/courtesy All Action)

Above: **The far from modest family house in Glendale, California, which Quentin moved back into just before making *Dogs.***
(Copyright © Wensley Clarkson)

Above: Flack and fiction. Quentin and the *Pulp Fiction* cast receiving the Palme d'Or at Cannes in 1994. *(From left to right)* Bruce Willis, Maria de Medeiros, John Travolta, Uma Thurman, Quentin, Samuel L. Jackson and Lawrence Bender (producer).
(Copyright © STILLS/courtesy All Action)

Right: Designer dudes. Quentin arriving at the Oscars in 1995 with his girlfriend, Grace Lovelace.
(Copyright © 1995 Malcolm Clarke/courtesy All Action)

Right: Together again. Quentin and Roger Avary receiving their Oscar for Best Original Screenplay.
(Copyright © Gary Hershorn REUTER/courtesy Popperfoto)

Above: Author Wensley Clarkson *(right)* and Quentin share a joke during a Horror convention in Los Angeles in May 1995.
(Copyright © Wensley Clarkson)

Left: Paradise found. The picturesque entrance to Quentin's current Hollywood home. He lives in a one-bed-roomed apartment in the building.
(Copyright © Wensley Clarkson)

During all those years of struggling, Cathryn had provided Quentin with a shoulder to cry on, a place to eat, a couch to crash on and years of advice, meetings and learning that undoubtedly helped him to cope with stardom when it finally came.

Cathryn had been the sort of manager/mother figure who bailed her clients out of jail, gave them ten bucks if they were broke, found them new apartments, booked their lunches with the studios, advised and nurtured them through numerous crises of confidence. But when it finally came down to it she was considered surplus to requirements.

Her biggest payday with Quentin had been when she earned a few thousand dollars from *Reservoir Dogs*. After that she had even agreed to take a cut in commission on his earnings to just five per cent. Cathryn had also been assigned the task of finding the apartment on Crescent Heights for Quentin. She had spent weeks hiring teams of real estate agents to search for the perfect place, after Quentin specified it had to have high ceilings and classic architecture. Cathryn had gone out with Quentin's mother Connie to buy him a futon bed, and Quentin had given his eccentric old waterbed to Cathryn when he moved out of his mother's house in Glendale.

She and Connie had also bought pots and pans and furniture for the apartment. He told her he just wanted to move straight in without having to be bothered 'by all that type of stuff'. She had arranged for him to purchase his new Geo Metro. She had even sent an electrician over to the apartment after Quentin knocked out the lights in the entire block when he was fiddling around with a plug.

After all this Cathryn's reward was to be dismissed a few hours after her house had been virtually knocked down by an earthquake.

Over on the other side of town, Hollywood auteur Oliver Stone was immersed in *Natural Born Killers*. The casting of Woody Harrelson as Mickey had brought a dry response from Quentin, who must have realized the movie had very little to do with his original screenplay. Stone was even considering casting real-life TV reporter Geraldo Rivera as himself,

in place of the Wayne Gayle character. John Malkovich had already passed on the part, although in the end Robert Downey Jnr. was cast as tabloid TV horror Gayle.

Quentin said he was 'real mad' about Harrelson because he was nothing like the Mickey he had imagined. He told anyone who would listen that Stone had butchered his script and he feared that it would end up being the complete opposite of the movie he had intended. Eventually he got so pissed off with the situation, he asked for his screenplay credit to be removed from *NBK*, and that was after only reading the first half of Stone's new version (written in collaboration with two other writers).

Quentin later explained, 'I really didn't want anyone to think I'd written some of the stuff that was in there!' In the end, the credit in the actual movie read, 'From a story by Quentin Tarantino'.

At one stage, a meeting between the two directors was arranged to try and patch up the problems over *NBK*. But it never really stood a chance of succeeding.

After an initial burst of polite conversation, Quentin got down to the nitty-gritty.

'You're a good film maker. Why don't you do something smaller – why don't you do a movie?,' said Quentin pointedly. He was trying to say that Stone should do a *Reservoir Dogs*.

Stone punched back rapidly. 'Well, that's what I'm doing with *Natural Born Killers*.'

'No, you're not. It's *Oliver Stone Takes On Serial Killers And Violence In America*.'

Stone did not look like a happy camper by this stage. But he was not going to take Quentin's attack lying down. '*Reservoir Dogs* is very good, but it's a movie. I make films and you make movies. Martin Scorsese, he makes movies. John Woo, he makes movies. But, after you've been working for fifteen years, you may look back and say, "Hey, all I've done is make a bunch of movies," and you might want to try and make a film someday.'

At that stage Quentin had absolutely no doubt that Stone meant to be highly condescending towards him. But when he thought about it later he realized that Stone was correct, and he concluded that he would rather make movies than films any day.

But Stone wasn't finished. He then told Quentin, 'You're in your twenties. You're making movies about movies. I'm making movies about the life I've lived to my forties. I've seen more violence than you've ever seen in your life. I've been in Vietnam. I've been shot. If you want to talk about violence, let's get real...'

In the back of Quentin's ever-inquisitive mind, as Stone delivered his battle speech, was a thought. 'I have the *Platoon* game back home. I really would love to play Oliver. But him and me are too much on the outs.'

Months later, Quentin tried to justify his attitude towards Stone's specific vision of *NBK*. 'You don't have to worry about seeing me in *NBK*, you'll only see Oliver Stone. His voice is so loud that, well, people who like it give him the credit. People who don't like it are nicer to me. It's like, "Who knows what Tarantino meant?"'

On a personal level, Quentin insisted he did not hate Stone but he did say, 'His biggest problem is that his obviousness cancels out his energy and his energy pumps up his obviousness. He's Stanley Kramer with style.'

Stone later shot some of the most disturbing scenes for *NBK* inside a real prison and even used four hundred and fifty inmates as paid extras on the thirty-million dollar production. Actress Juliette Lewis (Mallory) found the prison experience pretty far out.

'It feels like you're on amphetamines. Your heart beats fast. You're in danger.'

Lewis, then just twenty-one, got the part by convincing Stone she could be tougher than other actresses. 'I show pain as well as all this obnoxious stuff. I understand human nature. Screwed by her father – this can make Mallory cold and callous and want to blow people away.'

Stone had actually told Lewis to make Mallory sexy, but Lewis was thoroughly dismissive of the auteur's instructions. 'What makes her sexy

is a wig and high-heeled boots... I'm androgynous,' she said proudly. 'Without limits, I can be ugly or beautiful.'

In the end, Woody Harrelson was hailed for his acting as Mickey, complete with sinister shaved head, bare arms decorated with tattoos and sporting one tiny earring. He made the perfect boy-next-door-turned-psycho. Both he and Lewis clearly became wrapped up in their roles and were deeply affected by the atmosphere inside the prison where they were shooting.

'I definitely feel the weight of my violence a lot more,' said Harrelson at the time. 'There's a certain palpable tension. Playing hoops with these guys... There's a division between us and them. We can hang out. We can go home.'

Harrelson – still best known for his role as the barman on *Cheers* – scooped the role because Stone believed he had the eyes of a killer. His father Charles had been given two life sentences in a federal prison for conspiring to murder and murdering a federal judge in 1979.

But it was Stone's own comments about the way he saw the movie evolving that really niggled Quentin.

'It's like *Keystone Cops*,' Stone explained to one journalist. 'Really, I'm not saying I'm doing slapstick, but I'm looking for that edge, where the physical becomes humorous.' He went on, 'It's part of a larger canvas of modern America and crime and the media. We poke fun at the warden, the system, with a capital S... We poke fun at the idea of justice, at the idea of righteousness, the concept that in America there's a right way and a wrong way. I knew it would be a danger for somebody like me because there's no real upside. The subject matter is violent, and it doesn't have the broadest possible appeal.'

Stone then turned and stared hard into the distance. 'But fuck that', he said.

Meanwhile, at the funky, slightly rundown New Beverly Movie Theatre on Beverly Boulevard near the intersection with Fairfax, in West

Hollywood, *Dogs* was still showing at regular midnight performances. Quentin had always hoped that his movies would play at midnight and he sometimes made a point of driving past the cinema just to see how big the crowd were just before the theatre opened up for that final performance.

Much to Quentin's delight, the New Beverly had turned back into a regular movie house, after years as a porn theatre not unlike the Pussycat Theatre, in Torrance, where he had worked as a teenager. *Dogs* was still a big draw up until the summer of 1995.

On the work front, Quentin continued to satisfy his insatiable curiosity about other people's movies by performing the cameo role in *Sleep With Me*, directed by Rory Kelly, which Eric Stoltz had made him promise to do when they had met in New York more than a year earlier.

Quentin was even permitted to write his own dialogue on the basis that having him in the movie would add to its sales potential. In the end, he didn't just steal the scene, he walked away with the whole film.

His brief but electrifying appearance consisted of a motor-mouthed delivery of a monologue claiming that *Top Gun* (the box office success starring Tom Cruise and directed by *True Romance* helmsman Tony Scott) was not just a story about a bunch of fighter pilots but was actually about 'a man's struggle with his own homosexuality'.

According to Quentin, the reason *Top Gun's* hero is so on edge is that he can't decide whether he is straight or gay. Iceman (Val Kilmer) and his crew 'represent the gay man, and they're saying go, go the gay way, go the gay way.' Kelly McGillis represents heterosexuality, insisted Quentin. 'She's saying no, no, no, no, go the normal way, play by the rules, go the normal way.'

Quentin's first piece of evidence for this theory is when Cruise's character Maverick doesn't try to sleep with McGillis at the first opportunity. 'She's like, "What the fuck, what the fuck is going on here?"' The next time she is seen in *Top Gun* she is dressed as a man and Quentin

theorized that this was because she knew it was the only way to get him in the sack.

An even more conclusive piece of evidence, according to Quentin, is that in the penultimate scene in the film, after Maverick and Iceman have fought off the Migs, Iceman says to Maverick: 'You can ride my tail any time.' In *Sleep With Me*, the person Quentin is telling this to is so convinced that he says the line along with him, as if it is common knowledge. Actually, a brief look at a video of *Top Gun* shows that Iceman actually said: 'You can be my wing man any time.' But why ruin a good story?

In reality, it was all a set party piece which Quentin and his Video Archives friend Roger Avary had performed at parties and in restaurants with friends. However, respected critics like Pauline Kael in her *New Yorker* review had in fact described *Top Gun* as 'a shiny homoerotic commercial'. So maybe, in his own inimitable fashion, Quentin had actually nailed down the truth.

In April 1994, Quentin hosted *An Evening With John Waters* at Leammle's Monica Theatre, in Santa Monica, near LA. Director Waters' primary objective was to promote his latest flick, *Serial Mom*. This was followed by a question-and-answer session with the audience which ended up being completely taken over by Quentin.

'Waters was flabbergasted by Quentin's enthusiasm,' explained *Film Threat* writer Brian Williams, who attended the gathering. After the question-and-answer session Quentin was surrounded by fans. Most of them wanted to know one thing – would *Natural Born Killers* and *Pulp Fiction* be as good as each other?

Quentin paused for a second and then gave the only answer he could think of. '*Pulp* is the one you have to see.' A few weeks later, Quentin's people and Stone's people made a pact to stop criticizing each other's movies. It was a reluctant ceasefire on the part of Quentin as he was still seething about *NBK*.

But at least he had the satisfaction of knowing that *Pulp Fiction* was the first Disney movie to feature anal sex. 'It's hard to take credit for anal sex after that movie *American Me*. You can't really brag about anal sex until you've done it as many times as *American Me* does it.'

Every aspect of the movies mattered to Quentin...

'Live fast. Die young. Have a good-looking corpse.'

John Derek's philosophy of life in *Knock on Any Door*, 1949

Staying In Character

CANNES, FRANCE, SUNDAY EVENING, MAY. 1994

The palm-lined Croisette was jammed with gawking tourists, film flacks, journalists, producers, directors, would-bes and has-beens, hustlers of every conceivable stripe, exhibitors and exhibitionists, and starlets seeking ever more outrageous ways to strip off for the gangs of paparazzi. Quentin fought his way past a group of film financiers loitering on the sidewalk while discussing their dinner plans. Two hookers in skin-tight white tube dresses and stilettos puckered their lips in his direction, but he did not even notice them. This time Cannes did not seem such a cool place as when he had first visited the festival two years earlier with *Dogs*. The crowds seemed denser and the only person anyone really cared about was Festival jury chairman Clint Eastwood. His image was everywhere – on billboards, on window posters, on bronze busts and acrylic paintings in art galleries.

Quentin was also irratable because he was being treated with kid

gloves by timid junior studio execs. It wasn't like being the funky independent movie maker anymore. This trip seemed to be all about
networking and schmoozing.

Quentin blew into the reception area of the Majestic Hotel and
headed straight for the outside pool area, where he finished a rapid lap
around the bar before making a dash for the exit. The problem with
Cannes, he reflected, was that you spent most of your time wandering
from hotel to hotel looking for certain people to have a drink with. If they
weren't in one gin palace then you had to schlep to the next one.

A block east on the Croisette, he repeated his search-and-destroy
mission through another ornate hotel bar, fighting his way past a crowd
of bored French tourists. This time, he managed two sweeps of the drinks
area before settling down alone on a stool at the bar.

'Perrier *avec*... um ... with *les glaçons*...you know, ice?' stammered
Quentin at a puzzled-looking barman.

Here he was, director of the American entry for the prestigious
Palme d'Or award at Cannes and he was sitting solo at a bar without a
crony in sight.

Just then, Parker Posey (star of Hal Hartley's *Amateur* and director
Rory Kelly's much-panned *Sleep With Me*, also starring Quentin) and
friend Amaryllis Borrego (also in *Sleep*) approached. A look of relief
came to Quentin's face.

'Quentin Tarantino? You know there are signs up all over with your
name splashed as an ACTOR in *Sleep With Me!*' yelled Posey. 'What are
you doing at a bar alone – in Cannes?'

'Yeah, ya know, I was supposed to be meeting someone...but damn,
what time is it?' asked Quentin, revealing his long standing aversion to
owning a watch. 'Where the hell are they? he continued They must be
late.'

That seemed to be the story of his life at Cannes during the early
days of the 1994 festival.

The first night he had arrived in the town to find that his hotel room
had been given to someone else Then he had switched to the Hotel du

Cap, only to find his overnight bag was still back at the other hotel, so he ended up changing into a bag of *Colour of Night* (new Bruce Willis and Jane March film) stuff, including a promotional baseball cap and a dark blue sweatshirt.

However, the world movie premiere of *Pulp* a few days later turned Quentin from a lost soul into a man in demand.

Quentin and producer Lawrence Bender had decided it would be immensely hip and groovy to premiere the movie at Cannes since they had just managed to complete the final edit a couple of days before the festival opened.

The word was that it was an interesting return to LA lowlife for Quentin following the art house success of *Dogs*, but no one really knew what to expect. The critics were blown away by what they eventually saw on the big screen.

Jack Day in the *New York Newsday* wrote from Cannes, 'Tarantino's perversely inventive humour, his randy dialogue, and some sensational tongue-in-cheek performances give you little chance to regret your laughter.'

The respected Janet Maslin in the *New York Times* was low-key, but complimentary. 'Mr. Tarantino has devised a graceful circular structure that sustains his film's bold ambitions and two-and-a-half-hours running time. The storytelling is solid and the time flies.'

Literally overnight, *Pulp* became the hot ticket at Cannes. Suddenly it was the movie everyone was talking about.

Quentin faced 1,100 reporters and journalists who were lying in wait for him at the Palais du Festival, where one could almost see 2,200 nostrils quiver with *Pulp* Fever.

Also at the press conference following the world premiere, were John Travolta, Uma Thurman, Samuel L. Jackson, Maria de Medeiros, Bruce Willis and producer Lawrence Bender. But not one media enquiry during the forty-five-minute session was addressed to anyone other than Quentin.

Inevitably, the first few questions were about the violent content of *Pulp*.

Quentin shot back comfortably, 'Violence is just one of many things you can do in movies. People ask me, "Where does all this violence come from in your movies?" I say, "Where does all this dancing come from in Stanley Donen movies?" If you ask me how I feel about violence in real life, well, I have a lot of feelings about it. It's one of the worst aspects of America. In movies, violence is cool. I like it.'

Few people realized that Quentin himself was passionately in favour of gun control in America. He genuinely believed the level of street violence to be horrific, and travelling round Europe had shown him how pleasant it was not to face the threat of a gun on every corner.

But, for the time being, Quentin accepted that America would continue to pump out real-life violence at an even more prodigal rate than the movies. And as long as that climate existed there would be room for his type of movies.

Back at the Cannes press conference, Quentin was gracious when asked what he thought of one of the other Palme d'Or contenders, *Rouge*. Krzysztof Keislowski's final instalment of his *Three Colours* trilogy. 'That's a masterpiece, by the way,' he told the assembled wordsmiths.

Quentin was by no means confident of pulling off the prestigious Palme d'Or award. He seemed a little in awe of the panel of judges headed by chairman Clint Eastwood, French actress Catherine Deneuve, Italian film maker Pupi Avanti, Korean film maker Shin Sang Okk, Japanese writer Kazuo Ishiguro and Cuban critic Guillermo Cabrera Infante.

Of Ms Deneuve, he commented, 'Well, she did *Belle de Jour* so you never know.'

Quentin was really getting into his stride. He countered one question about *Pulp* by replying, 'The thing about this movie is that it's just a great fucking movie.' When asked if he had yet 'gone Hollywood' he insisted that the day he got a cellular phone the critics could write him off as a sellout. The journos loved it. They scribbled frantically, trying to record the exact words of the esteemed young film maker.

But Quentin then found himself on the receiving end of an awkward question about that old chestnut of the alleged similarities between *Dogs* and Ringo Lam's *City on Fire*.

Journalist David Bourgeois, from the satirical, and funky American movie magazine, *Film Threat*, had been sent to Cannes by his editor specifically to illicit a response to an article run previously in the magazine. This had highlighted shot-by-shot lookalikes between the two movies.

Halfway through the conference, Bourgeois got his chance.

'It was reported recently,' he began, as each tried to outstare the other, 'that you borrowed very heavily from the 1987 Hong Kong action film *City on Fire* to make *Reservoir Dogs*. It seems that both your movie and *City on Fire* are the same, and I was wondering if you'd like to make a comment on that and if you ever plan on making any financial restitution to Mr Lam?'

As Bourgeois sat down, there were a few nervous titters.

'None whatsoever,' came Quentin's reply. It was his shortest response to any question that day.

Then he seemed to rethink his strategy. 'I loved *City on Fire*. I got the poster framed in my house, so it's a great movie...uh...I steal from every movie. I steal from every single movie made, all right? I love it. If my work has anything it's because I'm taking from this and from that, piecing them together. If people don't like it, tough titty, don't go see it.'

No way was Quentin going to apologize for what he saw as a legitimate right to 'learn' from other people's movies.

Most Americans were actually in Cannes primarily to buy and sell territorial rights to movies although – despite the breathless announcements in the showbusiness trade papers – the majority of major deals had been made long before Cannes.

On the deal-making front, there was a small diversion away from the *Pulp* hype, when it was announced that *Killing Zoe*, Roger Avary's slick and violent directorial debut, had been picked up by New York-based independent October Films for US theatrical release.

The most significant aspect of this small deal was that it marked a reconciliation of sorts between Quentin and his old Video Archives buddy Avary. Avary did not want to get a reputation as a Hollywood trouble-maker, so he had not yet gone public about the dispute with Quentin over his contribution to *Pulp*. But Quentin continued to insist that the scene in the bathroom when Butch (Willis) is explaining everything to Fabienne was the only 'full-on' Avary-written scene.

This was just the latest chapter in a long-running saga of contention between Quentin and Avary over authorship of a number of projects. An earlier episode had culminated with Avary getting just one thousand for re-writing the ending of *True Romance* for Tony Scott. This time round, Avary was trying to be stronger, insisting, despite that earlier low-key deal between them, that he deserved more credit for *Pulp*.

'The relationship between Roger and Quentin is sometimes love, and sometimes hate,' observed Sam Hadida, one of the producers on both *True Romance* and Avary's *Killing Zoe*. 'They are like a couple: today she loves me, tomorrow she doesn't love me any more.'

The love-hate thing continued on into early 1995 when Quentin scooped a Golden Globe award for the *Pulp* screenplay. No mention was made of Roger Avary's role. Having accepted his trophy, he walked towards the Avary table, only to be greeted by Avary's wife Gretchen, with a sin-gle raised finger and a cry of , 'Fuck you, Quentin. How can you do this to us?' Gretchen then gave Quentin a kiss, while her husband agreed that even the best meant thanks can be forgotten under the glare of a spotlight.

A few weeks later, Avary's name appeared on the Oscar nominations for best screenplay Oscar.

But back at Cannes in 1994, competition for the festival's prestigious Palme d'Or award was intense. *Red* was seen as the movie to beat, despite the much talked-about *Pulp*. Everyone at Cannes was insisting that no American movie – especially a violent one – could win in a year when Europe had united to defend itself against the so-called cultural imperialism of Hollywood.

Quentin even jokingly tried to put himself up as a leading contender by insisting that when *Dogs* had won nothing two years earlier, 'I decided from that day fucking forth I'm not going to any awards unless I *know* I'm gonna win.'

When jury president Clint Eastwood announced *Pulp Fiction's* Palme d'Or victory on the last Monday evening of the festival, the elated Quentin leapt up from his seat in the auditorium and began negotiating his way through the audience. The jury had actually voted nine to one in favour of *Pulp* with the sole dissenter opting for Nikita Mikhalkov's *Burnt by the Sun.*

A few moments later, Quentin was joined on the podium by *Pulp* cast members Travolta, Jackson and Willis in an ecstatic group grope. Most of the black-tie crowd cheered the choice, but from the back of the hall an angry objector shouted her disgust at the decision. The irate woman yelled repeatedly, 'Scandal! Scandal!' in French. Smiling, Quentin countered this with an under-his-breath profanity. Then, as the woman continued her tirade, he raised his left hand and gave her the finger. Flipping her the bird seemed the ideal response and it brought an even louder cheer from the audience.

'I don't make movies that bring people together,' Quentin told the crowd. 'I make movies that split people apart.'

Then he held up the trophy and quipped, 'That's a big shield. When they throw bricks at me, that says I am not just about violence.'

At the post-ceremony press conference, Quentin got a much easier ride than he had a few days earlier. The only journalists who came close to any hardball questioning were a Russian and some Europeans, who asked him if he felt guilty about winning an art-film award for making mere popular entertainment. Quentin replied that he did not.

Following *Pulp's* runaway success at Cannes, Quentin set off for another round of film festivals in Europe during the summer of 1994. His favourite was the Taormina festival in Sicily, where he was president of the jury and brought along a selection of his favourite exploitation videos. Having time to show only one film, Quentin chose Jamaa Fanaka's *Soul Vengeance*, in which the hero, having been castrated by a sadistic cop, undergoes a voodoo rite and goes on a killing spree, strangling policemen with his penis.

The audience at Taormina came over deadly quiet as they sat and watched this schlock masterpiece.

Meanwhile, Quentin was rubbishing claims that he was planning a sequel to *Pulp*. However, he did retain copyright to all the main characters in the movie just in case he decided to do a film about their early days...

Thanks to *Pulp's* success at Cannes, movie execs at Miramax were faced with the dilemma of when exactly to release the film in the U.S. They were well aware that Oliver Stone's *Natural Born Killers* was slated for an early September opening and they could not decide whether opening *Pulp* at the same time would be a good or bad decision.

In the end, they pushed the release date back to mid-October and let the extraordinary *Pulp* hype machine continue to gather momentum. Magazines and newspapers all over America were serving up a daily diet of *Pulp*-related stories. The movie was being billed as Quentin's own take on contemporary lowlifes, criminals thieves, drug dealers and their girl-friends. It also seemed that weird black suits, white shirts and skinny black ties were still the order of the day for Quentin's sick and twisted heroes.

The release of *NBK* actually had the knock-on effect of giving journalists a further opportunity to mention Quentin and *Pulp*, especially since some writers had picked up on the friction between Quentin and Oliver Stone. Many critics revelled in the fact that some of *NBK*'s more gruesome scenes had been cut, including one sequence where the prisoners paraded around with warder Tommy Lee Jones' head on a stick. *NBK* went on to take more than fifty million dollars at the US box office, but it really acted as an effective free commercial for *Pulp*. Quentin eventually did very well out of *NBK* financially after being paid a three hundred and fifty thousand dollar bonus on the first day of principal photography,

plus ten thousand for every million the movie took above ten million at the US box office. Nevertheless Quentin's mother Connie boycotted *NBK* out of respect for her son.

Oliver Stone did have one dig at Quentin by using Kirk Baltz – one-eared police officer Marvin Nash in *Reservoir Dogs* – as tabloid hack Wayne Gale's cameraman. He even made Baltz use real tapes in his video camera during the gruesome finale of the movie.

But the most vitriolic comment in the bitter battle came from *NBK* producer Don Murphy. He said, 'I would openly celebrate Quentin's death. I never had a falling-out *per se*, but his actions since becoming Quentin Tarantino have been diabolical.'

The ill feeling between Quentin and *NBK* director Stone, as well as young producers Jane Hamsher and Don Murphy, continued to rumble on. Murphy – a plain-speaking character whose machine-gun style delivery is quite similar to Quentin's – was infuriated by Quentin's remarks in an interview with *Premiere* magazine during which he claimed the *NBK* script was stolen from him. Murphy immediately wrote off an indignant letter to the publication. Having pointed out that Quentin had signed numerous chain-of-title documents concerning *NBK* and was well aware of the sale of the project, he also laid into Quentin on a personal level:

> There is an interesting Quentin Tarantino story to be told. It would be the true story of a video geek from the South Bay who thought he could act, watched far too many videos, took the scenes and plots that other people came up with, worked them into scripts, and claimed them as his own. After lying his way through his resumé, he gets his foot in the door. He starts to believe his press. He dismisses most of the people who helped him get where he is going. Now, with the spotlight narrowing in on his lack of originality, everyone looks to see what he's going to do next. So all you readers out there, write in to *Premiere* what film you would like Quentin to copy next? I vote that he copy the old fairy tale *The Emperor's New Clothes*.

But in Hollywood, *Pulp Fiction* was being seen as a trend-setting, fashion-stealing event in the run up to its release. Costume designer Betsy Heimann explained the choice of wardrobe in typical Hollywood speak: 'I'm always thinking of the tone and colour of what people are wearing, particularly if they are going to get shot. Then you have to consider if you want to make a big statement or a small statement. When the kid gets tortured with gunfire, I didn't need to make it more visual because this is just the build-up for what comes next. So he wears a dark green shirt. You have to think of the important moments.'

Fashion scribes were particularly enamoured with Mia's (Uma Thurman's) top-dog high-style gangster wife look, complete with stylish black bob wig which was highly reminiscent of Danish actress Anna Karina. The simply elongated white shirt with protracted geometric cuffs, black bellbottoms, black bra and gold ballet slippers, rounded off with blood red nails and lips, were enthusiastically received. Mia's white shirt and bellbottoms were from the Agnes B chain, as was Vincent's suit, while Jules' suit was from Perry Ellis. The sex slave in the redneck torture scene got his leather all-in-one number from the West Hollywood store, the Pleasure Chest, on Santa Monica Boulevard.

On the punctured skin front, Travolta's earring was a clip-on job, as were Arquette's apparently vast number of rings on brows, ears, navel, nose and even (according to the dialogue) clitoris. Ving Rhames (Marsellus) was one of the few with an authentic piercing job in his left ear. But the Band Aid on the back of his neck which seemed such a sinister part of his make-up was in fact only there to cover a real life-scar. Quentin decided it looked kinda cool to leave it on.

The *Pulp* reviews were predictably glowing, but a few of them did pause for breath and actually try to analyze the content of the movie.

Anthony Lane, in the *New Yorker*, wrote, 'The architecture of *Pulp Fiction* may look skewed and strained, but the decoration is a lot of fun. I loved the little curls of suspense that kept us waiting for fresh characters, the details pondered by the camera in advance of a full-face shot:

the feet of Uma Thurman, the Band-Aid back of Ving Rhames's neck, and the smooth tuxedo of Harvey Keitel, who appears, rather stylishly, to be throwing a party at eight-thirty in the morning.'

Peter Travers in *Rolling Stone* pointed out, 'Tarantino refuses to patronize, glamourize or judge his band of outsiders. Instead, he lets us see the glimmers of humanity that emerge when they drop their masks of control.'

But a few commentators angrily claimed that excessively admiring write-ups for *Pulp* were sanctioning the violence and moral depravity highlighted in the movie. These critics lashed out at irresponsible executives for financing the film in the first place.

USA Today columnist Joe Urschel complained, 'Like contemporary tobacco chiefs who deny any link between cigarettes and cancer, Hollywood executives will be sitting before congressional committees ten years from now in adamant denial. They will continue to callously brush off the connections between their product and the violence in society – despite an avalanche of scientific studies showing the connection.'

Quentin was nothing if not thought-provoking. Each article or review of *Pulp*, sparked off dozens of letters from outraged movie followers who had a wide variety of opinions on the young film maker. Some of these letters were far from complimentary, but many of them were just as well written as much of Quentin's dialogue.

Ken Bash, of Malibu, wrote to the *Los Angles Times*, 'I had thought Quentin Tarantino a wildly overrated, plagiarizing, misogynist wimp who somehow got backing to make the Movie Mummy Didn't Want Him to Make. But now I know better. He is also a shallow, self-serving, puffed-up ignoramus who learned about life from a video screen. Wouldn't it be cool if a sadistic armed robber had walked into Video Archives years ago and subjected then-clerk Tarantino to a real-life dose of the butchery he has since so callously exploited on his way to the forefront of a new generation of film makers?'

But one thing everyone agreed on was that *Pulp* marked the return of John Travolta, even if he had gone soft – literally. In *Pulp*, his gut, breasts like a junior prom queen and skin as pale as a Norwegian vacationing in Greenland gave him a look reminiscent of late-period Elvis. But Travolta's flab was only skin deep – with his Prince Valiant haircut, the one-time teen heart-throb clearly wasn't afraid to be jeered at in order to bring a certain truth to the screen.

Spin-offs from the success of *Pulp* were also far reaching. At the Frankfurt Book Fair, in October 1994, the screenplay of the movie was one of the hottest properties on display. Agents who visited the annual fair – the biggest event in the publishing world – said that interest in the script eclipsed bidding on virtually everything else presented there.

'In my seventeen years at the agency, I have never seen the interest level so strong on any one work,' said Robert Gottlieb, head of the William Morris literary division and one of Quentin's personal representatives. Quentin even retained approval rights on all translations and his advance was in the region of two hundred thousand dollars.

The soundtrack of *Pulp* turned out to be just as successful, although music business execs were convinced that many customers were drawn as much by the priceless patter between Vincent and Jules about French quarter-pounders as by Urge Overkill's version of 'Girl, You'll Be a Woman Soon'.

Quentin's movies were naturals for such treatment. For all the criticism about blood and violence in *Pulp* and *Dogs*, the popularity of the sound tracks's dialogue proved that it was his words that truly stuck in the audience's mind.

The other key to the soundtrack success of *Pulp* and *Dogs* was that none of the music was specifically written to help sell the movies. It was there to serve the story. Quentin wanted to avoid criticism about just having an excuse for a soundtrack album.

'Directing is actually like making a mix tape of music,' he explained, 'because you're taking all these people's talents and adding an esthetic of your own, depending on what you've selected and how you arrange what you've selected.'

Pulp's blaring mixture of surf sounds, down-and-dirty funk, and atmospheric folk and rock songs actually spanned five decades of music. Much of the film's personality and rhthym came from the adrenaline drumming, evocative melodies and big, wet guitar licks of surf music instrumentals by Dick Dale, the Centurians and the Tornadoes. Quentin had first been introduced to the music of all these musicians by his old acting school buddy and home removal man, Rich Turner.

Surf music seemed a very unusual choice to score what was essentially a gangster movie, but no one doubted its effectiveness after *Pulp* was released.

'I never really understood what surf music had to do with surfing or surfers,' explained Quentin. 'To me, surf music always sounded like rock-and-roll spaghetti western music. That's what this movie is, more or less. It's like a rock-and-roll spaghetti western.'

But, unlike spaghetti westerns, the music in Quentin's movies is played by his characters on record players, car radios, restaurants, reel-to-reel machines – anything but CD players. *Dogs* was the same, held together in the beginning, middle and end by K-Billy's Super Sounds of the Seventies.

Quentin much preferred to find a score for his movies rather than commission music from composers or hip rock stars. 'People come to me from time to time and say, "The band really likes you; they'd really like to do a song for you". Well, I'm all nervous about that, because what if you don't like it? I won't want to use it, and then I'll have to hurt their feelings and everything.'

Meanwhile, *Pulp's* distributors Miramax were pumping up their marketing effort just before the movie's US theatrical release. The launch of what was essentially perceived as an art house movie into the mainstream market, on more than 1,300 screens across America, marked a rare promotional effort from Miramax, who had the advantage of having Disney behind them following their purchase of Miramax six months earlier.

The entire launch campaign was an expensive roll of the dice that Miramax chiefs feared could seriously backfire if *Pulp* did not get off to an outstanding opening. It actually opened with a whopping 9.3 million dollars, putting it firmly at the top of the US box office charts ahead of Stallone/Stone action flick, *The Specialist*.

Even the super-confident Quentin was astounded. That week, he called his friend Scott Spiegel at two in the morning and asked if he could drop by. Twenty minutes later, Quentin was pacing the floor of Spiegel's home re-enacting the entire *Pulp* sequence involving Wolf (Keitel) doing his James Bond thing with the body in the car and at the same time trying to explain why he was so knocked out by the movie's success.

But that runaway first weekend at the box office wasn't enough for Miramax. The following week they launched a new TV advertising campaign. 'We want to broaden out the audience to people who might like the movie but for whom it my not have been first choice,' explained Bob Weinstein, co-chairman of Miramax.

If the launch had flopped, Miramax would have been faced with pulling more than 1,300 prints of the film from movie theatres across America. Another risk lay in the violent content. After much discussion, they decided the promotion should concentrate on the humour of the film, and the posters featured John Travolta doing the twist. The Miramax marketing department coped with the fear of violence problem by using the slogan, 'You won't know the facts till you see the fiction.'

It was later disclosed that the promotional budget of *Pulp* was as high as the eight million dollars the movie actually cost to make. Disney – the family favourites – had provided Miramax with the financial clout to back the huge launch of *Pulp*.

But one aspect that Miramax had no control over was the response of audiences in the movie theatres. One man in New York passed out as he watched Vincent plunging the hypodermic into Mia. 'Is there a doctor in the house,' someone actually asked. The movie was stopped for nine anxious minutes before the announcement came: 'The victim is just fine.'

Quentin was called upon to defend the violent and graphic content of his movies by *Time* magazine. He decided on a new tactic this time round. 'I've seen what I've seen, and I've met people I've met,' he explained. 'I've been in weird situations. I'm not a hood, but I've seen fringe things here and there.' It was an interesting response, especially in the light of Oliver Stone's criticism of Quentin when they had met a few months earlier.

Quentin was getting so used to questions about his wholesale borrowing from other movies that had developed his response: 'People ask if my love of movies can be too much. What annoys me about the question is the snobbery; it treats movies like a bastard art form. Could a novelist ever read too many books or a musician listen to too much music? Well, I totally love movies.'

Bruce Willis hit the nail on the head when he said, 'You can say the most intellectual thing about *Pulp Fiction* and be right. But it also works for the trailer-park kids.'

Besides Willis, some of the other stars of Pulp were wheeled out to explain why they liked working with Quentin.

Uma Thurman insisted, 'Quentin is a great collaborator. He is extremely clear about what he wants, but he's not close minded; he's no bully.'

And John Travolta chipped in, 'He lets you put all the icing on the cake. For Vincent, I could mock up the hair, do the accent, the walk, the talk.'

Travolta later admitted he owed his revived career to Quentin, who had pushed him to take the lead in a movie adaption of Elmore Leonard's *Get Shorty* (Leonard being the same author whose book Quentin had tried to shoplift when he was sixteen).

Samuel L. Jackson probably summed up one of the major attractions of Quentin's movies by saying, 'Films are a show-me medium and Quentin makes tell-me movies.'

Meanwhile, Quentin managed to grab a few days in Ireland with his platonic friend, *It's Pat* star Julia Sweeney. He proclaimed it to be like a Merchant Ivory movie come to life.

Luckily for Quentin he hadn't yet been any place where *Pulp Fiction* had come to life...

'You'll never hear surf music again'

Jimi Hendrix on *Electric Ladyland*

Arrested Development

HOLLYWOOD. FALL, 1994

Quentin announced an exciting new project called *Four Rooms*, on which he was to collaborate with directors Robert Rodriguez, Alexandre Rockwell and Allison Anders. The movie was financed to the tune of five million dollars by his old friends at Miramax and consisted of four different stories – each individually directed – linked by an LA hotel concierge. Originally, Steve (Mr Pink) Buscemi was cast as the bellhop, but when he became unavailable, Tim (Mr Orange) Roth stepped in. Quentin directed the first segment in early November 1994, and it starred Bruce Willis, Seymour Cassel and himself. Both actors stepped in for scale salaries of around twenty thousand dollars each. One of the other segments starred Madonna as a witch.

The project had been around for more than two years since Quentin had come across it at the Sundance Film Festival in 1992 when he attended with *Dogs*. Then it was called *Five Rooms*, but the original producers were unable to raise the cash, so Quentin and Lawrence Bender

stepped in, bought off the founder member of the project and renamed it with one less room.

Four Rooms, which was also executive produced by Quentin, was expected to be premiered at the Venice Film Festival in September 1995.

In November 1994, Quentin loyally held a private screening of *Pulp* for all Video Archives employees. The store had actually evolved into an unofficial Quentin fan club with a huge painting of *Dogs* hanging over the front window and *Dogs* posters from Cannes on sale, as well as various other items of memorabilia.

Then, just before Christmas, Archives closed down its store only a short time after moving from Sepulveda Boulevard to a nearby beachside location.

All sorts of rumours about its demise circulated, including the story that Quentin had broken into the store one night and stolen all the videos! There was talk of him helping the owners stockpile their video collection so that angry creditors could not get their hands on them.

The truth was rather more prosaic. Video Archives auctioned off their collection of videos before actually closing down and Quentin bought six hundred videos at a total cost of approximately four thousand dollars. Video store-clerk-turned-director Roger Avary also put in a bid for certain cassettes and there was talk of the two rivals holding a bidding war for the majority of tapes.

Some locals were convinced that its connection with Quentin had made the store so popular that it had over-expanded and the owners simply could not provide the Blockbusters-style service that was now required.

Right up until it closed, Video Archives was regularly being raided by agents and producers so swept up by Tarantino mania that they actually believed there were more director/writers just waiting in the wings of the store. In fact, Quentin's success merely highlighted a whole new generation of video store clerks-turned-Hollywood-players, including Chuck Hogan, a Boston video geek who sold his first screenplay to New

Line for four hundred thousand dollars and Daniel Waters, whose screen-writing credits include *Heathers* and *Batman 2*.

Following completion of *Pulp*, Quentin let it be known that he was keen on doing unofficial and extremely well-paid re-writes on certain major films. In the summer of 1994, he earned a cool two hundred thousand dollars for a two-week polish on the action adventure yarn *Crimson Tide*. starring Denzel Washington and Gene Hackman. The submarine adventure was helmed by *True Romance* director Tony Scott, who actually persuaded the film's backers to stump up the cash for Quentin to inject some much needed humour into the dialogue. His input is instantly recognizable thanks to the characters' propensity for discussing old movies and TV series on at least three occasions. At the time of writing, *Crimson Tide* had edged over the hundred dollar million mark at the US box office.

Quentin was managing to become the most versatile talent in Hollywood, writing, acting and directing, and splitting those roles in a very lucrative manner if required.

Back in his acting persona, Quentin took a role in the Jack Baran-directed *Destiny Turns on the Radio*, which was released in America in April. 1995. Unfortunately, reviews for the movie were so lousy that some critics suggested Quentin should stick to his own projects in the future. In reality. Quentin's appearance only lasted about twenty minutes. But his name was deemed such a box office draw that every poster and trailer for the movie carried his image.

The *Los Angeles Times* branded *Destiny* as, 'so stultifyingly vacuous that pap would have been a godsend'.

In Britain, when the movie was released in June 1995, it seems to have seriously damaged Quentin's credibility. Again, the promotional posters attempted to cash in on his immense popularity, implying that Quentin was the only star of the movie. Audiences expecting to watch something as superb as *Dogs* or *Pulp* came out bitterly disillusioned. Quentin's defence was that he had only acted in *Destiny* and that did not make it a Tarantino project, but how were audiences expected to

understand that? They saw his name on posters and TV commercials and presumed they were going to be in for another movie treat, only to be very disappointed.

Then Quentin made a small appearance in director Robert Rodriguez's sequel to his incredibly low-budget, but widely admired *El Mariachi*. The two young directors had actually become close friends during the previous year and it was a relationship that would blossom into yet another major movie project by the spring of 1995.

In January 1995, the *Pulp* publicity machine continued to roll on, even though the movie had been out in the US for some months. Bruce Willis told columnist Liz Smith he loved *Pulp* so much that he had seen it five times. 'Each time I see it in a different way, and I like it better and better.'

Also, in January 1995, Quentin was chosen by the New York Film Critics Circle as the year's best director for *Pulp Fiction*. Quentin actually requested that Bruce Willis present him with the award and the star immediately agreed, only to discover that Circle Chairman Armond White had already booked Uma Thurman.

Quentin's second NYFC award for best screenplay caused equal strife. Miramax wanted Quentin's favourite novelist Elmore Leonard to present, especially as the studio had just shelled out a fortune for the rights to his novels for Quentin to eventually direct. But White had already asked for Camille Paglia to make that award.

After the ceremony Quentin was on good form in a room full of journalists. He was asked to describe how it felt to get an award and said, 'It's like going to a dance and actually being asked to dance – it's like, hey, cool.' He continued to entertain the reporters backstage with a rapid-fire, sometimes self aggrandising twenty-minute routine, complete with Elvis impersonations.

A few weeks later he scooped the two top honours for directing and writing from the Los Angeles Film Critics, and pundits were starting to predict Oscar success. But, interestingly, Quentin refused to allow video tapes of *Pulp Fiction* to be sent out for Oscar consideration.

Traditionally, studios seeking nomination in all categories make videos of the movies available even if they are still only on theatrical release. However, Quentin cleverly asked Miramax not to send out cassettes of his masterpiece because he believed the film would be compromised by not being seen on the big screen. The video version actually reduced the anamorphic widescreen theatrical print to a letterbix aspect ratio, even smaller than a conventional video image.

Many others in Hollywood were fast to condemn the move as a stunt. One source at Universal told the respected film business publication *Variety*, 'This is a transparent act of vanity and chutzpah.' Others claimed it would reduce the chances of lesser-known technicians being nominated because Academy members would not have a chance to see the final credits on the movie.

While the story of Quentin's apparently over-sensitive behaviour spread through Hollywood, he was taping a guest spot on a TV talk show and refused to be drawn into the row.

One member of the Academy of Motion Picture Arts and Sciences, who run the Oscars, commented drily to *Variety*, 'The irony is that Quentin Tarantino *started out* as a clerk in a video store. But maybe he's resistant to the idea because he's never been in an Oscar race before and he's so young and inexperienced.'

Quentin was denied eligibility for the Writer's Guild of America award nominations for *Pulp* because the companies that produced the film were not signatories to the WGA contract.

Also in early 1995, Quentin continued his hyperactive Hollywoodization by appearing as a guest on the US networked comedy series *All American Girl* with his friend Margaret Cho. It seemed like smart timing because *Pulp* had just been officially honoured with seven Oscar nominations, including Best Picture and Best Director. His role, playing virtually himself, was so 'in' as to be almost incomprehensible if any of the show's estimated eighteen million audience had not seen *Pulp Fiction*.

He played Desmond Winocki, a video-tape salesman, who is fixed up for a date with Margaret. Along the way, there were *Pulp* parody scenes, references and in-jokes, many of them fairly obscure. In one scene Quentin gives an old lady a portable TV and then recites a speech similar to that given by Christopher Walken in *Pulp*. Later, Desmond demonstrates the proper way to plunge a meat thermometer into a roasting turkey with definite shades of Mia (Uma Thurman) in that adrenaline injection scene. The programme also featured a club called Fantasy where Warren Beatty burgers were served by waitresses resembling the Ayatollah Khomeini. It didn't take a brain surgeon to work out the similarities to Jack Rabbit Slim's in *Pulp*.

Despite criticism that Cho was simply cashing in on Quentin's growing popularity by guest-starring him on her show, Quentin loyally defended his role and even revealed that he had dreamt up the part himself. 'I always wanted to be on a sitcom; I grew up watching them.' Quentin actually nursed a secret fantasy that he could become a recurring character on the show, much like Tom Hanks was on *Family Ties* many years earlier.

Much to Quentin's delight, *Pulp* officially became part of the Advanced Actors Craft class at New York University's Tisch School. NYU Professor Diane Gardner put it on her own curriculum and invited Quentin to visit the university to watch her students perform a number of scenes from the film.

In early 1995, Quentin received another distinction when a Usenet group was dedicated to the auteur. To join the fast talk all you needed was the Internet code: *alt. fan. tarantino.*

After painstaking analysis of *Dogs*, computer watchers turned to *Pulp* and began deconstructing every line of dialogue for some hidden meaning. At least one netter thought it had gone too far and put out a message: 'Give it up. Sometimes a cigar is just a cigar.

Around the same time, John Travolta announced that he was getting a fee of seven million dollars for appearing in the Twentieth Century Fox movie *Broken Arrow*. Not bad considering he got just a hundred and fifty thousand for starring in *Pulp*. A cheque for eight million was awaiting his agreement to do another movie called *The Lady Takes an Ace*. Travolta's next highest fee before he appeared in *Pulp* was just three million dollars. Quentin had singlehandedly revitalized Travolta's career.

Not content with reviving that and with giving Bruce Willis a cachet he had never previously enjoyed, Quentin's Midas touch extended beyond celluloid to the soundtrack for *Pulp*, which sold 300,000 copies by April 1995. Much of that was down to Dick Dale, the Californian surf musician, whose marvellous instrumental 'Misirlou' blasted the opening credits of the movie onto the screen. It was a track originally released the year before Quentin's birth in 1963.

The fifty-seven-year-old guitarist was suddenly transformed from what was a relatively regional musician into an international star and played several sell-out concerts in Britain in the spring of 1995. Two new albums, *Tribal Thunder* and *Unknown Territory* were also released under the High Tone label in early 1995.

One of Dick Dale's earliest bar bands played opposite Little Richard, whose bassist happened to be the teenage Jimi Hendrix. A fellow left-hander. Hendrix noticed Dale's unorthodox, upside-down Fender style, later adopting it as his own. It was also Jimi Hendrix, on Electric Ladyland, who said 'you'll never hear surf music again.'

NATIONAL FILM THEATRE, LONDON,
JANUARY, 1995

More than five hundred people had been waiting much of the afternoon for Quentin to personally sign their copies of his *Pulp Fiction* screenplay, which had recently been published in book form in Britain. Young girls gasped hysterically as they caught sight of their hero. City stockbroker-types in pinstriped suits surged forward and the crowd grew almost too big for the NFT bookshop to handle. Young, old, men, women – they all had a single objective: to meet their idol.

The twenty-minute book-signing session had followed an onstage

interview, coinciding with a season of Quentin's favourite films. The NFT
was usually the haunt of bookish, serious-minded cineastes, but this
occasion was different.

Just as Quentin started his marathon book-signing session, a pretty
fair-haired girl started screaming: 'QUENTIN! QUENTIN! QUENTIN!'
Others joined in, hoping he would at least look up at them. The same
girl became even more hysterical and tried to force a path through the
crowd. Shortly afterwards, she was removed from the shop by NFT
staff.

'We're accustomed to hosting celebrities at the NFT, but no one here
can remember anything like this,' explained a breathless Brian Robinson,
of the NFT. 'We've been having these interviews since 1981, and Robert
Redford didn't attract this intensity of following. Nor did Warren Beatty.
Or Gloria Swanson.'

On stage earlier, Quentin had worked the crowd brilliantly. He even
turned down the chance to present one of the Evening Standard Film
Awards that evening to stay and introduce each of his favourite movies
personally. Among his choices were Howard Hawks' *His Girl Friday* and
Rio Bravo, John Carpenter's *The Thing* and *Assault on Precinct 13*;
Douglas Sirk's *Magnificent Obsession* and Jean-Luc Godard's *Breathless*
and *Band of Outsiders*.

Quentin had achieved rock-idol status in Britain. His *Pulp* screenplay sold more than seventy thousand copies, more than double the next
best selling script. Screenplays of *Reservoir Dogs* and *True Romance* had
sold a combined total of more than fifty thousand.

Almost twenty thousand people had applied for the five hundred
tickets available for the NFT talk. And touts were selling the seven
pounds fifty tickets for four times their cover price in the hours leading up to his appearance. In the end, the NFT set up a video screen
link in an outside auditorium so a further thousand could see their idol
live.

Britain's more cerebral broadsheet newspapers devoted hundreds of
column inches to theorizing about Quentin's talent and celebrity. Even

his social engagements were reported endlessly, including his dinners with European directors Luc Besson and Bernardo Bertolucci.

British journalists seemed more open-minded about *Pulp Fiction* than many writers and critics in the United States.

Neil Ascherson, writing in *The Independent on Sunday*, described *Pulp* as 'a lurid farce, which is funny precisely because it manages to prevent the audience identifying with any of its cardboard characters.' He went on to say that *Home Alone* was a far more disturbing movie.

However he did conclude his lengthy article by saying, 'there has to be a bit of the nerd and wanker in every artist who invents a reality. The trouble with Tarantino is that his bit leaves little room for anything else.'

The decision by British censors not to award a video certificate to *Dogs* for the best part of two years simply had the knock-on effect of increasing Quentin's cult following in the UK.

The Prince Charles cinema, just off Leicester Square in London, became host to increasingly large numbers of passionate *Dogs* groupies, known as Doggies. Dressed in black suits and skinny ties and carrying plastic guns, the Doggies would shout Quentin's classic lines in unison with their favourite characters.

The Doggies even held a convention, in November 1994, in London, at which they each received a fake severed ear, complete with dripping fake blood. Each month the video ban continued, the movie became an even bigger success for the Prince Charles. It eventually became their most successful film ever. And in November 1994, the cinema put on a double bill of *True Romance* and *Dogs*. It was a sell-out.

Quentin's popularity in Britain was not just limited to London. In Manchester, more than half a dozen cinemas were showing *Dogs* and *Pulp* in the spring of 1995. When a three-screen cinema fifteen minutes from Moss Side, and in the heart of student-land, took off *Dogs* in mid-January 1995, the film was brought back within a week due to popular demand.

Cinema projectionist Kevin Lewis explained, 'The public want it, they want anything to do with Tarantino. The week we dropped it we had nothing but complaints, people asking for *Dogs* and *Pulp Fiction*. We are into a third year of showing *Dogs* non-stop; it's becoming an institution.'

The most remarkable aspect of this British Tarantino-mania was that *Dogs* actually took considerably more at the UK box office than in the entire United States.

Chris Fox, a 26-year-old lithographics systems operator, went to see *Dogs* three times, 'We talk about his films a lot at work.' He insisted that violence was not a major talking point. 'We are less likely to talk about the violence than we are about the music Tarantino has chosen to accompany the violence.'

Another Manchester-based *Dogs* regular, Chris Caldwell, said. 'There are no other films around that have the dark humour. The violence is comic book stuff. No other director captures my imagination like him.'

Others like Simon Broom, a 26-year-old unemployed man with a ponytail, reacted rather more disturbingly. He admitted liking *Dogs* and *Pulp* for their 'guns and swearing'. He often sat at home listening obsessively to the *Pulp* soundtrack trying to work out which song fitted which part of the film.

'I've seen nothing like it before. Nothing shows violence or humour like Tarantino. He gets to you, makes you think, and his characters have a black, dark edge to them which makes you shiver and laugh,' Broom confessed.

In Quentin's opinion, the fact that people still responded so overwhelmingly to *Dogs* more than three years after it had been completed, was the greatest compliment in the world. In some ways, it was better than getting an Oscar. The movie was about characters you would never want to meet in your worst nightmares but it was still hip, groovy and very cool.

Another extraordinary example of the way in which Quentin was affecting everyday life in Britain came when two schoolchildren, shunning Shakespeare and Shaw, chose to use some of *Pulp's* most chilling scenes in a school drama project for a mock GCSE exam.

Ben Marks and Emma Bell cleared the bad language with their teacher, borrowed replica handguns and stunned their classmates with a rendition of the five-minute scene in which Honey Bunny and Pumpkin discuss how they are going to rob the restaurant they are in. Their performances were followed by a discussion on the 'moral issues' raised by the scene and they eventually got an A-grade.

The influence of Quentin Tarantino seemed to know no bounds...

'I became the Catcher in the Rye of my generation. I almost became a prophet'

Mark David Chapman, killer of John Lennon

Born to Die

NEW YORK, MARCH, 1995

New York's Underground Film Festival announced they were going to show a short film comparing *Reservoir Dogs* to one of its major inspirations, Ringo Lam's *City on Fire*. The news created a media stampede, but neither Quentin nor his producer Lawrence Bender acknowledged the significance of the short movie which started with the following strap line: 'If either of these films teaches us anything it is that crime doesn't pay.'

Mike White, the 22-year-old film school grad and creator of the short film insisted, 'To see it [*Dogs*] had been taken from something else. I felt kind of cheated.'

The film – entitled *Who Do You Think You're Fooling* – intercut startlingly similar sequences from the two films. White said he never actually heard from Quentin, but admitted, 'If it was me, I would probably be mad. I don't hate Tarantino. I have a lot of respect for his work. I'm not trying to make him look bad, I'm just trying to point something out. I just wanted people to know. It's almost the people's right to know.'

Quentin told one paper in a specially prepared response, 'This has been the best year of my life ever, and nothing, nothing could be a distraction at this point.' But he claimed through his press representative that he was hoping to eventually see the film. And producer Bender insisted, 'Quentin's such an original voice, and of course, he's influenced by many film makers. I remember when my acting teacher gave that script to Harvey Keitel. Harvey said the characters had more originality than anything he'd seen, and that's what made it special.'

Shortly afterwards, as if to answer the mounting accusations of plagiarism, Quentin was nominated for the annual Directors' Guild awards alongside other formidable names, including Robert Redford (*Quiz Show*), Robert Zemeckis (*Forrest Gump*), Mike Newell (*Four Weddings and a Funeral*) and Frank Darabont (*The Shawshank Redemption*). Since the DGA awards began in 1946, all but three Best Director winners had gone on to win the Best Director Oscar.

Pulp fever continued to spread as the movie passed the hundred million dollar mark at the US box office. Talk-show host David Letterman got in on the act when he armed three members of his audience with camcorders and ordered them to go into their nearest movie theatre and shoot *Pulp* because his researchers couldn't get hold of a clip to show on his programme.

When they returned, the tape was cued up and aired on his show.

In February 1995, Quentin received what for him was the ultimate accolade, when *Pulp Fiction* backers Miramax announced they were launching a specialist US distribution label to be overseen by Quentin himself.

The label would distribute films chosen by Quentin. Most likely the first title in the series would be Hong Kong filmmaker Wong Kar-Wai's *Chungking Express*, a newly released movie which reminded Quentin of some of his favourite Chinese-based thrillers, like *City on Fire*.

In March 1995, Quentin made his first inroad into directing episodic television when he accepted an offer to helm an episode of the hugely successful medical drama series, *ER*. Even though he was paid just thirty thousand dollars for the job, he admitted getting a tremendous buzz out of working at the faster pace expected in television. Naturally, he insisted on altering the script a little to fit in with his vision of life in a hospital emergency room.

'Directing *ER* was a blast. It was pretty darned fast, man. You don't mess around,' he said.

ER star Anthony Edwards, who actually starred in Quentin's favourite homoerotic movie, *Top Gun*, was so taken by Quentin that he created a stand-up routine impersonating Quentin to perfection before the episode had finished shooting. Edwards compared Quentin to a playful, purple dinosaur called Barney, who appears on a children's television programme, saying, 'He's like Barney on speed.'

Quentin's episode included a gang member arriving at the hospital with an ear torn off, an apparent reference to the infamous *Dogs* sequence. But it was all a coincidence. However, Quentin was so convinced he would get the blame for the scene, he tried to get it cut.

Quentin also proved his loyalty to actors he had used in the past by casting Angela Jones, who played Bruce Willis's taxi driver, Esmarelda, in *Pulp Fiction*.

ER's style was already well established: an anxious camera trying to keep pace with each new trolley arrival; the co-ordinated lift from trolley to bed; the inevitable use of the electric paddles to restart a dead heart. It all proved perfect directorial fodder to Quentin. When the episode was shown in Britain, in July 1995, it was hailed by critics as a superbly executed piece of episodic television. Peter Patterson in the *Daily Mail* wrote, 'Hard to imagine anyone could put an extra fizz into the frenetic American hospital series *ER*, but guest director Quentin Tarantino managed it, stepping up the pace to the point where some scenes were like watching a video on fast forward.'

The only classic Tarantinoism in the entire episode was when a nurse entered the emergency room just after the medical team had been dealing with the mayhem. She asked, 'Everything all right here?' and received the reply, 'Hunky dory.'

A few days before the Oscars on March 27, 1995, Quentin showed up at the Independent Spirit Awards in Santa Monica and developed an 'instant crush' on actress Linda Fiorentino, whose brilliant performance in *The Last Seduction* probably helped more than anything else to make that movie the most talked about film of 1994/95 after *Pulp*.

Quentin – who won the Spirit award for best movie – had been loath to talk to any press until he spotted Linda being interviewed on camera by a reporter for the Bravo cable channel. He crept up alongside her, planted a big kiss on her cheek and then strummed her back like a flamenco guitarist.

A few minutes later, Quentin's long-standing girlfriend Grace appeared. He greeted her warmly with a 'Hey, baby'. Linda's back was instantly forgotten as Quentin and Grace clasped hands and walked off together.

Also in March, British film censors granted *Pulp* a video release certificate, despite the fact that they were still refusing to give *Dogs* one after almost two years of wrangling. The video of *Pulp* underwent one 'realignment' to change the angle of a shot in which Vince (Travolta) plunges the needle into his arm when fixing up heroin.

The granting of the certificate for *Pulp* helped push through a certificate for *Dogs* which was finally released on video in the UK in early June 1995.

In the magazine and newspaper world, editors like Paul Zimmerman at *Film Threat* were getting increasingly irritated by the vast number of Tarantinoisms creeping into every article, even when the subject was not directly related to Quentin. Classic examples would include daily reports of crimes in the *New York Daily News*. One actually read, 'Ionesco, the Marx Brothers and Quentin Tarantino together couldn't have hatched a more lunatic drama than the trial of Colin Ferguson.'

Paul Zimmerman explains, 'It got so bad that I had to ban my writers from mentioning Tarantino in anything other than a relevant subject.'

Back at his apartment on Crescent Heights, Quentin found it increasingly difficult to escape the glare of the public spotlight. Around 11.30 most nights he still loved nothing better than to lie on his couch and watch the TV talk shows on his wide screen, flipping between presenters because all the programmes came on at the same time.

Sadly, the once obligatory taco chips and beer were no longer a part of Quentin's staple diet. Occasionally, he allowed himself some Cap'n Crunch cereal or Bill and Ted's Excellent Cereal but his agents and managers had advised him to cut down on fast food. It was so difficult for Quentin to resist such junk that he even wrote a message to himself which he pinned up by the fridge. It read, 'Stay away until you absolutely have to go there. Then enjoy it. But don't get used to it.'

Quentin even tried to step up his healthy food intake by replacing certain meals with a bizarre concoction of Mountain Dew, crushed ice and packets of diet drinks all blended together for a cocktail from hell.

Ever-increasing quantities of movie memorabilia were turning the one-bedroom apartment into more and more of a pop-culture playground. These included kitschy artifacts such as the razor from that infamous ear-slicing scene, a frighteningly lifelike head of B movie diva Barbara Steele, a pack of genuine Texas Chainsaw chili, a Zorro knife given to Quentin by Jennifer Beals, and dozens of cases of bottled Pepsi. On the mantelpiece there were now dolls – an Ilya Kuryakin doll from *The Man from U.N.C.L.E.*, a John Travolta doll, a Boy George doll – and some awards, including two bronze horses from the Stockholm Film Festival.

Framed vintage movie posters were hanging everywhere and there was a large bookshelf in the dining room as well as an even larger bookcase in the bedroom packed with video tapes. Quentin had also started collecting even more lunchboxes which were on one shelf, plus the neatly stacked obligatory board games, including new additions like *Thunderball*, *I Spy* and *Baretta* as well as a *Grease* game. It was still his dream to get a *Reservoir Dogs* game going. On the wall was another poster of *True Romance*, this one signed by Tony Scott, 'Quentin: This is the best script and best movie I have ever done. Give me more.'

Quentin deliberately kept the lighting in the apartment dim because the main function of the place was to serve as a mini-movie theatre where he could sit for hours watching whatever films took his fancy. He still had a late-night penchant for Roger Corman's Women-Behind-Bars movies. Quentin considered *Night Call Nurses* to be a fine example of the Corman oeuvre because it contained the classic mix of sex, nudity and political consciousness. There was always a blonde, brunette and an ethnic minority amongst the busty Corman women. Quentin's favourite scene in *Nurses* was when the brunette nurse tells a prospective lover, 'Maybe if we went someplace else, someplace where I felt more comfortable, more at home.' And then her would-be boyfriend replies, 'Like your home, for example.' Quentin cracked up every time he heard that scene.

Out on the streets of Hollywood, Quentin had become almost like a patron saint of video stores, although sometimes it got a real drag: like the time he was mobbed outside his local Blockbusters. But the thing he found really hard was that he could no longer just go and hang out at a movie theatre, something that had been a way of life for him since his childhood. He'd thought about donning a cap and dark glasses, but knew that would look dumb, so he began seeing more and more private Hollywood screenings of movies.

Quentin desperately wanted to live his own life again. During the making of *Pulp* he'd only had that movie to think about, but he didn't want to be on call the whole time. He needed a year off, but could not resist some of the acting roles and executive jobs on other people's movies that were being offered to him virtually every day. He reckoned he could juggle all these jobs pretty easily without letting them take over his life. His priority was still to take a year off from actually directing and writing his own movies. He genuinely believed that it was the only way to retain his artistic integrity.

When he did get to a movie theatre, a lot of films caught his attention. But his undoubted favourite of 1995 was *Ed Wood*, the eccentric story of a failed movie director. Directed by *Batman's* Tim Burton, the movie had a real-life feel and it highlighted the plight of a man who would not give up trying to do the thing he loved most – making movies. In many ways, the central character's determination reflected the attitude that had taken Quentin to the top of his profession in such an incredibly short space of time.

There was another ingredient in *Ed Wood* that caught Quentin's eye; the ornate 1940s-style theatre featured in many of the sequences was the Pussycat Movie Theatre in Torrance where he had kicked those perverts and sickos out on their ears during seedy porn film shows.

On the domestic front, Quentin made a couple of concessions to Hollywood tradition by getting a trainer and an exercise machine, thanks to some regular reminders from his mother, Connie.

She bought him a health rider with bar seats, powered by pedals which pushed and pulled it. Connie was worried that Quentin would put back on the 30 pounds he had managed to lose after he finally made it with *Dogs* in 1991. The only problem was that Quentin did not have a clue how to operate the machine and he got his assistant to call Connie to ask her for the guarantee because he wanted to send it back. Then it transpired that he had forgotten to put the batteries in the mileometer measurer on the handlebars.

Quentin is still very close to Connie, since each considers the other to be the only true relative they have in the world. But these days Connie does spend a lot of time playing telephone tag with her famous son.

She is bemused by his current rock star status, especially by the huge crowds that seem to gather at events where he is billed to appear. 'I cannot imagine why anyone would get in a frenzy about anybody. We all put our pants on the same way. No-one is really that different. I mean, I was one of Elvis's biggest fans but I would never scream over him or the Beatles for that matter.'

The most recent memento Connie has of her son is a huge stuffed green Loch Ness Monster that Quentin brought back from England for her in January 1995. 'It's a cute little toy and is typical of Quentin. He just took a fancy to it and decided I would like it and ended up walking it through customs and onto the airplane and then out the other end, all just for me,' adds a proud Connie.

Reports that Quentin would direct a movie version of the TV series *Man From U.N.C.L.E.* were scotched by the man himself who insisted he had only been talking to producers about the job, although he did admit it would be 'a cool movie to do'. Some Hollywood insiders believed that it would be an ideal opportunity to test out Quentin's abilities the stricter environment of a major studio-financed project.

Quentin signed up for yet another acting role in March 1995, when he agreed to star in *Hands Up*, a thriller to be directed by Virginie Thevenet. Quentin's character was slated as low-life bootlegger. To Quentin, it was very appealing because it sounded a bit like life back at his grandmother's trailer in Tennessee.

His character also manages to fall in with a young woman (played by Charlotte Gainsboro) who just happens to be linked with an S and M parlour dominatrix. The movie is set in a nightclub called *The Black Lizard* and shooting started in LA in July, 1995.

If this was Quentin's idea of getting a life after *Pulp*, then the mind boggles as to what he'd do if he got really busy.

'Let's not start suckin' each other's dicks quite yet'

Harry Keitel as the Wolf in *Pulp Fiction*

Man on a Mission

OSCAR NIGHT, DOROTHY CHANDLER PAVILION,
LOS ANGELES, MARCH 27, 1995

As Sir Anthony Hopkins ripped open the envelope to announce the winner of the best original screenplay award, there was a hum of expectation in the audience.

'Quentin Tarantino and Roger Avary for *Pulp Fiction*...'

While the opening track from *Pulp* played, a spontaneous round of applause began. It went on and on. Quentin and Avary met just on the lip of the podium and hugged. It was a slightly mechanical manoeuvre, maybe even slightly over-rehearsed. An underlying tension between the two men was still apparent.

Quentin accepted the statuette and held it in one hand as he leaned towards the microphone. It felt much heavier than he'd expected. But then it *was* made from pewter, draped in layers of nickel, copper, silver and, finally, gold. At thirteen inches and eight and a half pounds, it is the most valuable commodity in Hollywood.

'Thanks. This has been a very strange year,' Quentin told the star-studded audience. 'I can definitely say that. Ummm. I was trying to think this is probably the only award I am going to win here tonight. So maybe I should say a whole lot of stuff right here right now and get it out of my system. Everything building up and blow it all tonight and say everything. but I am not going to say it.'

Roger Avary started on a more traditional note. 'I want to thank my dear wife Gretchen, whom I love more than anything in the world [a beat of silence] and I really have to take a pee right now so I am going to go.'

Quentin was right. By leaving the obvious unsaid, he had retained a measure of respect from those who did not approve of his movies.

Applause and laughter followed as the two former video store clerks left the Oscar stage. But their speeches in front of an estimated worldwide audience of two billion people threw a smokescreen over some careful Hollywood wheeler dealing behind the scenes. Quentin and Avary still had mixed feelings about each other's contributions to *Pulp*, even though they had formed a legal agreement about them months before.

After numerous letters and phone calls between lawyers, managers and agents representing Quentin and Avary, it had been exchanged until it was agreed that Quentin and Avary would share the prize if *Pulp* won. Quentin still insisted that only a brief amount of Avary's actual dialogue was used in the version of *Pulp* that had made more than one hundred million dollars at the American box office alone.

But the director was actually more annoyed by the way the Academy did not give *Pulp* best picture and best actor, for which John Travolta had been nominated for the first time since *Saturday Night Fever*. He also felt it deserved recognition for art direction and costume. But then no-one could have countered the enormous success of Tom Hanks and *Forrest Gump*. which took the prizes for best picture, best actor and best director, besides four other lesser categories.

Quentin's disappointment was fuelled by the fact that *Pulp* had been nominated in seven categories, yet only ended up with one award. One critic noted that 'in a cooler, hipper world, one with a sense of humour and of the outrageous in everyday life, *Pulp Fiction*, would win.' But the

Hollywood old guard were not yet quite ready to acknowledge Quentin as a genius.

As Jay Carr predicted in *The Boston Globe* before the ceremony, '*Pulp Fiction* won't win the best picture Oscar on Monday. It's fresh, surprising and entertaining, the most dazzling and exhilarating reinvention of the gangster movie since Martin Scorsese's *Goodfellas*. This, of course, amounts to the kiss of death in an Oscar race. The Academy of Motion Picture Arts and Sciences – which means people who work in the film biz – favours long movies about uplift. And though it's hip and kicky, *Pulp Fiction* isn't exactly preoccupied with redeeming social values or whooping it up for the American dream.'

Jay Carr concluded, '*Pulp Fiction* will resonate through our culture longer than *Forrest Gump*. It's not a sick movie; it's a healing movie, an attempt to work through some troubling stuff that's in the air – and in the streets. It's more than clever. It's cathartic. It airs stuff that needs airing, leaving us less alone. Didn't *Hamlet* leave the stage littered with corpses of everybody but Fortinbras? And what about *Oedipus Rex*, with its tragic hero standing at the end with blood pouring out of the eye sockets he mutilated? You can't generalise about violence. Context is all. *Pulp Fiction* takes an irreverent stance toward some deep-seated fears and taboos and that will cost it at Oscar time.'

Earlier that day Quentin and girlfriend Grace Lovelace had reluctantly agreed to go first class to the Oscars' ceremony, both wearing outfits loaned by designers, as has become a Hollywood tradition in recent years. Grace wore a long black Armani evening dress and Quentin managed a tuxedo, care of Hugo Boss. Grace and Quentin's relationship had grown steadily closer since their decision to link up again the previous year. Quentin's mother Connie says she wouldn't be surprised if they got married. 'Quentin does not have any doubts about Grace's intentions because she has been around since before he made it,' she explains.

Grace had been Quentin's first serious girlfriend in his mid-twenties. They had then split up while he went off and discovered that girls were interested in him because of his fame. But, all through that period of sexual experimentation and one-night stands, Quentin could not get Grace out of his mind. And once he had settled back in LA after that extended stay in Amsterdam, he knew that he needed to get back on track with Grace, a down-to-earth university lecturer.

Back at the Academy Awards, even Quentin's producer Lawrence Bender got in on the Oscar glamour act when his girlfriend was loaned a hundred thousand dollar necklace by Harry Winston.

But perhaps the best comment about Oscar night came from Quentin's only British Dog, Tim Roth. He said, 'If you were a white guy, and you played a black sixty-five-year-old lesbian single mother of four who was crippled with multiple sclerosis, and you directed yourself, you'd get an Oscar – you'd get several.'

At the Miramax Oscars party held at Chasen's restaurant, in Beverly Hills, Quentin and Grace, plus a group of their friends, had a special private room set aside for them. Quentin's old friend Scott Spiegel was invited, although he barely had a chance to speak to Quentin who was mobbed every step of the way.

'Quentin was being swallowed whole,' was how Spiegel put it later.

MUSSO AND FRANK'S RESTAURANT, HOLLYWOOD BOULEVARD, SUMMER, 1995

Nestled in a nondescript strip, Musso and Frank's is as intimate as a speakeasy, but without the attendant gloss. There is no discernible decor: just portraits of a handful of movie stars, a string of table lights, and some polished dark oak lining the ceiling over the cocktail bar.

As one regular says, 'Hip doesn't last, so Musso and Frank's caters for everyone. There is only one master – the atmosphere.' The talents who have dropped in over the years include Charlie Chaplin, Bob Mitchum, Spencer Tracey and some more recent appearances from Madonna and Springsteen.

On this particularly hot evening, Scott Spiegel handed Quentin a

Manhattan Martini and he swallowed half of it in one gulp. This was a rare opportunity to escape the agents, producers and execs who seemed to be stalking his every move.

Quentin sank a little deeper into the red leather banquette seat and smiled across at his companions, Tim (Orange) Roth, Tim's girlfriend and Scott Spiegel. Across the room, a lively entourage were laughing and munching on steaks and chicken. Quentin longed for a plate of fast food. He'd had enough of picking at perfectly sculpted nouvelle cuisine meals in some of the city's most expensive restaurants.

Just then a buxom gal in a leopard print vest, and complete with flame-coloured hair the texture of lawn-mower clippings, strutted past and give him the wink. He smiled at her brazen behaviour then took out his wallet to order another drink. His three companions sniggered when they saw the message on the front: 'Bad Motherfucker'. It was the same wallet that Jules had used in the final diner scene in *Pulp* and Quentin had kept it as a memento.

Musso and Frank's was just one of a small number of hang-outs that Quentin still tried to get to occasionally when he wanted to get back to the real world. He had been a regular at the perpetually cool restaurant, The Olive, on Fairfax, until it closed down in late 1994 and he loved the margaritas at The Three of Clubs, a hole-in-the-wall bar frequented by some of the coolest cats in town.

Quentin's all-time favourite eating establishment was still the Toi Thai restaurant on the corner of Sunset and Gardner, but he was getting fed up with the rubbernecks who seemed to turn up there with alarming regularity. Some nights it didnt seem to matter where Quentin hung out – he would be forever facing a barrage of congratulations from members of the public and other Hollywood players. He always tried to treat them in a gee-gosh-golly-thank-you kind of way, but the lack of privacy was beginning to wear him down.

Quentin's disappointment at not winning the two big Oscar prizes was forgotten a few weeks later when he won the Edgar award for best picture. The annual Edgar awards, sponsored by the Mystery Writers of America and named after the great Edgar Allan Poe, were given out in New York in April 1995.

'I got real excited about winning the Edgar, but he looks real sorry on the trophy. Like, I'm sorry I won, you know,' explained Quentin afterwards.

On May 2, 1995, Quentin made his third appearance as a guest on the *Tonight Show* with Jay Leno. Tarantino-fever was apparent from the moment host Leno came on screen. As he announced his guest list, a cheer went up at the sound of Quentin's name and the camera cut to placards being held up by young women that read: 'WE LOVE YOU QUENTIN.'

Quentin's mission that night was to plug his starring role in *Destiny Turns on The Radio*. He walked on the stage in a black suit, black patent lace-up shoes, black shirt and a healthy covering of two-day-old stubble.

Leno and Quentin laughed away like old friends and he flirted outrageously with the attractive dark-haired girl who played drums on the *Tonight Show* band. When Quentin admitted he had a 'crush' on her, she was brought over to sit next to him for his entire segment. The audience hung on Quentin's every word.

The programme screened an interview with one of the actors who had worked with Quentin on the episode of *ER* which he'd directed. Leno presented Quentin with a doll of *Baywatch* star David Hasselhoff and revealed to the world that he was a big fan of the series. Hasselhoff then called in by phone and spoke to Quentin. Hasselhoff even invited Quentin to join the cast of the show.

Quentin chipped in, 'I'd like to do a little of that mouth-to-mouth stuff. I am totally into that.'

The extraordinary thing about Quentin's appearance on the *Tonight Show* was that so much effort had been made to anchor the entire programme around him. Other celebrity guests Tori Spelling and Naomi Judd only got brief coverage in comparison. Quentin was definitely the star performer.

Even when Spelling, of *Beverly Hills 90210* fame, came on stage in the briefest of hot pants and started talking about how she had not worn any panties on her previous appearance with Leno, the audience seemed less interested than when Quentin explained to America that *90210* was girlfriend Grace's favourite TV show.

On Sunday, May 14, 1995, Quentin remembered to call his mother Connie to wish her happy Mother's Day for the first time in years. 'He saved his life for another year,' says Connie.

However, Quentin was still refusing to wear a watch. Connie believes that her son now has enough people around him to make sure he only needs to ask, so the chances of him purchasing such a device seem slim.

Elsewhere in Hollywood an inevitable spin-off of Quentin's success first with *Dogs* and then *Pulp* was that increasing numbers of copycat movies were starting to come. Some, like *Killer* and the Jason Priestley vehicle *Cold Blooded* were quite good, while others (like the big budget *Kiss of Death* failed) to hit the mark. But they all shared that same film *noir* feel as well as very downbeat endings.

In other movies, Tarantinoisms were being dropped into screenplays like confetti. In Keenan Ivory Wayans *Low Down Dirty Shame*, one of the villains refers to Hong Kong actor/hero Chow Yun-Fat. In *Demolition Man* with Sylvester Stallone, Jackie Chan got a mention. Co-star Wesley Snipes even told the audience about the character he played in the earlier *New Jack City*, who enjoyed watching Brian de Palma's *Scarface*. Suddenly, it was acceptable to have 'in' jokes and references in movies.

In early summer 1995, Quentin found himself on the receiving end of some fame-induced problems. A man was discovered in the grounds of his apartment block and the police were called. The character turned out to be obsessed with meeting Quentin and he was far from stable. It emerged that the man was infuriated by certain violent elements of *Pulp Fiction* and wanted to 'deal with' Quentin.

It then transpired that the man had made a number of threatening calls to Quentin, prompting him to change his phone number four times in two years. One friend said that Quentin was 'extremely freaked out' by the stalker incident, especially as Hollywood has a disturbing history of similar incidents, two of which have actually resulted in the deaths of movie stars.

Quentin became quite paranoid about vetting anyone who wanted to meet him. To his friends, this was not surprising, for Quentin had always been very careful not to take risks. His car was ordinary and low- key; he did not own anything of any great value; he liked to dress very plainly. Now a stalker was threatening the low-profile lifestyle he had so carefully nurtured.

Following the stalker threats, Quentin hired bodyguards for the first time. It was a sad but necessary development, the first real evidence that perhaps certain Hollywood trappings were actually more vital than he had at first realized.

By the summer of 1995, Quentin had grown tired of the entire *Pulp* fever scenario. As far as he was concerned, *Pulp* was like a former girl-friend who had to be put behind him and forgotten so that he could get on with his next project – another crime-riddled movie about some more lowlifes or other. As he told one journalist, 'I'm sick of talking about *Pulp Fiction*. I don't want to talk about it, hear about it or see it again.'

Unlike the rest of the world, Quentin believed that he was only as good as his next movie and time would tell if that was going to be an even more impressive film than the last one...

'To a new world of gods and monsters'

Ernest Thesiger, raising a toast in *The Bride of Frankenstein*, 1935

A Smart Motherfucker

THE SHERATON HOTEL, LOS ANGELES AIRPORT,
MAY 7, 1995

The familiar sound of jumbo jets thundering overhead heralded Quentin's arrival at Fangoria's Weekend of Horrors, featuring the Fourth Annual Fangoria Chainsaw Awards. He had agreed to make a personal appearance at the horrorfest to promote the green-lighting of *From Dusk Till Dawn*, to be directed by Robert Rodriguez from the script Quentin had first been commissioned to write back in 1990.

As more than two thousand horror film geeks queued for the chance to sit in the auditorium and listen to Quentin and his pals holding forth about the meaning of life and his first attempt at producing a horror movie, the man himself was nowhere in sight.

Orderly queues of autograph hunters were formed by the horrorfest organizers who assumed that Quentin would stop and sign his name for fans after his scheduled one-hour chatathon.

'He's a great guy. I met him last year and we had a beer together. I'm sure he'll stop and have a chat,' said one hopeful, who had encountered Quentin at the 1994 horror fest and found him most accessible.

Another gothic-looking fan wearing black from head to toe, chipped in, 'He's a cool guy. He's one of us.'

Meanwhile, the minutes ticked away towards Quentin's scheduled 1.30pm appearance and the crowd of autograph hunters and fans grew steadily longer until it snaked out of the auditorium and right into the Sheraton reception area. By 2.20pm there was still no sign of him.

'We've never seen anything like it. I hope he turns up soon or else we'll have a riot on our hands,' explained a deeply harassed hotel manager.

One fan had flown specially from New York that weekend to meet his idol and get his signature on a glossy black and white photo. It had cost him six hundred dollars in air fares alone.

By 2.50pm the crowd was getting restless. A feeling of impending doom was working its way through the auditorium. At the rear exit, two heavies with walkie-talkies and a blonde in four-inch heels who described herself as one of his assistants waited tensely for Quentin's black stretch limo to appear.

'It's kinda weird. Last year he turned up in his Geo Metro,' explained one film geek called Ron, from San Diego.

Just after 3pm Quentin appeared as if by magic on the podium alongside director Robert Rodriguez and Bob Kurzman, the special effects wizard who had originally commissioned Quentin to write the script for *From Dusk Till Dawn* for just fifteen hundred dollars. The crowd went ecstatic and greeted Quentin with a standing ovation. He hadn't even said anything yet, but they didn't care. They were so pumped to see Quentin that they had been applauding him before he even arrived when the MC made brief reference to *Pulp* and *Dogs*.

Quentin bowed, grabbed the mike and began his spiel about *From Dusk Till Dawn*. As usual, his delivery was classic machinegun style, even though his waspish New York tasseled loafers, and white socks, gave him a distinctly preppy look.

Quentin explained that the movie would co-star himself and *ER* principal George Clooney as two bank-robbing brothers called Seth and Richard Gecko.

'I have just broken out of jail after robbing a bank. We kill cops,' he proudly informed the audience. 'We kill everybody, we kill civilians. George's character will kill anyone who gets in his way because he has to rob. Me, I'm not like that, I am a psychotic asshole. I am a racist. I am a killer. I don't give a fuck, alright?'

'Yeah,' screamed the audience in appreciation.

It was a remarkable performance by Quentin. The crowd had been baying for his blood just two minutes earlier. Now they were eating out of his hand.

Then Quentin and his friends showed the audience a very rough-looking video of the special effects that were being planned for *From Dusk Till Dawn*. It was wobbly vision at its best, but the crowd didn't care. They latched onto every image and gave gasps of approval. What he did not mention was that Rodriguez and himself had thrashed out deals for $2.35 million EACH.

Occasionally, Quentin would hand the mike to one of his friends to explain some of the background to the movie, but they seemed happiest when he was doing the talking.

'It's goin' to be really weird because they are one-part vampire, one-part rat, one-part just big monster. You won't even know what's coming.'

Quentin explained in breathless terms that he and George would be on the run from the cops when they stumble into a bar called The Titty Twister (snigger, snigger from the audience) 'and then we are fighting ten thousand bat creatures. It's really cool.' Naturally, the strippers in the club are vampires.

A brief question-and-answer session followed and the subjects thrown at Quentin included *The Man from U.N.C.L.E. Four Rooms* and 'whatever happened to that movie you were supposed to write for John Woo?'

Quentin's reply was a little predictable for once. 'I have been too damn busy. Life's too short.'

Just then he leant over, asked someone the time and immediately got up to call a halt to the proceedings.

Outside the auditorium, the hundreds of fans who had formed a quarter of a mile queue for Quentin's autograph after his appearance, were still convinced he would see them once the show had wrapped.

Suddenly, a white-faced horrorfest official approached the front of the line and announced that Quentin wasn't going to sign any autographs because he hadn't got time.

The guy from New York looked angry. 'But he always stops to sign autographs.'

'Not any more he ain't. He's a superstar and they do what the fuck they want...'

Quentin now insists he does not 'want to be known as the gun guy for ever'. He says he has a host of different movie ideas floating around in his head, including a very atypical screenplay about 'how a guy feels about his ex-girlfriend and a girl who wonders whether she is my first love or my true love, which one was she.' There is a definite romantic edge to Quentin that has not yet been fully exposed. Undoubtedly his primary source for this idea is his relationship with girlfriend Grace Lovelace. After all, movies are real life to Quentin.

In the summer of 1995, Sean Connery fascinatingly revealed that he had advised the producers of the latest Bond flick, *Goldeneye*, to hire Quentin. They dismissed the idea out of hand. That decision may prove costly as Quentin's input would have expanded the appeal of 007 to beyond Bond's traditional and rapidly dwindling middle-of-the-road audience.

Director Terry Gilliam, whose encouragement was so important to Quentin at that difficult session at the Sundance Film Institute shortly before *Dogs* was shot, says the next few years will be crucial in his development. 'The interesting thing will be if he can develop beyond movies and beyond writing about them and handling this stuff out here because he's got to. We keep talking about what is Quentin going to do next. He's gotta stop being this cinema freak kid who is so clever and wild.'

In a candid interview with *The Times* weekend magazine in October 1994, Quentin said, 'I guess I do look at things differently. I don't think my films are hard to follow. The only thing that's required is that you have to commit to watching them, you have to engage with them totally. I don't make films for the casual viewer.'

But how would he like to be remembered, *The Times* asked him. 'As a good storyteller. That's the bottom line. Ultimately, all I'm trying to do is merge sophisticated storytelling with lurid subject matter. I reckon that makes for an entertaining night at the movies.'

When Hollywood heavyweights David Geffen, Jeffrey Katzenberg and Steven Spielberg announced their intention to form a new studio, Spielberg, was asked what movies they would like to make. He replied, 'We'd love to have a *Pulp Fiction* from talent like Tarantino.'

But Quentin's main priority is the exact opposite of most of Hollywood's. He wants to keep the budgets of his movies modest, and pick and choose precisely what he wants to do. With his low rent apartment, compact car and scant concern for his appearance, he can afford to take another two years off if it takes that long to create his next masterpiece.

Above all, Quentin Tarantino is a movie buff who, like Buster Keaton's projectionist in *Sherlock, Junior* or Jeff Daniels in Woody Allen's *Purple Rose of Cairo*, has gone from his seat in the dark to penetrate the world up there on the big screen.

He considers the classic lines of dialogue between the action in his movies to be 'my little kisses, my valentines to the audience. I think that's the way they take it, and that's the way they accept it'.

If Quentin's work does survive the test of time, it will owe a lot to the performers who flock to him and match his ceaseless energy with their own. One can catch a hint of the conflict to come in the climactic speech of *Pulp*, magnificently delivered by Samuel L. Jackson. 'You're the weak, and I'm the tyranny of evil men,' he declaims. 'But I'm trying, Ringo, I'm trying real hard to be the shepherd.' Will Quentin try as hard? Only time will tell.

End Credits

Roger Avary is directing a new project after getting fresh interest in his material following the acknowledgement of his role in *Pulp Fiction* and the subsequent Oscar. He now also shares publicists and agents with Quentin. The two former video store clerks seem to have reached a truce.

Jamie Beardsley still speaks to Quentin on a regular basis and is hoping to develop a project through his production company, A Band Apart. But she concedes that she and Lawrence Bender still do not see eye to eye.

Lawrence Bender has at least half a dozen movies in development with various directors attached and he will undoubtedly produce whatever project Quentin decides to write and direct next.

Steve Buscemi's acting career was given a huge boost by his role in *Reservoir Dogs* and he is considered one of Hollywood's brightest stars, with appearances in a number of recent movies plus a regular gig in the first series of the much-praised TV cop show, *Homicide*.

Richard N. Gladstein continues to be involved in Quentin's career, having carved out a role for himself as a movie executive that Quentin and Lawrence Bender are prepared to put all their trust in.

Craig Hamann still lives in the San Fernando Valley and remains a client of personal manager Cathryn Jaymes. He has had numerous near misses with screenplays which have been optioned by major studios, but then not produced. One day he'll get lucky...

Monte Hellman still lives in the same picturesque house in the Hollywood Hills that played such an important role in the development of *Reservoir Dogs*. He earned the respect of Quentin and Bender through his involvement in *Dogs* and currently has a project he hopes to direct, with Bender as executive producer.

Samuel L. Jackson's career goes from strength to strength and he is currently contracted to do four major Hollywood movies back-to-back.

Cathryn Jaymes still lives in the house that was almost destroyed by the LA earthquake in January 1994. She is currently helping develop the careers of other director/writers.

Harvey Keitel continues to pick and choose the most extraordinary variety of movie roles. Some, like *The Piano*, seem inspired while others, like *The Bad Lieutenant*, have his followers somewhat confused.

Grace Lovelace has managed to keep an impressively low profile despite the fact that she is Quentin's only true love and he continues to worship her.

Jack Lucarelli has graduated from teaching actors at the James Best Acting School to directing his own low-budget feature film, which he was trying to sell at Cannes at the same time as Quentin was basking in the glory of *Pulp Fiction*.

Stanley Margolis sticks mainly to personal management and operates from his home in the San Fernando Valley. But he is always on the lookout for another Quentin.

Don Murphy and his producing partner **Jane Hamsher** are enjoying immense success in Hollywood. They are producing Oliver Stone's next big project, *Planet of the Apes*, and they have numerous other movies in development at major studios.

Tim Roth continues to make brave and interesting choices as an actor. He even managed something more commercial in *Rob Roy*, but admits he prefers small, non-studio productions because they are more of a challenge.

Scott Spiegel has just written a new project he hopes to direct through Lawrence Bender. He still collects cereals from around the world and reads an average of twelve superhero comics each week.

Tony Scott went back to mega-action star vehicle flicks like *Crimson Tide* and has seen his bank balance shoot up by tens of millions of dollars.

Eric Stoltz continues to specialize in off-beat roles that tend to be a little intense. But he has built up an interesting following amongst the under-thirty-five designer café society crowd.

Oliver Stone is a law unto himself and has just directed Sir Anthony Hopkins as Richard Nixon in his latest wide scope filmic statement, this time about the life of the most disgraced American president in the history of the United States.

Quentin Tarantino is set for a long and powerful career as the most unusual film maker to emerge in the history of Hollywood. He still drives a red Geo Metro.

Lawrence Tierney hasn't done much since *Reservoir Dogs*, but he now has a fan club and his own sign on the Internet, which is a shame since he cannot operate a computer.

John Travolta is about to be paid seven million dollars for his next movie and continues to tell anyone who will listen that his revived career owes everything to Quentin. Throughout all this, he has remained a Scientologist.

Rich Turner's career as an actor has been slow to take off and he works in a nine-to-five job near his home in the South Bay. He still drives that Chevy pick-up and is waiting for a call from Quentin when he decides to move to a mansion in the Hollywood Hills.

Harvey and **Bob Weinstein's** Miramax company continues to go from strength to strength thanks to the backing of Disney. It seems certain that they will be financing Quentin's next project, whatever that turns out to be.

Bruce Willis went back to *Die Hard, With a Vengeance*, and it became one of the hit movies of the summer of 1995. But he still longs for another *Pulp Fiction*...

Connie Zastoupil is working very hard as an executive in the health-care industry and has moved to the east coast because of professional commitments. She talks to Quentin at least once a month and is still nagging him to buy a bigger car.

Curt Zastoupil now lives back in Southern California and has remained on good terms with Connie and Quentin. He still has a goatee.

'He stands at the Hollywood crossroads where guilty laughter and sadistic brutality merge'

Writer, Clancy Sigal

Filmography

Reservoir Dogs

Harvey Keitel	Mr White
Tim Roth	Mr Orange
Michael Madsen	Mr Blonde
Chris Penn	Nice Guy Eddie
Steve Buscemi	Mr Pink
Lawrence Tierney	Joe Cabot
Quentin Tarantino	Mr Brown
Eddie Bunker	Mr Blue
Kirk Baltz	Marvin Nash
Randy Brooks	Holdaway

Released by Miramax Pictures in 1992. *Director* Quentin Tarantino. *Producer* Lawrence Bender. *Executive Producers* Richard N. Gladstein, Ronna B. Wallace, Monte Hellman. *Screenwriter* Quentin Tarantino. *Cinematographer* Andrzej Sekula. *Editor* Sally Menke. *Costumes* Betsy Heimann. *Music* Karyn Rachtman. *Production design* David Wasco. *Running time*: 1 hour, 39 minutes.

Pulp Fiction

Samuel L. Jackson	Jules
John Travolta	Vincent
Uma Thurman	Mia
Bruce Willis	Butch
Amanda Plummer	Honey Bunny
Tim Roth	Pumpkin
Maria de Medeiros	Fabienne
Harvey Keitel	Wolf
Christopher Walken	Captain Koons
Eric Stoltz	Lance
Ving Rhames	Marsellus
Rosanna Arquette	Jody
Quentin Tarantino	Jimmy
Angela Jones	Esmarelda

Released by Miramax Pictures in 1994. *Director* Quentin Tarantino. *Producer* Lawrence Bender. *Executive Producers* Danny De Vito, Michael Shamberg, Stacey Sher. *Co-executive Producers* Bob Weinstein, Harvey Weinstein, Richard Gladstein. *Screenwriter* Quentin Tarantino. *Cinematographer* Andrzej Sekula. *Editor* Sally Menke. *Costumes* Betsy Heimann. *Music* Karyn Rachtman. *Production Design* David Wasco. *Running time*: 2 hours 33 minutes.

The Strictly Unofficial Quentin Tarantino Coolest Movies-of-All-Time List

1. **Rio Bravo** (1959)   Howard Hawks
2. **Taxi Driver** (1976)   Martin Scorsese
3. **Blow Out** (1981)   Brian de Palma

The rest not in any order and subject to change daily:-

One-Eyed Jacks (1961)	Marlon Brando
Breathless (1983)	James McBride
His Girl Friday (1940)	Howard Hawks
Rolling Thunder (1977)	John Flynn
Badlands (1973)	Terrence Malik
Casualties of War (1989)	Brian de Palma
Used Cars (1980)	Robert Zemeckis
It's a Mad Mad Mad Mad World (1963)	Stanley Kramer
The Life and Times of Judge Roy Bean (1972)	John Huston
Where Eagles Dare (1969)	Brian G.Hutton
The Dirty Dozen (1967)	Robert Aldrich
Bringing Up Baby (1938)	Howard Hawks
The Killer (1989)	John Woo

The Driver (1978)	Walter Hill
Blood Simple (1983)	Joel Coen
Long Good Friday (1980)	John Mackenzie
Mona Lisa (1986)	Neil Jordan
The Hit (1984)	Stephen Frears
The Killers (1964)	Don Seigel
Comfort and Joy (1984)	Bill Forsyth
Local Hero (1983)	Bill Forsyth
Le Petit Soldat	Jean Luc Godard
Vivre Sa Vie	Jean Luc Godard
Breathless (1964)	Jean Luc Godard
Bande à Part (1964)	Jean Luc Godard
Pierrot Le Fou (1968)	Jean Luc Godard
Shaft (1971)	Gordon Parks
The Good The Bad and The Ugly (1966)	Sergio Leone
The Killing (1956)	Stanley Kubrick
The Asphalt Jungle (1950)	John Huston
Rififi (1955)	Jules Dassin
The Taking of Pelham 123 (1974)	Joseph Sargent
City on Fire (1989)	Ringo Lam
Kiss Me Deadly (1955)	Robert Aldrich
Pope of Greenwich Village (1984)	Stuart Rosenberg
A Clockwork Orange (1971)	Stanley Kubrick
Fandango (1985)	Kevin Reynolds
Days of Thunder (1990)	Tony Scott
Night Call Nurses (1972)	Roger Corman

Jules et Jim (1962)	Francois Truffaut
A Girl in Every Port (1928)	Howard Hawks
The Guns of Navarone (1961)	J.Lee Thompson
Dead Poets Society (1989)	Peter Weir
Frogs (1972)	George McCowan
Willard (1971)	Daniel Mann
Night of the Lepus (1972)	William F.Claxton
Dark Passage (1947)	Delmer Daves
The Last Boy Scout (1991)	Tony Scott
Indiana Jones and the Temple of Doom (1984)	Steven Spielberg
Year of the Dragon (1985)	Michael Cimino
Scarface (1984)	Brian de Palma
Topkapi (1964)	Jules Dassin
The Thomas Crown Affair (1968)	Norman Jewison
Once Upon a Time in America (1984)	Sergio Leone
Abbott and Costello Meet Frankenstein (1948)	Charles Barton
Abbott and Costello Meet the Mummy (1955)	Charles Lamont
Hi Mom! (1969)	Brian de Palma
Back Street (1961)	David Miller
Maniac Cop Two (1990)	William Lustig
Intruder (1989)	Scott Spiegel
The Vigilante (1947)	Wallace Fox
Perfect (1985)	James Bridges

Mad Love (1935)	Karl Freund
The Trip (1967)	Roger Corman
The Last Seduction (1994)	John Dahl
Ed Wood (1994)	Tim Burton
Salvador (1986)	Oliver Stone
For a Few Dollars More (1965)	Sergio Leone
Le Doulos (1962)	Jean Pierre Melville
They Live by Night (1949)	Nicholas Ray
The Long Goodbye (1973)	Robert Altman
Coffy (1973)	Jack Hill
Magnificent Obsession (1954)	Doulgas Sirk
Savage Seven (1968)	Richard Rush
The Thing (1982)	John Carpenter
Caged Heat (1974)	Jonathan Demme
Silver Bullet (1985)	Daniel Attias
Kansas City Confidential (1952)	Phil Karlson

Index

*'Then I saw that there was a way to hell,
even from the gates of heaven'*

John Bunyan, *Pilgrim's Progress* (1678)

Fade to black...